Beef Production

Cattle coming down from the hills *Frontispiece*

BEEF PRODUCTION

M.M. Cooper
Professor of Agriculture, University of London

2014
BIOTECH BOOKS
Delhi - 110 035

ISBN 81-7622-145-7

Published by : **BIOTECH BOOKS**
1123/74, Tri Nagar,
Delhi - 110 035
Phone: 27382765
e-mail: biotechbooks@yahoo.co.in

Showroom : 4762-63/23, Ansari Road, Darya Ganj,
New Delhi - 110 002
Phone: 23245578, 23244987

Laser Typesetting : **Classic Computer Services**
Delhi - 110 035

Printed at : **Chawla Offset Printers**
Delhi - 110 052

PRINTED IN INDIA

Acknowledgements

I am deeply interested in land utilisation, more especially in those aspects which are related to animal production. I have also had the benefit of critical advice from Dr John Hammond, and I would like to acknowledge this valuable assistance as well as his permission to use photographs. There are many others who have helped me with valuable criticisms, in particular John Montgomery Esq., George Maxted Esq., Dr Alan Stewart and Dr A.E. Henderson. I would also like to thank my colleague "Canada" Davis for his contribution on hill-country development. I have quoted freely from many authorities, and I trust that I have suitably acknowledged all these in the text.

I am particularly grateful to the *Farmers' Weekly* for assistance in getting together one of the attractive features of the book, namely the plates, and to the several people who have given me permission to use their photographs. Mr. Norman Davis and Mrs. Jean Jordan have earned my special thanks for their assistance in the preparation of figures and in the typing of my illegible handwriting. My wife, too, has done her share in checking manuscripts and proof reading, and she has suffered all the backwash of the growing and production pains which are inevitable in such an effort as this.

M.M. Cooper
Wye College
(University of London)

Foreword

It is evident from recent events that this country will in the future have to be more self-supporting in all agricultural products than it has been in the past. While the milk industry in recent years, thanks to the application of science and a body of progressive producers, guided by the Milk Marketing Board, has been able to lift production considerably, the same cannot be said of the beef industry.

The methods now employed in milk production are very different from those which existed fifty years ago, but the methods employed in beef production have shown little change during this period. In this book Professor Cooper has attempted to focus attention on some of the problems of beef production which will have to be solved before it regains its position in the economy of British agriculture. All may not agree with the solutions he offers to these various problems, but the problems have been put, and if one does not agree with the solution offered then it is up to those in the industry to offer a better solution. It is evident that radical changes in methods of production will have to be made if the beef industry is to be able to stand on its own legs. Science has shown that the young animal is a much more efficient converter of feeding stuffs into meat than is an old one, and in these days of high costs of concentrates, it might well pay the Eastern Counties farmer better to fill his yards with yearlings during their first winter rather than to fatten older bullocks.

The general situation in British agriculture has changed during the last fifty years, and the dairy industry which was at that time practically non-existent has risen to one of primary importance. As Professor Cooper has indicated, one of the present problems of beef production is how to make use of these advances in the dairy industry so as to lower costs in the beef industry. This can be done by the production of colour-marked, beef bull-dairy cow crosses by A.I. and by multiple suckling to supply the raw materials for beef at lower costs than in the past. Other problems, unfortunately at present outside the province of the producer in the absence of a marketing board, also need to be solved before the beef industry can be efficient, such as, for example, the provision of sufficient cold-storage hanging-space to mature our beef properly and to provide a carry-over in times of peaks of production.

John Hammond

Contents

List of Plates

Chapter 1

Beef Production as a Component of British Farming

Eighty years ago the pattern of a prosperous farming industry in Britain was well defined. On the better and more tractable land there was intensive arable production, which was generally associated with some intensive animal production, in particular the folding of sheep and the yard fattening of bullocks. The profitability of this was measured not just by the returns from meat, but also by the contribution the fattening animal made to soil fertility. The poorer country which was incapable of intensive arable production was the traditional source of store cattle and sheep, because such land was not so valuable that farmers had to farm intensively in order to derive a return commensurate with the capital they had invested. The whole constituted a very effective system of land utilisation. The poorer country which was admirably suited for the production of store cattle and sheep, but which was incapable of fattening them, provided the raw material for the better-land farmers, who were able to utilise by-products of wheat and barley production such as the restorative clover crop, the cleaning root crop, straw and tail corn, and, at the same time, maintain their land in good heart for corn production.

The pattern was largely destroyed by the development of agriculture in the New World and by the rise of Britain as a manufacturing country, where prosperity was based on exports and on capital investments in the new countries. Primarily the domestic demand was for cheap food-wheat, meat, butter and cheese–which the new countries could provide to pay for the services their economies demanded. This two-way trade was fostered by the development of cheap and rapid transport by sea which brought countries much closer together, and by the application of refrigeration to ocean transport to make possible the carriage of perishable foodstuffs such as meat from one side of the globe to the other. No longer was the home farmer secure in the practical monopoly of a home market. He had to compete with the American prairie farmer, who was producing wheat at an absurdly low figure because he was farming virgin land and he was using mechanical aids such as the reaper which McCormick had developed. The Dane was capitalising on the cheap grain which at one time had threatened to ruin him by using it to produce butter, bacon and eggs, which he exported to Britain. New Zealand was in a process of rapid development, and pastoral sheep production was providing mutton and lamb at a price with which the sheep-fold could not compete. The Argentine with its huge areas of natural grassland was beginning to realise on this tremendous natural asset, and frozen beef of low quality was gradually replaced by chilled beef of the highest quality which was to the liking of the English housewife. Under the impact of these forces British agriculture went into a decline. Hundreds of thousands of acres of arable land tumbled down into grass, and much of it tumbled even further into a complete state of dereliction and abandonment. Gradually in the face of the inherent conservatism of the British farmer, who was loyal to his traditions of sound rotations and high farming, the character of agriculture began to change. The grassland ewe flock replaced folded sheep, and the dairy cow took the place of the fattening bullock on many farms. Liquid milk was a product which was entirely free from overseas competition, and from the turn of the century it gradually became the sheet anchor of British farming. The development of dairying was to a large extent based on the utilisation of cheap imported feeding-stuffs, which were used too for pig and poultry production, and also played an important part in the production of baby beef, a quality product which was able to withstand overseas competition.

This substantially was the position at the outbreak of the Second World War, which marks the end of a phase of British agriculture characterised by decline and a very slow revolution to meet the demands of the changed trading circumstances. It is true that there were pioneers who were defining the shape of things to come-the proponents of ley farming, the large-scale corn growers, who were applying mechanical aids to reduce costs of production, and the down-land dairy farmers, who were using the mobile dairy on land which had hitherto been regarded as suitable only for grassland sheep. There had been vast advances in the techniques and materials of agriculture. Nitrogenous fertilisers were becoming freely available, the plant breeder had developed new strains of cereals, grasses and forage plants, there was a better realisation of the fundamentals of pasture management and utilisation, and there was a vast increase in the possibilities of mechanical aids in agriculture.

The immediate demand of the war-time situation was the maximum degree of self-sufficiency in respect of food and raw materials which were products of the land, and the policy of British war-time agriculture was framed with this end in view. It was not self-sufficiency on the pre-war basis, for priorities were established for certain products which were considered to be essential, *e.g.*, grains, potatoes, sugar-beet and milk. Subsidies and the price-fixing mechanism were used to encourage the production of these items and to discourage such lines as eggs, pig-meats and beef. The relative decline in beef production as compared with milk was hastened by these direct measures, and, indirectly, by taking grassland, albeit much of it of inferior quality, away from the grazing bullock for arable production. Ley farming became the fashion, and the dairy cow the favourite animal in the utilisation of the ley.

War-time conditions put British agriculture in the melting-pot. The dog and stick man had to turn his hand to the plough, and the dairy farmer who used his land as a source of roughage and as leg room for his cows had to produce the nutrients he formerly ordered from his cake merchant. The horse had to give way to the tractor, for the labourer's time had become too expensive and the magnitude of the cultivation task too great for old methods to persist. Fortunately farmers were paid a price for their produce which made such changes possible. At the end of the war, not only were farmers in a frame of mind to adopt innovations, but they had the where-withal to put them into effect, at least on the better-class land.

There were many who thought that with the end of the war British farming would return to its former pattern. That was the experience following the First World War, which provided only a temporary boost for agriculture, which soon returned to its previous status of a depressed industry as Britain strove to retain her old international position as an exporter of manufactured goods paid for by cheap imported food. But the Second World War had been a longer and much more expensive affair, and it had brought about changes in the manufacturing potential in countries such as Canada and Australia, which formerly bought our goods in large quantities. Overseas investments, particularly in America, had virtually disappeared because they had been used to finance the war. Britain had become a debtor country, very conscious of anew phenomenon known as the 'Dollar Gap.'

Considerable as the changes in British agriculture were during the war and immediately after, there were vastly greater changes in the social and political outlook of Britain. There had been a great levelling of incomes and a huge rise in the purchasing power of the mass of the people. The nation had set its face against the depressing years of the middle thirties when Boyd Orr had shown that a high proportion of the nation subsisted on a below-optimum diet. Rationing has persisted for a much longer time after this last war than it did after the 1914–18 war, not because of any great reduction in the supply of particular items of food, but because of the larger demand for them. Liquid milk, for instance, was still rationed when its supply was virtually 40 per cent higher than it was in 1938-39. With certain foods, of course, the maintenance of rationing has been the direct result of a policy of conserving foreign exchange, and meat, particularly beef, to some extent comes under this limitation. It is not just a question of payment for imported meat but also payment for feeding-stuffs which could be converted into meat in this country.

Plate 1: Dereliction does not Encourage Investment in the Absence of Security

Plate 2: The Scatter of Fertiliser by Aerial Top-dressing

Our national problem of enlarging our standard of living, so far as food supplies are concerned, in the face of restricted conditions of world trade as a result of our overseas indebtedness, is to a large extent tied up with our capacity to increase t the productivity of our limited farming lands, which are continually being encroached upon by demands as diverse as open-cast mining and the building of arterial roads. If the traditional roast beef of old England is going to be something more than a memory of the older generations, then it has to be produced in greater quantities from our own farming lands, but it cannot be produced at the expense of the other essential products such as milk. It is probable, though, that we are approaching saturation paint so far as the liquid-milk market is concerned. Increases in production, more and more, will have to be diverted to processing, and this will mean a lower return to the producer. The price pooling system will spread the effects of these lower returns, which are buffered by the predominant position of the higher-priced liquid milk. Without entering into any detailed discussion of this point, it seems that the expansion in dairying will come less from increased numbers of dairy cattle than it will come from higher output per dairy cow, which at a figure of approximately 600 gallons is much too low to be accepted in a country whose land resources are so limited. There are national movements, which are gathering momentum operating to raise this figure, in particular herd recording, artificial insemination and breed-improvement schemes.

Now let us consider where we can get leg room and sustenance for our bullocks. The fattening bullock competes with the dairy cow for land and for food, and if domestic beef production is to rise we have got to make available more food to beef cattle. This can only be done by a general raising of our standards of all competing and contributing branches of farming. In East Anglia, where yard fattening of bullocks was more firmly established than in almost any other part of Britain, there are now many farms where bullocks have disappeared from the scene and have not been replaced even by dairy cows. The story here is that grain and sugar-beet have been profitable and bullocks have been a losing proposition. Fertility can be restored by artificial fertilisers, and increased tractor forces have made the cultivation problem much less formidable. Land can be handled if it is worked at the right time even though it has lost structure. One cannot be side-tracked by the soil issue here, but one can regret the burning or ploughing-in of crop residues which would make good stock feed. Work at Sprowston has shown, for instance, that the sleeping of sugar-beet tops as opposed to ploughing-in does not depress subsequent yields, and there is a harvest of mutton to boot. Numerous trials also show the benefit of good muck in enhancing yields. The feeding animal, whether it be in the sheep-fold or the bullock yard or on the restorative ley, is a concomitant of first-class arable crops.

One cannot blame the individual who finds bullock feeding relatively unprofitable and decides to drop it from his farming. It would be stretching a man's loyalties to the State a little too far to suggest that he should lose money in order to raise the national meat ration. But we are looking at this as a national problem, and we can regret a set of conditions which result in a lowering of the national food supply because potential feeding-stuffs are wasted.

One of the most pressing of the problems facing the beef industry is the supply of stores. In the old days when dual-purpose cattle dominated this was relatively straightforward, and there were large numbers of steers of dual-purpose breeds, particularly Shorthorns. Today specialised dairy cows, in particular Friesians, are beginning to swamp the dual-purpose breeds, and every cattle market has its quota of dairy-bull calves which are not considered worth while for fattening and are sold for baby veal. Annually at least a million calves meet this fate in Britain. There have been suggestions that the Friesian steer is not without merit as a beef animal, and the outcome of current work at Cambridge, for which Mansfield and Brooks are responsible, is being awaited, with considerable interest, for it will provide the first definite information on this point. Colour-marking crosses with dairy-type cows is another practice which has been encouraged through a free A.I. scheme and through calf-rearing subsidies. The intention here is that low-producers should be mated, not to produce herd replacements, but to provide calves for rearing as beef stores. This can be a two-edged sword, however, in a country characterised by very small dairy herds, for it may result, as a consequence of unfavourable sex ratios. In beef-cross heifers being drafted into dairy herds. However, the practice undoubtedly does promise to be of first-rate importance in increasing our supplies of fattening cattle, for it mans that store raising can be associated with dairying on the smaller marginal farms where the monthly milk cheque is a very important consideration.

The second possible source of stores is land which is either neglected or used much below its potential for stock production. There has been much wishful thinking about our hill country, and there has been a tendency to make rather unrealistic estimates of its capacity to produce cattle for fattening. Later we shall be dealing with this topic in suitable detail, but it may be said at this juncture that we cannot look for spectacular increases in the output of cattle which on this land are not only products from but also agents in the land improvement plan. In order to offer reasonable prospects of profit the hills have to be farmed in large units in order to spread the overheads of capital invested and labour costs. In other words the land has got to be ranched, but this does not mean that the possibilities of improvement should be neglected. Aerial top-dressing, increased fencing, the improvement of limited areas of tractable land by reseeding and fertilising to provide sustenance for the winter months, and better methods of grazing will unquestionably make very big differences in carrying capacity over a period of time, but we will have to think of it still as country which will carry a cattle beast to ten or twenty acres and a sheep to three or four. The poorest of this land cannot be used for breeding, for initially it will carry only fairly mature cattle, which must be regarded primarily as mowing machines contributing to land improvement. Their quality for beef production will not be enhanced by their prolonged sojourn on the hills.

Even a limited realisation of the potentialities of the poorer land will probably demand something in the nature of what Americans call pump-priming on the part of the State. Capital investment will be hazardous if returns, measured in shillings and not pounds per acre, are endangered by market fluctuations. One could not today conscientiously recommend a private individual to pour thousands into land which carries the marks of former occupation in the shape of improvements which have fallen into decay because depression in the good farming areas made hill farming unprofitable. The State must offer some security of investment, and it must provide much in the way of the overall settlement services such as adequate communications and electricity and water supplies. The benefit of money spent in the development of marginal and beyond-marginal land is not confined to these areas alone, for a plentiful supply of store cattle and breeding ewes will permit the potential of our better farms to be realised.

One does not picture, in any such development of beef production, the specialised production methods of the South American or Queensland cattle ranches. British farming is bound to preserve its diversified character, and with few exceptions production of beef is likely to remain integrated with other farming enterprises. On the hills it is likely to be the junior partner of sheep-raising, and on the small marginal farms the raising of stores is more likely to remain a by-product of dairying. When one examines the budgets of the dalesmen, or similar farmers, one is immediately impressed by the great importance of the monthly milk cheques. It is not reasonable to expect them to change to the rearing of stores alone so far as cattle production is concerned, even though the multiple suckling of calves at the present time is a fairly profitable undertaking. It would, however, be more logical to expect that such farms in remote districts should sell cream instead of milk. On the one hand there is the heavy expense of daily transport over long distances of bulky perishable milk which, converted into cream of only one-tenth the volume, could be collected only every other day. On the other hand the feeding of large quantities of whole milk in calf-rearing represents a needless waste of the most valuable animal fat. Twenty gallons or so of whole milk will give a calf a very good start in life, and it will continue to thrive on separated milk and a cream substitute such as a cereal mixture which will cost only a fraction of the value of the cream it replaces. Apart from calf-rearing, separated milk in small quantities on such farms can provide an extremely valuable animal protein for poultry and pigs, especially in the early stages of development.

However, on many farms, not so much the small marginal farm as the larger holding with some other main line of income such as arable production, multiple suckling of colour-marked or dual-purpose calves is likely to increase. It constitutes an alternative to dairying on ley farms where buildings and layout are not easily adapted to dairying, and, properly organised, it does not involve any heavy demand on labour.

Unless there are radical changes in the relationship between concentrate costs and realisations for carcass beef, it seems likely that once the early-rearing stage is completed the emphasis will be on bulk feeding of one kind or another, *e.g.*, pasture and its derivatives, forage crops such as the kales, and straw. The emphasis, too, will be on *in situ* utilisation in order to reduce labour costs which are liable to become disproportionate where cattle are kept in comparatively small numbers. If pasture is to be the main feeding-stuff it is inevitable, because of the seasonal nature of its growth, that the killings will be mainly concentrated in the late summer and autumn. Yard fattening will survive, particularly where valuable crops which require dung for heavy yields are grown, *e.g.* hops, market-garden and greenhouse crops, but the indications are that on most farms where bullocks are used to tread straw into muck, feeding will be based more on good quality hay and silage, roots and very limited quantities of home-grown concentrated foods.

The preceding discussion anticipates, to some degree, aspects which will be dealt with in greater detail in subsequent chapters. They have been mentioned here to give perspective. One can only hope that our future will be a relatively normal outcome of the trends which are being manifested not only in our domestic affairs but in the world as a whole. Apart from the short-term aspect of a diminished capacity to buy food from abroad, necessitating greater reliance on our own land resources to maintain our material standard of living, there is the wider long-term issue of a rapid increase in the world's population. It has been estimated that every three seconds there are two more mouths to feed, and year-by-year these mouths are opened wider in their demands for more food. We in Britain have been accustomed to a standard of feeding well above that of the great majority of people, but we have no right to expect to maintain such an advantage if our own land resources are not fully utilised. Year by year a greater pressure is being exerted on our land and more and more we shall have to rely on our own agriculture for our food supplies. In this respect beef is no exception, and so the keynote of the chapters which follow is a more intensive use of our land, with beef cattle playing their part in securing an integrated and highly productive system of agriculture.

Chapter 2

The Development of British Beef Breeds

Robert Bakewell

The rise of British breeds of beef cattle to a predominant position in countries where specialised beef production is an important element of agricultural economy is one of the most fascinating stories of farming. In the United States, Argentina, Brazil, Uruguay, and in the Commonwealth countries Shorthorn, Aberdeen Angus and Hereford cattle and their crosses are numbered in tens of millions, and yet barely a hundred and fifty years ago there were no distinct and recognisable breeds in the sense that we know them today. The central figure in the chain of events which took British cattle from an assorted motley of no-purpose cattle to their present position of eminence is Robert Bakewell (1725–95), a Leicestershire, farmer who is unquestionably the founder of the British, pedigree livestock industry. This remarkable man, with concepts a hundred years in advance of contemporary biological knowledge, established a procedure of breeding which the modern science of genetics can explain but not improve upon to any substantial degree.

Bakewell was not himself directly responsible for any of the three breeds mentioned above. They were the achievement of men who followed his methods–Watson of Keillor, who pioneered the Aberdeen Angus, the brothers Colling, pupils of Bakewell, who founded the Improved Shorthorn breed and Tomkins and others who worked with the Hereford. Later we shall see in a more detailed study the common quality of the Bakewellian approach in the methods of these men and those who followed them. Bakewell worked with the Longhorn breed, which he improved to a considerable degree, but unfortunately he developed an animal with indifferent milking qualities and a spread of horns which rendered it unsuitable for yarding, and it could not compete with the breeds which his successors founded. Bakewell made his greatest contribution with the Leicester sheep, which was used to improve practically all the British longwool breeds that we know today, and that share with the British Down breeds the international standing of British beef cattle.

Enclosure of Farms

In order to understand properly the significance of the vast changes which Bakewell initiated, the logical starting-point is a brief account of medieval English agriculture which was based on a village community centred around common grazing land and arable fields farmed in strips on a three-course system. Two crops of corn were followed by a year of fallow, and the volunteer growth on this land provided scanty keep for cattle and sheep which derived most of their sustenance from the grazing of common land. The level of nutrition was miserably low except in the early summer. Cattle numbers were reduced by slaughter in the autumn a convenient balance of breeding and young stock and working bullocks which were wintered on straw and poor quality hay derived from enclosed meadows. Red clover had not yet been introduced into English farming, nor were there any roots or similar forage crops. Cattle were prized less for their meat and milk qualities than for their draught performance. Length of leg was an important attribute in animals which had to traverse miry lanes and roam miles in search of food, and size of bone served the ox in good stead when he had to draw, a heavy plough through stiff soil (Ernle, 1936). Virtually it was a period of survival of the fittest. The lean, slab-sided, late-maturing beasts of those days could survive under conditions of near starvation which modern improved breeds cannot endure.

Improvement of livestock was not possible with this system of collective farming. The village cattle, severally owned, grazed together, and stock breeding, in Ernle's words, 'was the haphazard union of nobody's son with everybody's daughter.' Following the Black Death there came a series of economic and social changes which, over the next four centuries, altered completely the character of British farming. One of the most far-reaching of these changes was the enclosure movement which was initiated in the Tudor period, and was substantially completed by the beginning of the nineteenth century. Instead of an agriculture based on small scattered strips of land cultivated in conformity with the village pattern, holdings were consolidated into compact blocks as we know them today. No longer was the occupier of land forced to follow the traditional scheme of farming–he was free to vary his programme of cropping and he was able to control the mating of his livestock. In the first instance the enclosure movement received its momentum from the expansion of sheep-farming, for wool in the Tudor period was one of the most important and profitable products of farming. Gradually, however, the force behind enclosures changed as Britain became an industrial country. Particularly in the Midlands and the northern counties, villages changed to towns and cities, while important centres of Tudor days such as Winchester, Norwich and Ipswich were left far behind. Britain's urban population was exerting an increased pressure on the countryside for food, and this could be supplied only by the improved conditions of agriculture possible on enclosed farms.

Meanwhile a contributory cause or possibly an effect of enclosure was operating, namely the introduction of new crops, notably clover and turnips, which became the basis of the Norfolk four-course rotation which spread widely through Britain. The second half of the seventeenth century and the first half of the eighteenth century was a period of widespread agricultural changes, and it was at the height of this agrarian revolution in 1760 that Bakewell entered into possession of his father's farm. As a young man Bakewell had travelled widely in Britain, and he was conversant not only with the changes occurring in agricultural methods, but also with the changing demands on agriculture. The urban population in heavy industries required not only bread corn but animal protein in the form of meat derived from animals which could be driven to the point of consumption and slaughtered there. The expanding demand for milk was to be satisfied much later when means of rapid transport and distribution were available.

Expansion of meat production was consistent with an expansion of crops for direct human consumption. We see this illustrated clearly in the methods which Lord Townshend (1674–1738) used in the sandy wastes of Norfolk to give substance to the old farming proverb, 'A full bullock yard and a full fold make a full granary.' Farmyard manure and the treading and dunging of folded sheep restored structure and fertility to worn-out land which had been depleted by successions of corn crops. To Coke, another Norfolk pioneer, more than to anyone else can be attributed the rapid development in the arable districts of England of a system of farming based on the yard fattening of bullocks which provided fertility to grow heavier crops of corn. It was the spread of this system which gave direction and incentive to Bakewell; and the men who followed in his footsteps. The urban demand for both meat and bread could be satisfied because agriculture had developed a technique in which the two lines of production had complementary roles.

Improvements in the level of nutrition of livestock, consequent upon enclosures and the introduction of new crops, made another and rather more direct contribution to livestock improvement. It enabled the breeder to distinguish the culls by nature from the culls by nurture. Under hard conditions of feeding the inherently good and the inherently bad are not easily distinguishable, but where reasonable conditions of feeding obtain, the animals with superior genetic qualities for such a characteristic as meat production can manifest the advantage. When Bakewell commenced his breeding work he was in a position to distinguish outstanding animals for his foundation, whereas a century earlier stock of similar genetic quality might have passed unnoticed. Later when we consider the impact of nutrition on the development of the carcass animal the force of this point will be more deeply appreciated.

Some idea of the extent of the changes which occurred in carcass animals as a result of improvements in breeding and nutrition can be derived from the following figures quoted by Ernle (1936). In

Plate 3: No Sight in Farming is More Satisfying than a Yard Full of Good Cattle

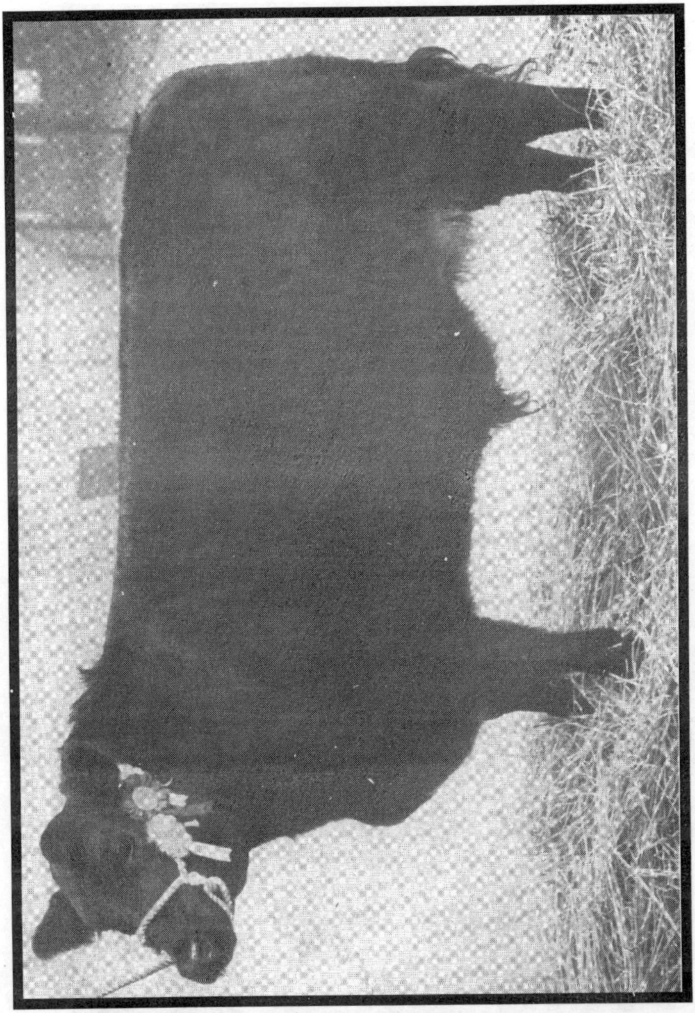

Plate 4: A Modern Smithfield Winner

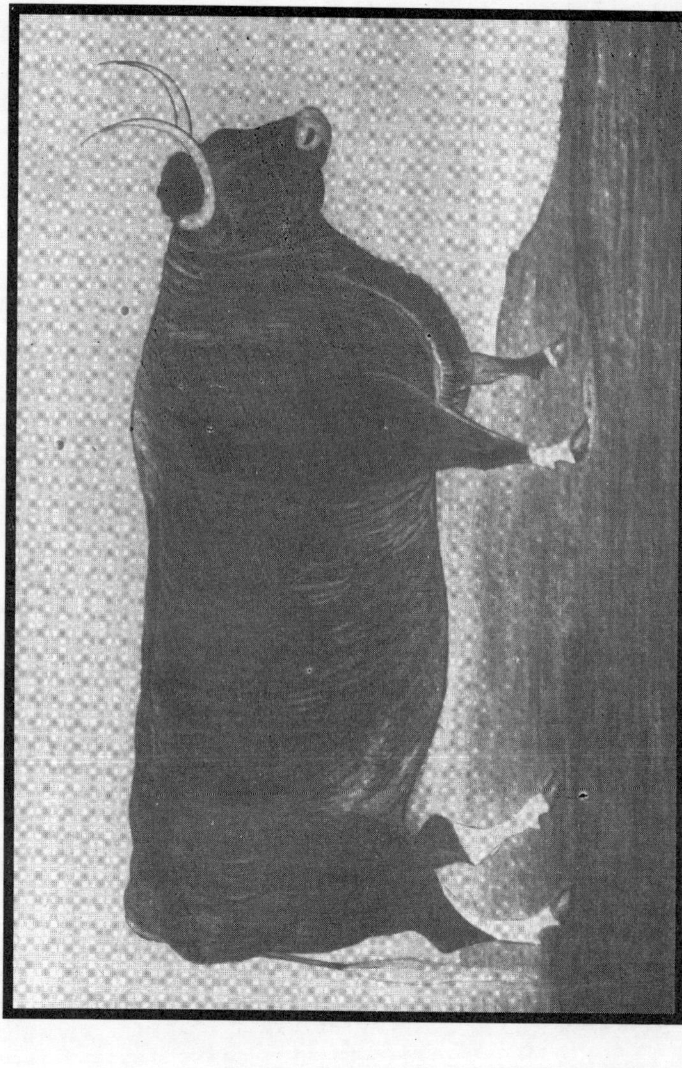

Plate 5: The 2-ton Bullock is a Curiosity Today

1710 the average weight of beef cattle sold in Smithfield market was 370 lb., while calves averaged 50 lb., sheep 28 lb. and lambs 18 lb. In 1795 beef cattle had risen to an average of 800 lb., calves to 148 lb., sheep to 80 lb. and lambs to 50 lb[1]. Figures given for animal production over this period are sometimes unreliable, possibly because weights and measures were not sufficiently standardised, but even allowing for possible extravagances in the above estimates, it seems abundantly clear that the eighteenth century witnessed remarkable changes in the production of meat animals.

The Raw Materials of Breed Development

By 1760 there were quite substantial differences in the cattle stocks of Britain, and though they could not be sub-divided into breed groups as we know them today, they could be recognised as local cattle tribes. The general characteristics of these tribes, in a large measure, could be accounted for by the various invasions of Britain and the cattle which the succession of invaders introduced. These have been described in some detail by Wilson (1921). The Britons had a small light-bodied type of cattle, generally black in colour, which was known as the Celtic Shorthorn. It was too small a breed for the heavy draught duties of a military occupation, and the Romans introduced a heavy breed of their own, which Wilson (1909) described as white with black points, and wavy upturned horns. In all probability these introductions were not unlike the draught cattle one sees in Italy today. Wilson suggests that these Roman cattle, mated with the Celtic Shorthorns, were the progenitors of the White Park Cattle now preserved in a few herds. It is believed, however, that the main survivals of the Celtic Shorthorn are to be found in the Welsh, Kerry and Highland breeds.

The next cattle invaders were those which the Anglo-Saxons introduced, and it is probable that the red colour of many British cattle comes from this source. Little is known of these, but they were probably a larger type than the Celtic Shorthorn, and had been used for draught purposes in their country of origin. Then came the Norsemen with their cattle which were small, short-legged, narrow-backed, big-bellied creatures, with scythe-shaped hind legs, usually light dun in colour, and hornless. It is believed that they are

---

[1] Presumably these are dressed weight figures, but the authority Ernle quotes does not make this clear.

responsible for the polled character of the Galloway, Aberdeen Angus and Red Poll, three breeds which originated in areas occupied by Norse invaders. Breeders of polled cattle today will acknowledge only the polled character of the above rather unattractive foundation.

The fourth invasion was a peaceful one during the latter part of the seventeenth century by Dutch cattle which, even in the days of Caesar, were noted for their milking qualities. Probably they were introduced by Royalist landowners who, during their exile in the Low Countries at the time of the Commonwealth, recognised the merit of Dutch cattle and their suitability for the improved conditions of British agriculture. It is practically certain that these Dutch cattle contributed to the Holderness and Teeswater cattle from which the Shorthorn breed has been developed. It is probable, too, that the broken colour of some British breeds has been derived from these imported Dutch cattle, and undoubtedly they have contributed in a large measure to the milking propensities of the Shorthorn and Ayrshire breeds.

This completes the list of sources from which British cattle breeds have been derived. We can picture the existence in the early eighteenth century of local cattle tribes with certain superficial characteristics attributable to their original foundation. Of genetic variation there would be plenty, though the inherent variability of cattle in respect of such economic considerations as milk and meat production would be masked by the levelling effect of an inferior environment. The situation then, in many respects, may be compared with that obtaining today in countries with unimproved native stocks where forces of agricultural progress are beginning to take effect.

We cannot, however, regard Bakewell as the complete pioneer. Kelley (1946), for instance, mentions that methods of inbreeding which Bakewell adopted had been used prior to 1760 by the breeders of thoroughbred horses and of English gamecocks, while already in certain districts local cattle races had developed reputations for milk or meat production. Notable among these were the Teeswater and the Holderness cattle, the former because of their milking qualities and the latter because of their fleshing qualities.

Bakewell's Methods

The salient features of Bakewell's methods of breeding about which he was very reticent, probably deliberately because he did not wish to share trade secrets or perhaps to disclose that he was adopting incestuous breeding, were as follows:

1. Assembly of foundation stock from several sources to introduce genetic variability and to give scope for selection on the basis of new gene combinations.
2. Restriction of ideals in order to speed the progress of selection towards a given goal. Bakewell's goal was carcass quality, *i.e.* quick-maturing beasts with a capacity to fatten and a high killing-out percentage, in contrast to the slab-sided, late-maturing sheep and cattle of his day. (There were complaints that Bakewell bred sheep which were too fat for a gentleman's palate. He replied that he was catering for the working man's needs.)
3. Mating of like to like in the belief they would beget like.
4. The adoption of close inbreeding to fix desired characteristics.
5. Intense selection in an environment in which animals; could give full expression to their inherent qualities. Restricted use of sires and letting them out until such time as he was able to determine whether they were of sufficient breeding merit that they should be returned for service in the herd or flock.

The foregoing is an impressive list, and it has been remarked previously that it embodied certain scientific principles which were not properly established even a century later. What prompted him to adopt inbreeding cannot be established. Perhaps it was a logical outcome of the concept that like will beget like. Perhaps when he bred Twopenny there was no better bull available in the herd, and so he was mated back to his mother (*see* Figure 1), and by a stroke of good fortune the offspring conformed to Bakewell's ideals. It is interesting to conjecture what the present position of British sheep and cattle would have been if failure instead of success had resulted from Bakewell's inbreeding. We can only be grateful that Bakewell was successful to the point with his inbreeding that he was able to inspire the work of the Colling brothers, Booth and the others that followed.

By inbreeding Bakewell isolated his stock from surrounding stock, and in so doing he increased the relationship of his herd to

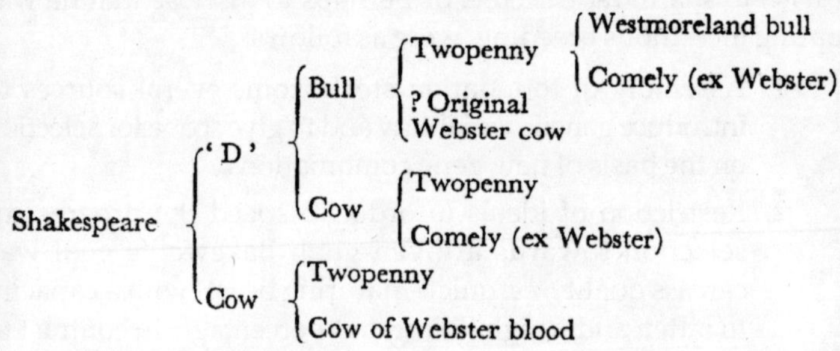

Figure 1: Pedigree of Bull Shakespeare Bred by Fowler, who Used Bakewell's Stock (Kelley, 1946)

outstanding favoured ancestors such as Comely and Twopenny. Because he selected rigidly and because he used the progeny test to ensure that his reduction of genetic variability was consistent with the attainment of his ideals, he established a breed of sheep and a breed of cattle which were consistently different from and superior to the sheep and cattle which surrounded him. The logical outcome of his work was the development of the pedigree concept, *i.e.* the identification of animals by their parentage. He created a nucleus of superior identified animals which were capable, because of the effectiveness of his selection and the reduction in heterozygosily, of improving the stock on which they were used. Possibly their merit as improvers was due to hybrid vigour.

The Development of Shorthorns

The bull Shakespeare (*see* Figure 1), according to Marshall (1784), was 'the best stock-getter the Midland district ever knew.' Unfortunately the Longhorn, because of its poor milking qualities, no doubt a result of the single-purpose nature of Bakewell's selection, and because of its spread of horns, did not rise to eminence as a British breed, Bakewell, however, had followers who were working with other localised cattle groups, and perhaps the most notable of these were the brothers Charles and Robert Colling who commenced farming on their own account in 1782 when Bakewell was approaching the zenith of his fame, and when visitors from all over Britain and Europe were coming to see his farm and his livestock. In

1783 Charles Colling joined these visitors, and spent some considerable period with Bakewell, whose confidence he must have won, for the imprint of Bakewell's methods is firmly impressed on those adopted by the Collings. They too began with the best stock they could find, but apparently they did not subscribe to the like-begets-like theory, for there is evidence of contrasting types in the foundation stock. Kelley (1946) records the following descriptions of stock which appear in the ancestry of Favourite (*see* Figure 2), the most famous of the bulls which Charles Colling bred:

Hubback	A small neat early fleshing bull
Haughton	A neat fine cow the reverse of R. Barker's bull
R. Barker's Bull	A large, coarse, wire-haired beast with a large head, dark horns and a black nose. His dam a big coarse cow
Lady Maynard	The beautiful Lady Maynard
Dalton's Duke	Brindle and coarse
Foljambe	A useful thick beast, good handle, dark face
Phoenix	Handling particularly soft and mellow in appearance, the reverse of her dam, the beautiful Lady Maynard
Bolingbroke	Remarkable inclination to fatten, handsome hind quarters, fine head and muzzle
Favourite	Large massive animal of good constitution, had remarkably good loins and long level hind quarters

Favourite
- **Bolingbroke**
  - **Foljambe**
    - **Richard Barker's Bull**
    - **Haughton by Hubback**
  - **Young Strawberry**
    - **Dalton's Duke**
    - **Lady Maynard**
- **Phoenix**
  - **Foljambe**
  - **Lady Maynard**

Figure 2: Pedigree of Favourite bred by Charles Colling (Kelley, 1946)

We see in this pedigree and description definite evidence of the heterogeneity of the foundation stock of the Shorthorn breed and of the system of compensatory matings which the Collings adopted. Evidently they were trying to combine the neatness and early maturity of such animals as Hubback and Lady Maynard with the substance of Dalton's Duke and Richard Barker's bull. They appear to have succeeded, for Bolingbroke retains a propensity to fatten and Phoenix has good handling qualities, while Favourite seems to have approached their ideal because this bull was used very widely in the herd. Figure 3 shows just how intensively the Collings inbred to him, and shows how in one major respect at least they subscribed to their master's precepts. The bull Cecil has a 75 per cent blood relationship to Favourite, and this represents an intensity of inbreeding which is not normally encountered in modern stud breeding. Favourite himself was inbred, being a double grandson of Foljambe. The greatest tribute which could be paid to the bull was the degree to which they endeavoured to intensify relationship to him.

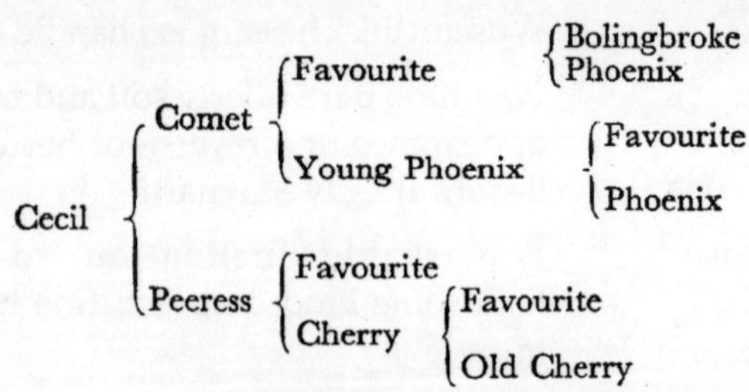

Figure 3: The Collings' intensive use of the bull Favourite (Kelley, 1946)

The next great name in Shorthorns is that of Thomas Booth, who used Teeswater foundation cows and from 1790 onwards employed Colling-bred bulls. The Booth herd was maintained for 105 years through three generations of the family, and it affords one of the best examples of herd continuity to be found in stud breeding. It contrasts strongly with the average duration of modern pedigree Shorthorn herds which Donald and El Itriby (1946) state to be 14.3 years. A contemporary of the Booths was Thomas Bates of Kirklevington, who somewhere prior to 1810 bought the first Duchess from the Collings. In 1816 he bought her daughter at the Collings' dispersal sale, and with these two animals as a basis he developed some of the most intense inbreeding that the British pedigree industry has seen. Wright (1923) states that the average degree of relationship between members of the Duchess family was 60 per cent, which is somewhat higher than the 50 per cent of ordinary full brother and sister. The average intensity of inbreeding was equivalent to two generations of brother-sister matings.

Bates's objectives contrasted with those of the Booths. 'Boots for the butcher and Bates for the pail' summarises the differing ends of the two breeding groups. Bates endeavoured to maintain the dual-purpose function of the Shorthorn, while the Booths made carcass quality a primary consideration. This divergence of endeavours has a very, important significance in the evolution of the Shorthorn breed. The Booths catered for the earliest developing demand, namely animals capable of making rapid and economical live-weight gains, while Bates met the requirements of a growing body of farmers who produced both milk and meat. Over the 150 years which have elapsed since the first Booth commenced breeding, the demands on British cattle have evolved gradually from the Bakewell ideal through to the Bates ideal and beyond to the single-purpose ideal of the specialised dairy-cow. Currently, we see the progress of this evolution in the rapidly increasing importance of the Friesian and Ayrshire in the national herd. In maintaining the milking propensities of Shorthorns, Bates, and those who adopted his aims in selection, rendered a signal service to the breed, for they, retained within the pedigree group sufficient genetic flexibility for it to be moulded in accordance with the changing demands of British farming.

If everyone had subscribed to the Booths' plan and had practised inbreeding and selection aimed at fixing fleshing characteristics, inevitably genes for milk production would have been lost to the breed. As it happened, both Booth and Bates cattle were registered in the same herd book, first published by Coates in 1822, and it was possible for subsequent breeders to secure genetic variability within their herds by fusion of the distinct strains without losing 'breed purity.' Both dairy and beef type Shorthorns have continued to be registered in Coates's *Herd Book*.

The next great figure in the evolution of the Shorthorn breed was a Scot, Amos Cruickshank of Sittyton. Fortunately Cruickshank, when he established his herd from 1837 onwards, did not subscribe to the current craze for animals of pure pedigree, *i.e.* tracing back through fashionable lines to the breed's foundation. He bought from many sources cattle which individually conformed to his requirements of ruggedness, good constitution and deep-fleshing, for he was breeding bulls for farmers whose cattle had to make economic gains on oat straw and turnips. Cruickshank returned the breed to the melting pot and restored heterogeneity which had been lost by inbreeding. During the first twenty years of the herd's existence he adopted a policy of wide outcrossing without any regard for family lines, and the criterion in selection and mating was that animals individually conformed to his requirements. New gene combinations were created and the horizons of selection were greatly widened.

In 1858 Cruickshank bought for thirty guineas an eight-year-old bull, Lancaster Comet, which was double grandson of Will Honeycomb, whose description indicates that he was a deep-fleshed low-set bull conforming closely to the modern requirements of a Scottish Shorthorn (Kelley, 1946). The transaction was completed by correspondence, and Cruickshank was so disgusted with the bull's wide spread of horns that he banished him to a remote farm, where he was given a number of cows which had proved difficult to get in calf. The bull was dead before the year was out. So little did Cruickshank value him that he was left out so late in the autumn that he developed rheumatism and had to be destroyed. But he had fulfilled his function in the Sittyton herd, for he sired one of the most outstanding bulls the breed has known, Champion of England, which Cruickshank bred to very intensively in the remaining years of the herd's existence. Champion of England was used for ten consecutive seasons, and many sons and grandsons were used to carry on the line. Cruickshank established firmly what is now known as the Scotch type of Shorthorn, predominantly beef animals, characterised by early maturity and short thick bone with a deep covering of flesh. They have been exported widely, particularly to North America and to the Argentine, where they are considered the improver breed *par excellence*. The Sittyton herd was disposed of in 1889, but its blood lines were carried on notably by William Duthie of Collynie and Deane-Willis of Bapton Manor (Kelley, 1946).

The Aberdeen Angus, Hereford and Other Foundations

The evolution of the Shorthorn breed has been described in some detail, partly because it is the oldest of the British beef breeds, and partly because it illustrates the general policy of mating and selection adopted in respect of the other British breeds. We see this illustrated for the Aberdeen Angus breed in the pedigree presented in Figure 4. Young Jock was bred by Hugh Watson of Keillor, who was the pioneer breeder of Aberdeen Angus cattle. He commenced operations with a selection of black cattle from the multi-coloured stocks of the Angus district. The original Angus cattle varied in colour from duns, reds and brindles to blacks. Some specimens were horned, others were polled. McCombie of Tillyfour who followed with cattle bought from Watson, was so concerned with the appearance of red recessives from the mating of heterozygous black parents that he erected a high wall to cut his breeding stock off from the sight of red cattle. As an added precaution farm buildings were painted black because of the supposed importance of maternal impressions. Though one may regard McCombie's precautions with some scorn in the light of present knowledge, one can only marvel the more that men equipped with so little knowledge of the mechanism of heredity should have achieved so much in the

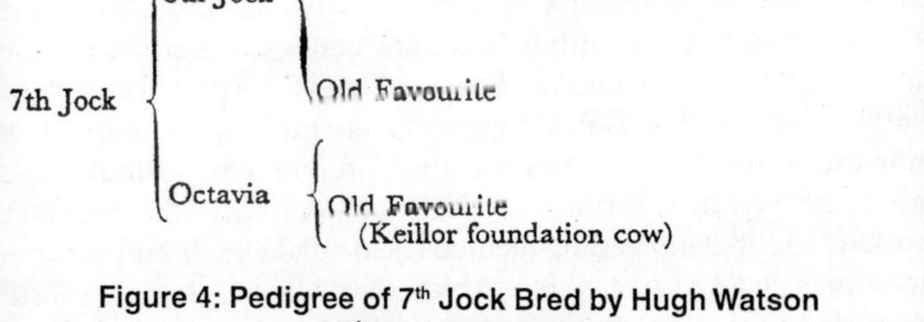

Figure 4: Pedigree of 7th Jock Bred by Hugh Watson of Keillor (Kelley 1946)

amelioration of a primitive local breed. Again, as in the case of the Short-horns, there were several breeders working contemporaneously with animals, some of which were derived from the original Keillor foundation. Again we see the amalgamation of lines isolated by inbreeding to restore flexibility in selection for objectives which were gradually evolving in response to the changing demands on agriculture.

The history of the Hereford reveals another example of a characteristic breed type being evolved from an assortment of foundation cattle, which were probably an admixture of Dutch and Welsh cattle, and possibly animals of a Devon type. The original Herefords in their home district were prized as draught animals, but bullocks, superannuated from the plough, at 5–6 years of age were transferred to the Midland areas for fattening on grass. The movement of Herefords to fattening areas outside the county is therefore a practice of considerable antiquity, and unquestionably this has been an important contributory factor in establishing the reputation of the breed. Similarly, the demand for Scottish cattle for fattening in East Anglia in the eighteenth and nineteenth centuries provided a stimulus for the development of the Aberdeen Angus and the Scotch Shorthorn. In contrast, many breeds which continue to have a limited local importance or which have died out completely, probably have suffered in their development because they were not subjected to the stimulus of outside demand. The Hereford, Shorthorn and the Aberdeen Angus, on the other hand, spread beyond their native borders, and their qualities were remembered by migrating British farmers when they settled in the countries of the New World.

The Hereford differed from the Shorthorn and Aberdeen Angus in that it was essentially a farmer's breed, and there was much more decentralisation of breeding effort in the early formative days of the breed. Though the original breeders generally agreed on the functional attributes of the breed, they differed in respect of the colour characteristic, and so isolated groups were built up in accordance with the individual breeder's colour preferences. Within these groups inbreeding was practised (Kelley, 1946, records that the elder Tomkins adopted inbreeding methods before Bakewell), and so some measure of genetic isolation was achieved. Fortunately breeders were reconciled to the standard Hereford colour pattern around about the middle of the nineteenth century, and so matings between isolated lines could be planned to combine good points and to secure a wider genetic basis for selection without the disadvantages involved in effecting amalgams with strains which had been evolved under widely differing environmental circumstances. The Hewers, Tomkins and Jeffries, the great names in the history of the breed, all aimed to produce a beef animal adapted to fattening on grass. In this important respect the material for the breed's foundation was uniform, and its evolution was expedited through the absence of any need to go outside of the original lines to secure necessary breeding material.

Of the history of other British beef breeds such as the Sussex, the North Devon and the Galloway, much less is known. Their history in the areas where they were evolved is a long and confused one. Primarily they were farmers' breeds, and in this respect they are to be compared with the Hereford rather than the Shorthorn, which became the main breed in the fashionable development of pedigree cattle breeding which was such a feature of British farming in the nineteenth century. The first herd book for the Sussex was published in 1879 and separately for the Galloway in 1877, whereas Shorthorn pedigrees have been published since 1822. The first herd book of the Aberdeen Angus, in which Galloway pedigrees were also included, was published in 1862, and the Herefords' was published for the first time in 1846.

That some of the British breeds have neither the long standing of pedigree of the older breeds nor their international importance can in no sense be interpreted that they are generally inferior. On the contrary, they probably have peculiar adoption qualities which render them particularly valuable for certain conditions of beef production. It is significant that the Galloway, evolved under the hard grazing conditions of south-west Scotland, has recently been exported in considerable numbers to New Zealand because of an expectation that it will be well suited to the task of arresting deterioration of third-class hill country devoted to sheep farming. In the hands of New Zealand stud breeders the Galloway may be evolved even further to meet special local needs in the same way as Romney sheep in that country have been greatly changed from the English type in accordance with differing local demands.

In no sense can one regard the 'type' of any of these breeds being fixed despite the long history of segregation and close breeding which has aimed at confining variation within certain desired limits. Despite the breeders' best efforts sufficient genetic variability has been retained within breeds to permit of progressive evolution of breed types in accordance with the changing demands of farmers. Fifty years ago the requirement of the trade was for large joints. Today the small family unit, accustomed to a much greater variety in food, demands small joints with a limited amount of fat that are derived from early-maturing animals which produce a tender and not very strongly flavoured meat. In order to retain popularity each breed has had to change its basis of selection towards the breeding of the smaller earlier-maturing types. One cannot forecast what the ideal may be in cattle selection in twenty or thirty years' time. Contemporary agriculture sees a changing emphasis in feeding from concentrates to grass and its derivatives. The outcome of this may be an enhanced demand for scavenging types of grassland feeders such as the Sussex, which may yield an important by-product in the form of beef which will be bought eagerly by a public which can no longer afford the luxury of baby beef.

We see another change in the function of the specialised beef breeds in the growing use of their bulls, through artificial insemination, on dairy cows not considered good enough to breed dairy replacements. There seems to be little doubt but that Britain will have to derive much other home-produced beef from the dairy industry, and the bull breeder's aim may be primarily one of providing sires which will correct effectively the legginess and leanness of the specialised dairy breeds, very much in the same manner as Down rams are used to correct the carcass deficiencies of hill-country sheep whose main virtue is that of surviving on scanty grazing. When we admire the perfection of a Smithfield winner we cannot assume that we have witnessed the acme of perfection in breeding, and that the breeders' efforts are merely to be directed towards the uniform attainment of such a type. Changing of standards is one of the most permanent characteristics of farming, and in no branch is this better exemplified than it is in cattle breeding.

Chapter 3
Breeding: Variation and Its Basis

In Chapter 2 an account was given of the evolution of modern breeds from nondescript types. The achievements of the pioneer breeders are even more remarkable when one remembers that genetics, the science which explains hereditary differences, is one of the newer branches of learning. The practice of breeding has been far in advance of its theoretical concepts for nearly two hundred years, and even today the practising geneticist can offer little in the way of advice in planning a breeding programme, beyond that which Bakewell would have given to one of his favoured students. It is true that many fallacies, such as maternal impressions, telegony and the like, have been exploded, and that there is some explanation for the mode of transmission of characteristics, while it is now possible to forecast what will happen in a number of simple genetic situations, but the most that a breeder can expect from genetics, at our present stage of knowledge, is some understanding of the complexities and difficulties of his problem of breeding, and some guidance on the mating and selection methods he should adopt.

THE MECHANISM OF INHERITANCE

In order to understand the mechanism of inheritance it is necessary to know something of the structure of the cells of the animal body. Each body cell has a nucleus, and within this nucleus there is material known as chromatin, because of the dark appearance it takes when it is stained for examination under the microscope. Normally the chromatin exists as a tangled mass, but just before a cell divides, in the course of growth, the chromatin is broken up into a number of paired rods known as chromosomes. The number of chromosomes is characteristic for each species l of plant or animal. Pigs, for instance, have 19 pairs of chromosomes (Krallinger, 1936), while cattie are believed to have 30 pairs (Krallinger, 1931). At cell division each member of a pair of chromosomes reproduces itself so that each of the two daughter cells which result from a cell division is provided with exactly the same chromosome make-up as the mother cell. As a result all the cells of the animal body, with a notable exception which will be discussed later, have the same chromosome make-up, which is identical with the chromosome make-up of the original fertilised cell which was the starting-point of the complex adult body.

The chromosomes are important because they carry the hereditary units which, singly or in combination, help to determine the characteristics of a plant or an animal. These hereditary units are known as genes, and it is convenient to think of the chromosomes as 'strings of genes.' It is not necessary for us to deal further with the nature of genes, for it is sufficient for the purposes of this discussion to realise that each makes some contribution to the genetic make-up of an individual.[1]

It was mentioned previously that certain cells do not have the full complement of paired chromosomes. These are the reproductive or germ cells, the spermatozoa produced by the male and the ova produced by the female, which are characterised by a half number of chromosomes. The spermatozoa produced by a bull, for instance, contain only one member of each pair of chromosomes, and therefore has only thirty chromosomes. This situation is brought about in the following way: At cell division, leading to the formation of germ

---

[1] The reader is advised to consult one of the standard textbooks on genetics, such as *Principles of Heredity* by L.H. Snyder (Heath).

cells, instead of each chromosome splitting so that a replicate goes to each daughter cell, one chromosome of each pair goes to a daughter cell. The situation will be clearer if we think of a body cell of only two pairs of chromosomes, A_1 and A_2 and B_1 and B_2. When a germ cell is formed A_1 goes to one cell and A_2 to the other. Similarly B_1 goes to one cell and B_2 to the other. The assortment of the members of two pairs is entirely at random, so that in the resulting germ cells we may find anyone of the following combinations:

$$A_1 B_1, A_1 B_2, A_2 B_1 \text{ or } A_2 B_2$$

This random assortment of chromosomes is one of the primary causes of variation. One can realise the almost unlimited variety of combinations which may be obtained in cattle if they have thirty pairs of chromosomes.[1] This, however, is anticipating another problem in breeding, namely genetic variation.

We are now in a position to discuss the inheritance of contrasted characters such as black and red colour in cattle. If we postulate a pair of genes which control the appearance of the two colours we can define a true-breeding black as one that carries a factor for black on each member of the appropriate pair of chromosomes. When reduction division (*i.e.*, at the formation of germ cells) takes place, each germ cell will always have a chromosome which carries a gene for black. In the case of the impure blacks, *i.e.*, blacks which will occasionally produce red calves, one of the chromosome in the appropriate pair carries a gene for black while its mate carries the alternative gene for red. Because, the black gene has the power to dominate the red gene, the animal with the mixed gene pairs is black in appearance and is indistinguishable except by breeding performance from a true-breeding black. Half of the germ cells it produces will carry the gene for black colour, and the other half will be lacking this gene which is replaced by one determining red colouration. When impure blacks are mated together there is a possibility that a proportion of the offspring will receive no black factor from either parent, and will therefore be red in colour.

The situation is illustrated in Figure 5. In the first instance a true-breeding black bull and a true-breeding red cow are mated together. The black bull produces spermatazoa, which always carry

[1] The number of combinations is 2^{30}.

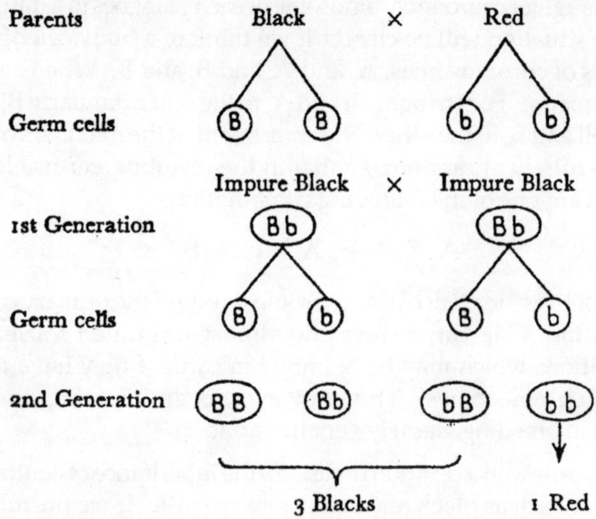

Figure 5: Inheritance of Red and Black in Cattle

the black gene, while all ova produced by the red cow carry the red gene. Union of such germ cells gives a combination Bb, which results in a black animal because of the dominance of black. If one mates such hybrids they will produce germ cells of two kinds, and it is seen that there is one chance in four that a red animal will appear, and three chances in four that a black animal will be the product of mating. Only one of these three blacks on an average will be true-breeding (BB).

Dominance in some respects makes breeding much more difficult in that it tends to confuse the genetic picture. Animals may look alike or behave in a similar way, but their cargo of genes and hence their power to pass on desirable characteristics to their offspring may be vastly different. In other respects dominance may be a decided advantage, *e.g.*, horned is recessive to polled in cattle. A true-breeding polled bull (PP) mated to a horned (pp) herd will effect a desired absence of horns in the next generation, but it will not of course eliminate the horned factor, for this will still be carried by all first-cross beasts (PP). If ever they are mated to a bull with a similar make-up there will inevitably be a proportion of horned calves.

It must not be imagined, however, that all character pairs exhibit dominance or recessiveness. In Shorthorn cattle, for instance, when whites and reds are mated invariably we get roans which have a mosaic of red and white hairs. Here an intermediate type is secured. When roans are interbred we get segregation into reds, roans and whites generally in a 1 : 2 : 1 ratio. The inheritance of colour in Shorthorn cattle is not quite as simple as it was first thought to be (Shrode and Lush, 1947), and there are some exceptions to the above rule, but it can be taken for our present purposes that roan is an intermediate expression of a gene combination involving factors for the contrasted colours red and white. The Blue Andalusian fowl is another example of intermediate expression. Blue Andalusians carry a gene for black and a gene for white, and when bred together in sufficient numbers a ratio of 1 black : 2 blues : 1 white will be obtained. It is impossible, therefore, to fix a true-breeding Blue Andalusian.

Inheritance of Two Characters

We will now consider two pairs of contrasted characters of which are inherited independently, *i.e.* characters which are determined by pairs of genes carried on different chromosomes. A suitable example is provided by the Hereford colour pattern, which is dominant to plain, and polled which is dominant to horned. If we mate a Hereford bull to Red Poll cows, all the offspring of the first generation will be polled with the Hereford colour pattern. Mating these hybrids together we get segregation of all the possible combinations in the ratio of 9 Hereford-polled : 3 plain-polled : 3 Hereford-horned : 1 plain-horned. This ratio is the mathematical expectation. It will not be achieved except where there are very large numbers to iron out freak possibilities. The explanation for this is as follows: The Hereford parent may be represented by HH pp and the Red Poll by hh PP. Both parents are true-breeding for the characters in question, and genetically they are said to be *homozygous* because each produces only the one sort of germ cell in respect of these characters. In the case of the Hereford it is Hp, and in the case of the Red Poll it is hP. The resulting hybrid must always have the combination Hh Pp. These are impure for both characters, and so they are said to be *heterozygous*. When these hybrids produce germ cells there are equal chances of anyone of the four following types being produced:

HP, hP, Hp and hp

When conception is effected there are equal chances of these different types of germ cells combining together in the manner illustrated by the 'checker board' shown in Figure 6. There are sixteen possible ways the germ cells can unite, and gene combinations when hybrids (Hh Pp) are mated together can range from HH PP to hh pp. In nine cases there is an H and a P present, and in such instances the resulting animals will be polled and Hereford patterned like their parents. In only one instance (HH PP) will the animal be true breeding for both these two characters. The factor P is present in three combinations with the double recessive hh. In one of these we have the combination (PP hh), and here we have an example of a true-breeding (homozygous) polled plain which takes us back to the Red Poll parent. It would not be true to say, however, that we had secured a pure-bred Red Poll once again, because this animal is bound to have many other genes, apart from those we are considering, which have been derived from its Hereford grandparent. Similarly, there are three chances in sixteen of animals carrying pp in combination with H. In one instance (pp HH) the animal resulting is true breeding for the horned and Hereford combination. Again we cannot say that this is a pure-bred Hereford, for other characteristics dependent on genes derived from the Red Poll grandparent will be expressed in this animal. Finally, there is one chance in sixteen of obtaining the double recessive (pp hh) which is a true-breeding horned and plain red animal. We have, in fact, obtained an entirely new character combination which was not apparent in the polled-Hereford hybrids of the first generation.

Genes	HP	Hp	hP	hp
HP	HH PP	HH Pp	Hh PP	Hh Pp
Hp	HH Pp	HH pp	Hh Pp	Hh pp
hP	Hh PP	Hh Pp	hh PP	hh Pp
hp	Hh Pp	Hh pp	hh Pp	hh pp

Figure 6: Diagram Illustrating Possible Gene Combinations when Hybrids (Hh Pp) are Mated

The above example provides another illustration of the source of genetic variation in livestock. If we breed from crossbreds differing in respect of only two simply inherited characters it is possible to get nine different gene combinations (genotypes) as follows:

PP HH, Pp HH, pp HH, PP Hh, PP hh, Pp Hh, pp Hh,
Pp hh and pp hh

Only four of these genotypes are true-breeding, and the balance are likely to give rise after appropriate matings to animals with characters not expressed in their parents.

Though one does not advise mating of crossbreds, nevertheless cross-breeding has been an important element in the moulding of new breeds. For example, the New Zealand stud-master Little, who was largely responsible for the evolution of the Corriedale breed of sheep combined certain qualities of the fine-wooled Merino with those of English Longwools, notably the Lincoln. It took many sheep generations and much rigid selection to eliminate unwanted variation due to new combinations, but today the Corriedale breeds as true to type as most of the recognised pure breeds of sheep. More recently America has provided us with two examples of new breeds of pigs, the Minnesota No. 1 and the Minnesota No. 2, which in each instance are amalgams of two existing breeds. The Santa Gertrudis, which is described in Chapter 6, is an example of a breed of cattle which has been evolved from British and Zebu types to suit sub-tropical conditions in the southern United States.

Three Character Combinations

The degree of genetic variation increases as we bring extra characters into our considerations. For instance, if we mate an Aberdeen Angus bull with Hereford cows we are able to consider another pair of characters in addition to horned and polled and Hereford and plain. This is black and red. The first cross would be as follows:

Hereford × Aberdeen Angus
(HH pp bb) ↓ (hh PP BB)
Hh Pp Bb

The three dominant characters Hereford, polled and black will all be expressed in the hybrids. The hybrids, in turn, are capable of producing eight different kinds of germ cells–HPB, HPb, HpB, hPH, Hpb, hPb, hpB and hpb. Combination of germ cells from males and females is at random, and so the genotype of the second generation can range through all possible combinations from HH PP BB to hhpp bb. The expected ratio of the combinations is:

27 black – Hereford – polled

9 red – Hereford – polled

9 black – plain – polled

9 black – Hereford – horned

3 black – plain – horned

3 red – Hereford – horned

3 red – plain – polled

1 red – plain – horned

There are 27 distinct genotypes in the above combinations, but only eight of these–(HH PP BB), (HH pp BB), (hh PP BB), (HH PP bb), (hh pp BB), (hh PP bb), (HH pp bb) and (hh pp bb)–are true-breeding in respect of three of the alternatives of the character pairs.

We will not proceed much further with these multiple character combinations because the situation becomes more and more complex. If, for instance, we were dealing with twenty pairs of contrasted characteristics, each independently inherited and each set of character alternatives dependent for expression on the presence of only one pair of genes, we would have 3^{20} different genotypes of which 2^{20} would be true-breeding combinations. Multiplied out, these figures become 3,486,784,401 and 1,048,566 respectively. Breeders of beef cattle would be very fortunate indeed if the animals with which they were working differed in respect of only twenty pairs of genes. The probability is that many more gene combinations are involved–just how many no-one may even hazard a guess. It is not surprising in these circumstances that the attainment of perfection is such an elusive goal.

Multifactorial Inheritance

So far we have considered situations where each pair of genes has been responsible for the expression of one alternative of a pair of contrasted characters. There are many characteristics, however, whose expression is dependent not on a single pair of genes but on a number of genes which act in concert, *i.e.* in an additive fashion to give continuous variation. Most of the important economic characteristics such as longevity, fertility, fleshing capacity and so on are believed to be influenced by the action of many genes, which each make a contribution to the total heredity of the animal in respect of the characteristic in question. For instance, milk production in a cow is dependent on many factors such as ability to ingest and digest food, the rate of flow of blood through the udder, the concentration of milk precursors in the blood stream and the individuality of the mammary gland. It is inconceivable that only a few pairs of genes determine the ceiling in respect of all attributes contributing to milk yield. Similarly, with fleshing qualities we encounter not a simple but a very complex genetic situation.

One may illustrate multifactorial inheritance by a classical study of inheritance in colour of wheat carried out by Nilsson-Ehle, a Swedish geneticist about thirty years ago. 1n the colour alternatives red and white in grain he found by appropriate breeding that three pairs of factors were involved. True-breeding red wheat may be labelled RR SS TT, while true-breeding white wheat may be labelled rr ss tt. When red and white are crossed we get grain intermediate in colour between that of the parental types for which the following genotype may be written: Rr Ss Tt. When this hybrid wheat produces another generation there is almost continuous variation from the extremes of the two original parental types. As in the case of the three independently inherited characters there are 27 distinct genotypes of which only eight are true breeding. Nilsson-Ehle classified the resulting wheats into several colour categories which showed barely perceptible differences from one to the other as one progressed from white to red. If there had been any more genes involved there would have been continuous variation. Within each colour classification he established that there were distinct genotypes. For instance, in his main colour group which he labelled intermediate red, there were seven different genotypes, all of which produced the same colour effect but gave different breeding results.

THE NATURE OF GENETIC MERIT

This example from wheat illustrates a very common problem in breeding–namely that though individuals may look alike or behave in a similar way they may give vastly different breeding results.

Apparent similarity may be due to different genes adding up to the same hereditary result, as in the case of the wheats described above, or it may be due to the modifying influence of environment. Before we go on to discuss this aspect of the problem–the contention that 'half the breeding goes down the throat'–it is necessary to have a better understanding of what constitutes genetic merit.

Most breeders of livestock are familiar with the outstanding merit of first-cross animals. There are numerous examples of how the virtues of the first cross are exploited in animal production–Down-cross fat lambs, the famous blue-grey-cattle which are the product of a white Shorthorn bull on Galloway or Aberdeen Angus cow, and numerous first crosses in poultry which exhibit those most important attributes, a capacity to live and to lay a large number of eggs. These first crosses exhibit what is known as hybrid vigour, the exact nature of which is not understood. Many theories have been advanced concerning its manifestation, but none are completely satisfying. The breeder can only accept it as a phenomenon of very great importance in the first generation, but he can do nothing to maintain it in the second generation when the hybrids are bred together. At this point not only do we get segregation out into the extreme parental types, but also we get new combinations of genes which result in some individuals that are undesirable and relatively worthless.

The complete outcross within a breed also often results in animals of very high quality in respect of their own performance, but when it comes to breeding they often prove very disappointing. The author at the present time has a considerable head of poultry under progeny test. Some cockerels when mated to certain hens produce a family of full sisters which are outstandingly good. Under ordinary field conditions an unselected sample of ten daughters submitted to a laying test may all survive and produce an average of 180 eggs or more before they are 17 months old. In other instances the same cock mated to other hens of similar breeding may produce families where the sample of daughters shows a high casualty rate, and those that survive may not average 150 eggs apiece by the time they reach 17 months. Now it cannot be accepted that because certain hen families are of outstanding quality in respect of their own production, they will be outstanding breeders. This breeding work is partly designed to test the efficiency of hen family selection as an aid to improving the merit of a flock, but it is quite conceivable that some of the merit in a hen family is due to something which may be explained in terms of hybrid vigour.

In other words, it is quite possible that it is not just the number of genes or the magnitude of each gene's influence that matters in inheritance, for there may be a question of gene combinations. The point can be illustrated by comparisons with various games of cards. Poker players will know that a run of five cards all of the same suit is a very powerful betting hand. If we were to take three cards at random from a hand that was all diamonds running from the five to the nine and combine them with two cards drawn from another hand which had a run of spades from ten to the ace, we would get a hand that did not even have a pair of deuces to grace it. Perhaps it is rather far-fetched to liken gene combinations to fortuitous card combinations which make a hand very valuable, but often the behaviour of succeeding generations in comparison with their parents can quite plausibly be explained on such grounds. On the other hand, gene action in respect of some characters may be more akin to the action of high- ranking cards such as aces and kings in games like whist or bridge. One cannot go very far with a collection of twos and threes in these games. If we have two very good bridge hands and take a half sample from each and combine them, the chances are that we will get a better than average hand. Similarly, if we mate an outstanding ram in respect of wool production with ewes of the same calibre we will generally get offspring which are above the breed average in this respect. However, they will not be as much in advance of the average of the breed as one might expect, for we are up against what geneticists call 'regression to the mean.' It is estimated that with Romney Marsh sheep, mating of rams and ewes with fleece weights–a readily measurable character–4 lb. above the breed average will result in offspring only ¼ lb. higher in production than the average of the breed (McMeekan, 1943). This falling back to the average may be due partly to fortuitous gene combinations not being reproduced in the next generation. The outstanding sires and dams, judged on their own wool production, are our better hands at poker, and have therefore been favoured by good fortune in their hand-out of genes, but they are relatively inefficient in transmitting their superior qualities. On the other hand, the fact that they have offspring appreciably better than the average indicates that additive effects have some importance, *i.e.* that they have some aces and kings in their make-up.

The Masking Effects of Environment

It is appropriate at this stage to discuss the manner in which environment can mask genetic expression, for undoubtedly environment is a very important factor in determining regression to the mean. Why were the parent sheep referred to in the previous section 4 lb. better than the breed average? The chances are that their advantage was only partly the result of a superior genetic make-up. Give a sheep every gene that matters for wool production and cut off its food supply for a few days, and all its promise will be for naught. Naturally one does not starve a sheep to death and then expect it to produce wool, but less drastic environmental influences can have a profound effect on subsequent; productivity. Henderson (1950) has shown that lambs reared on a low plane of nutrition at twelve months of age produced only half the wool that was produced by their half-sisters which had been given all the food they could eat. These sheep, subsequently all on the same favourable plane of nutrition, are retaining marked differences in size and conformation. The individuality of the low-plane ewes apparently has been affected for life. In an ordinary flock individuals are subjected to all sorts of ups and downs. The fact that a lamb was a twin and not a single, that it suffered from worms or lameness at a critical stage may mark it down as a wool producer for the rest of its life. The dairy cow that gives much more milk than its herd mates may have relatively little in the way of genetic superiority, but it may have been grown without check, it may have dodged such bullets as acetonaemia or mastitis, it may have calved at the right time of the year, and it may have been the favourite of the dairyman, who was inclined to be just that bit more liberal with her at ration time. The chances are that her daughter is not going to inherit all this good luck. Because a man wins a football pool, this does not mean that his son is likely to be more successful than the son of an unlucky neighbour. When one views a collection of beef bulls lined up before the judge can one say that the best-balanced and deepest-fleshed bull would have been awarded the championship over the meanest looking if the herdsmen attending the two bulls had been reversed? Pedigree breeding abounds with examples of parents whose own performances were mediocre, but which have produced high-quality offspring, and the converse also holds.

A failure to recognise that environment plays such an important part in determining excellence in an individual has been responsible for more disappointments in breeding than perhaps any other cause. Though genetic make-up puts a ceiling on the possibilities of an animal, its actual performance is limited by environment which comprises feeding, management, freedom from disease and so on, Some very good animals pass unrecognised because they do not have a chance to develop. Conversely, mediocre animals are given such a. good chance, either deliberately or accidentally, that they appear to be so much better than their contemporaries which are more highly endowed genetically. It is true, however, that one cannot make a silk purse out of a sow's ear. For an animal to appear good it must have the right genetic make-up, but, because of gene, interactions this does not necessarily mean that it will consistently produce offspring with these characteristics.

Chapter 4
Selection

PHENOTYPIC AND GENOTYPIC SELECTION

In Chapter 3 use has been made of the expression 'genotype' to describe the genetic make-up of an animal in respect of a particular characteristic. For instance, a bull which begets only polled calves even when mated to horned cows has the genotype PP. Another polled bull which sires a proportion of horned calves has the genotype Pp. Such bulls in appearances are indistinguishable, but their different genetic make-ups are revealed by their progeny. They are said to have the same phenotype–a term used to describe the appearance or the performance of an animal. Its value is an expression not only of the genes which the animal has received from its parents, but of its environment as well. In cattle we occasionally encounter identical twins which have arisen through the cleavage of a fertilised ovum, and the subsequent development of two individuals which have precisely the same genetic make-up. They differ from the more common fraternal twins which develop from two ova which have been fertilised by two different spermatozoa. Both the ova and spermatozoa involved individually have different sample halves of their parents, genotypes, and, genetically, fraternal twins are no more alike than brothers or sisters born at different times. Though identical twins start off in life with the same inheritance, they can develop very differently according to the circumstances of their nutrition, management and exposure to risks of infections. One identical twin may achieve 10 cwt. at two years, while its mate is only 7 cwt. Their phenotypes so far as growth is concerned are very different but they have the same genotypes.

Conversely, one can have animals of equal productivity and yet their breeding performances are not comparable. A breeder looking through a line of yearling heifers may make certain decisions as to which he will retain for entry into the breeding herd. He judges them on the criteria of size in relation to age, depth of flesh, body proportions and breed type, and discards as many as he can of those which do not come up to his standards of excellence. He hopes that by such rigid selection he will improve the quality of his herd. It is true that he may succeed, provided he has enough scope for his selection, in securing a uniform line of females which will be attractive to look at, but he will still find that in the next generation of calves there will be the usual proportion which are disappointing. Quite possibly if he had taken his cast-out heifers and bred from them he would have had very few more disappointments and a lot of welcome surprises. Many famous herds and flocks have been built up on a foundation of discards by established breeders. In dairy cattle, where there is a more precise measurement of performance because of milk recording than one finds in beef cattle, where assessment of quality is rather more subjective, there are numerous examples of how selection on phenotype can be misleading. Very often the best daughters a bull has come from his low-producing mates and vice versa. This does not mean, however, that selection on phenotype is valueless, but simply that it does not give the results that one fondly hopes for. Various investigations in several parts of the world have shown that only 25 to 30 per cent of the apparent superiority, or inferiority, of a dam in respect of milk production is due to additive genetic factors. If a bull is mated to two groups of dams which differ by 400 gallons in production, the expectation, if the whole of this superiority were inherited, would be daughter groups differing by 200 gallons. In actual fact, the difference would be closer to 50–60 gallons, *i.e.* 25–30 per cent of 200 gallons. High-producing cows, it has already been pointed out, are generally very fortunate cows in respect of environment. Furthermore, their merit may in part be due to favourable gene combinations which are not reproducible (our poker hand analogy), and so we get this regression to the mean. That regression is not complete is an indication that additive gene effects (our aces and kings) are also important, but the progressive breeder of dairy cattle finds that he has to adopt other criteria than the milk backing of his stock to determine whether parents are transmitting these factors in an appreciable degree. This in effect means progeny and testing or, more pedantically, genotypic selection.

Heritability or Strength of Inheritance

This fraction, 25–30 per cent, is a measure of the heritability or strength of inheritance of milk production. It is a measure of the differences between dams that can be attributed to heredity, and will be reflected in the next generation, *provided the same sort of environment is maintained*. To the breeder of dairy cattle it is a figure of considerable practical importance because it gives an estimate of how much progress can be expected from selection based on productivity of dams. Estimates of heritability for many characteristics of livestock have now been made by research workers all over the world, particularly in the United States, from which country the following figures relating to heritability of various characteristics of beef cattle have been obtained (Knapp and Clark).

Birth weight	53 per cent
Weaning weight (age corrected)	28 per cent
Final feeding weight (15 months)	86 per cent
Gain during feeding	65 per cent
Weaning score	28 per cent
Slaughter grade	45 per cent
Carcass grade	33 per cent
Area of eye muscle	68 per cent.

These estimates were made at the U.S. Range Livestock Experiment Station in Montana, which maintains over 1,300 pure-bred Herefords. Every year a number of bulls are mated to 25–30 females, and careful records are kept of the produce of these matings. Eight steer calves, selected at random from each sire's get, are fed in record-of-performance trials to standard ages. The heritability figures given above are derived from the correlations between the performances of half-brothers in the groups. If the half-brothers resemble one another very strongly as they do in respect of final weight after feeding, then there is a high heritability figure–in this instance 86 per cent.

What do these figures mean to the breeder, and what use can he make of them? Final feeding weight at a given age, following a standard system of feeding, is a characteristic which will respond to phenotypic selection because it is strongly inherited. If we are particularly interested in securing stock which reach heavy weights at an early age, we shall make very good progress by selecting parents which display this characteristic to a marked degree. This is exactly what the Montana workers are doing. Each year they keep, 40–50 selected bull calves, which are prospects for progeny testing, under standard feeding conditions for a period of 196 days from weaning. The 12–15 heaviest bulls which have shown the highest rate of gain are then checked for conformation points, and those that pass this inspection will go on to progeny testing. In this way the most worthwhile prospects are sorted out for the expensive progeny test, which provides the only reasonably certain means of determining the sires which have a good transmission performance in respect of weakly inherited characters such as weaning weight (28 per cent), which is very dependent on the milking capacity of the dam and carcass grade (33 per cent).

The measure of success which the Montana Station has achieved by these methods of selection is illustrated by the following figures in respect of one of their lines. Over the period 1936–40 the offspring of the foundation bulls averaged daily gains of 1.75–2.0 lb. during feeding. Three generations later in 1950 the rate of gain of steers varied from 2.0 to 2–4 lb. daily.

It will be noted that weaning score has a relatively low heritability at 28 per cent. This assessment is made by three competent judges who score animals independently and their results are combined. The assessment is the usual one in beef stock judging, and points are given for such characters as width and depth of chest, thickness of flesh, smoothness, thickness over the loin, straightness of back, character of head, balance and symmetry and so on. This substantially is the only method by which beef cattle are assessed for breeding in most countries and particularly in Britain.

We look at a young bull and he passes muster on conformation, and we accept him as half the breeding herd. These Montana results, however, show that in respect of conformation as a whole we need not expect like to beget like in anything like the degree which we would hope. Here we have a character not unlike milk production in its strength of inheritance. We are reminded that progressive breeders of dairy cattle who have been disappointed so often by impressive milk records-in the near ancestors of their annual intake of heifers have had to augment this system of selection with progeny testing. They use all the available information they can in selecting a young sire, buying the son of a proven sire out of a cow, preferably the daughter of a proven sire, which has a high life-time production, but they do not use this new bull intensively until they are assured by a sample of his offspring that he is breeding the way they want a bull to breed. It slows up the rate of turnover of generations, and is very much more complicated than just looking at a bull and his dam, examining his pedigree and making an assessment, but it is the only sure way of determining the genotype of an animal which might make or mar a herd.

One interesting side issue of this Montana work in respect of type score at weaning, based on a judgment of 613 steers by 83 different sires, is that there was no relationship between scores and subsequent rates or economy of gain during feeding (Knapp, 1950). This does not mean that an undesirable animal can be expected to gain more rapidly or more efficiently than the more desirable animal, but that future gains or efficiency of feed utilisation cannot be predicted from usual examination of stock. This is a rather surprising result, as most stockmen hold that type and fattening ability are associated, and so they select wide-muzzled beasts which are deep and thick, have plenty of chest room and a roomy middle, in the expectation that they will be economical feeders. This does not imply, however, that certain type features are not important in influencing the final quality of a carcass.

Progeny Testing

How can a breeder when he is concerned with weakly inherited character avoid being misled by that ephemeral thing we call phenotype and establish some knowledge of the genotype of the animals he uses to produce the next generation? There is no simple physiological test for doing so. One cannot examine a sample of semen under a very high-powered microscope and say that the spermatozoa therein are packed with the right genes. Neither are there any worth-while correlations between outward physical features in a parent and the performance of the offspring. There are breeders of Guernsey cattle who like to see yellow pigmentation in the ears of their bulls, because they believe they will be more likely in consequence to have daughters whose milk is rich butter-fat. Unfortunately it is not as easy as this. The best method one has of getting some estimate of the genotype of a bull in respect of character with a low heritability is by an examination of the performance of sample offspring.

Judgment of a parent in this way is known as progeny testing. It is no new device in selection, for it was widely practised by Bakewell nearly two hundred years ago. It has, however, received a new emphasis in the past ten or fifteen years because selection of breeding stock on appearances or on pedigrees, especially pedigrees consisting merely of fashionable and impressive sounding names, has been so disappointing in that it has done little more than preserve the excellence of breeds and has not enlarged it.

There are several points to be observed in conducting a progeny test. The first is that there must be a reasonable number of offspring. The mere fact that a penny tossed four times comes down heads on each occasion is not conclusive proof that a double-headed penny is being used, but twelve such tosses would make one highly suspicious. This is the case with progeny testing. Four or five offspring provide useful evidence, but not until there are ten or a dozen does one really get a fair idea of what the parent is passing on. It must be remembered, too, that one parent's contribution is not the sole determinant of excellence, for another parent is also making a contribution, and this has to be allowed for. The Danes, who are very knowledgeable in animal breeding, require twenty daughters of a bull to be recorded in their testing stations in order that they can make a fair assessment of his breeding capacity. In practice, one is limited to taking just as many daughters as is convenient according to the size of one's herd. In a very small herd a bull may be used for two or three years before there is sufficient evidence to make an assessment of his genotype. In larger herds a bull may be tested in a relatively short time by mating him to only a proportion of the breeding cows. In this respect large herds have an advantage over small, for they have the scope to use a bull relatively sparingly and yet get some line on his breeding ability before a decision is made to use him widely or discard him. The small breeder is very much at the mercy of his herd sire. This of course is an argument in favour of co-operation among small breeders in the proving and use of sires– a very desirable arrangement which is, nowever, not easily put into practice.

In cattle breeding one generally thinks of progeny testing as applying to sires alone, because it is seldom that individual dams have sufficient offspring to constitute a sufficient test sample. In this connection, however, beef breeders have an advantage over dairy men, for carcass quality is expressed in sons and daughters whereas daughters alone produce milk. One is more likely to encounter a proven breeder among beef cows on this account. It is important, however, to have offspring from such a cow sired by several bulls in order to test properly her effectiveness as a breeder.

The second important feature about progeny testing is that all available offspring should be considered in a test. In some breed societies ratings of excellence in sires are based on a minimum number of daughters which have exceeded certain levels of production. No mention is made of the other daughters which may have failed miserably. Such standards are both illogical and misleading. It would be just as sensible to reckon up the success of a day at the races by considering only the wagers placed on winners and disregarding those that failed to yield a dividend. Such standards of course have a value to the breeder for sales purposes, but it may be suggested that any breeder who is honest with himself would not practice such self-deceit. Unfortunately, such are the frailties of human nature, many are impressed by quite possibly worthless initials behind a bull's name. Furthermore, the occurrence of a few outstanding offspring may fill the mind's eye so effectively that quite unwittingly the breeder is misled. This is more likely to occur in the breeding of sheep and beef cattle than it is with dairy cattle, for with the latter there are more definite production standards, and a few recorded yields of only 400 gallons or so are likely to make more impression than a proportion of indifferent lambs or calves which may not be debited against a sire whose reputation stands high because he has produced occasional winners at a county show.

The third important factor in progeny testing is that one must provide an environment for stock which permits them to give expression to their inherent qualities. There are two sorts of culls– culls by nature and culls by nurture. There was a time, for instance, when the Argentine was an important buyer of British bulls in order to arrest the deterioration which occurred in their pure breeds after several generations of breeding. Today purchases abroad are on a very limited scale- and this is not surprising in view of the present high quality of Argentine beef herds. The explanation for this improvement is quite a simple one. Hammond's classical studies at Cambridge on growth and development of carcass animals have revealed that if improved animals are underfed and generally mismanaged there is a reversion to the primitive unimproved type with a high proportion of bone, large heads and relatively heavy shoulders and a poor development of the loins and hind quarters. It cannot be assumed that poor treatment impairs a bull's transmitting powers, for there is no evidence that acquired characteristics are transmitted, but it prevents discrimination between inherently good and inherently bad types. Despite thirty or more generations of careful selection and breeding there is still a great deal of variability in our pedigree stock, and parents which are rated highly as specimens of a breed are quite liable to produce offspring which are inherently poor. If they are given every opportunity to develop they reveal their lack of quality, but if nutrition is poor their deficiencies are masked. This was the situation in the early days of the Argentine cattle industry, before breeders had acquired the skill of British breeders in stock rearing, and a truly bad bull was likely to be used because his parentage was good. The only corrective available to a breeder was an imported bull which was able to show that he at least carried the desired genes even though he might not be particularly good at passing them on. Today, not only do Argentine breeders bring their stock out to full advantage, but also, in doing so, they are able to distinguish the lines which are consistently transmitting the qualities that are wanted.

Top-line pedigree breeders, therefore, apart from any consideration of presenting their stock in the best possible condition for sale, must rear their stock on a plane of nutrition which allows them to give full expression to their powers to develop along the lines which will be described in Chapter 7. Sometimes this feeding is carried to excess, and quite commonly one encounters nurse cows of a dairy breed suckling young bulls which are practically as heavy as their foster mothers. This is not so serious in the highly improved breeds such as the Aberdeen Angus or the Beef Shorthorn if they are used for top crossing, in the manner that Down breeds of sheep are used on mountain crosses in order to improve carcass quality, but in those pure breeds where breeding stock are raised under very stringent range conditions, then such pampering may have a very detrimental effect on the breed. Previously reference has been made to the fact that New Zealand has imported a considerable number of Galloway cattle. This has been done because there is a body of opinion which considers that the existing improved breeds have no longer the capacity to survive and thrive on high hill country grazings where cattle are essential for proper land utilisation. It is part of a function of a beef breed to perform satisfactorily under such conditions then selection must be conducted in an environment that distinguishes the satisfactory strains. Because power to live on hard commons is associated with a low rate of maturity and a tendency towards primitive types, there is something of a conflict in breeders ideals. This point will be discussed more fully in Chapter 6, which deals with the problem of adaptation. At this juncture it is only necessary to establish the point that selection must be related to the objectives, and if progeny testing is one of the methods of selection that are being adopted, then the system of feeding and management must be such that the test sample can express its inherent capabilities.

To summarise, three important features of satisfactory system progeny testing are:

1. An adequate sample to reveal the parents breeding powers;
2. An environment which allows the full expression of the desired characteristics; and
3. Absence of bias in the sample so that it does not give a false impression.

In regard to this latter point the beef man is at disadvantage as compared with the breeder of dairy cattle in that he has no precise measurement such as milk yield or butter-fat, but he has the compensations that both sexes express their breed function, and assessment can be made at an earlier age. At two years of age in the 'improved' breeds the animals have reached carcass maturity, but dairy stock even at three years provide only very meagre data upon which the breeding worth of their parents may be assessed. One may have some inkling of yield and test of milk, but very little of wearing qualities except in so far as this can be gauged by type assessments.

To overcome his difficulty of precise measurement the breeder can at least assemble all the available offspring of a particular bull when they have sufficient maturity, and make some usual estimate of their worth. At least one can see production in the shape and size of a beef animal, whereas in a dairy heifer one can only attempt an educated guess. If the herd is large enough there should always be some young bulls under test so that there is a potential successor for the old proven sire that is currently heading the herd. It would be a very great help, especially for young breeders, if an experienced panel of judges were made available by breed societies to make an impartial assessment of progeny groups, somewhat along the lines that type classifications are made for dairy cattle in certain countries, notably the United States and New Zealand.

The Importance of Ancestors[1]

Pedigrees are normally set out to third and sometimes the fourth generation when an animal is offered for sale. Breeders may even go back further to seek out favoured and fashionable ancestors upon whom they may place an undue emphasis. In this connection it is important to remember both the sampling nature of inheritance and the great residual of genetic variability even in our modern breeds. If one could be certain that our cattle were relatively homozygous for the important characteristics no very great harm would come from what someone has cynically called 'ancestor worship', but too often events prove that this is not the case. Consider a pedigree such as that presented in Figure 7. Substantially the animal A has derived 50 per cent of its inheritance from each of the two parents B and C. One of the parents may appear more important than the other because of manifestation of dominance, but dominance is not generaliy held to be particularly important in economic characteristics such as carcass quality where additive gene effects are believed to be of much more consequence. The grandparents D, E, F and G each on an average contribute a quarter, and if D were a particularly valuable sire one could be justifiably pleased about his presence in the pedigree, because on an average A will have derived

1 For a fuller discussion read Chapter 14, *Animal Breeding Plans* by Lush (Iowa State College Press, 1947).

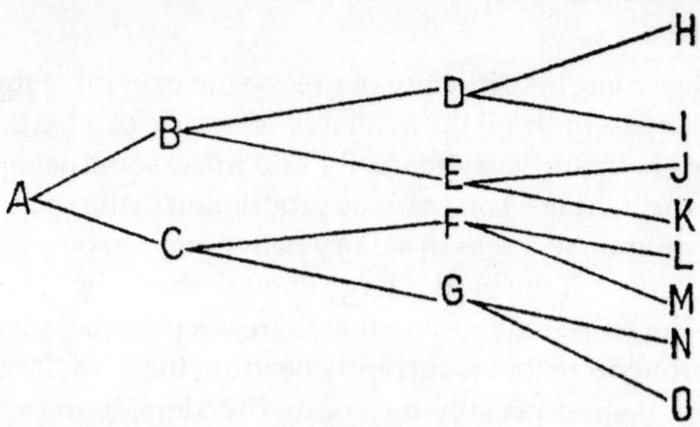

Figure 7: Pedigree to Illustrate the Relative Importance of Ancestors

25 per cent of his inheritance from him. Further back the contribution becomes progressively less, and great-great grandparents contribute on an average only one-sixteenth apiece of the genes which constitute the sum of A's inheritance. It is quite true that certain characteristics from ancestor J may be observed in A, *e.g.*, J may be the only polled great-grandparent, but this characteristic may have been expressed in the direct line through to A. Bull J could not be described as a prepotent bull simply because of this, for every gene that is his contribution will, in the absence of effective selection, be accompanied on an average by seven genes derived from the other ancestors of his generation. The operative phrase in the preceding sentence is 'effective selection,' for notable ancestors are meaningless unless their good qualities have been preserved in their descendants. In the random assortment of genes that occurs in the formation of germ cells it is quite possible that a well-below-average sample half can be passes on. If this is repeated over a couple of generations then mediocrity and worse may follow in the succession. So often one encounters in justification for the retention of an indifferent animal for breeding an assertion that because it traces back to such and such a sire or dam its blood lines are such that it is bound to give results in the long run. This is quite possible if the lack of quality in the animal can be accounted for by environmental influences, but if on the other hand a beast has shown that it is poor when fairly judged on the performance of its progeny, that then all the famous names from the herd book back in its ancestry cannot redeem it.

This is, in no sense, a suggestion that pedigree is without value. To the contrary, a great deal of aid in selection can be obtained from a pedigree where full information is given. Particularly is this true where precise measurements can be made of characteristics as they can in the case of egg and milk production. In beef cattle one is up against the difficulty that there is no objective assessment of quality. The grading of unselected progeny groups by an independent panel, along the lines suggested previously in the section dealing with progeny testing, would do much to convert a pedigree from a collection of high-sounding names to a document which has some meaning in selection. We know from dairy cattle that the best bet in bull selection is the son of a truly proven sire out of a cow with along and consistent life-time performance. It seen reasonable to suggest that the position will not be very different with beef cattle.

Cow Families

One cannot leave this question of the importance of pedigree without making some reference to cow families. Each breed seems to have its favourites, and which are bonded by the one magical name. Daisy 83rd may have a smaller degree of relationship to Daisy 82nd, because the two cows have come down different lines of descent from the original foundation, than she has to Prudence 101st because of a sire and a maternal grandsire they have in common, but, despite this, in many breeders minds a Daisy is a Daisy and a Prudence is a Prudence. It would be just as logical for a breeder to attribute all the good qualities of his own daughter to his great-great-grandmother-in-law. Family only becomes of real importance beyond two to three generations when there has been a plan of breeding which preserves the intensity of relationship to the ancestor in question. Probably the most notable example of this is the famous Duchess family of Shorthorns in which Bates preserved a coefficient of relationship higher than that of full sisters. Where, however, cow families are derived from a succession of outcrosses, then the situation is that of the pedigree presented in Figure 7. Quite possibly the notable success which attended Bates with his Duchess strain has helped to perpetuate the female family concept in British livestock breeding, though it is true also that the Collings placed a great deal of emphasis on their female lines.

It is often advanced in answer to the above arguments that certain qualities are preserved through many generations along a female line. In the mechanism of heredity there is nothing which will deny this possibility. A simple dominant if can be preserved in the face of continued matings with animals carrying the recessive over generations *ad infinitum*, provided that at each step one parent is selected which expresses the dominant. The author recalls one succession of four generations where each cow in the line exhibited a characteristic looseness of the bowels. It was not established, however, whether the various sires used did not also make some contribution to the perpetuation of this weakness. A point about the female in most species which is relevant to this discussion, is that one pays rather more attention to her as an individual. The sire, in his polygamous state, is regarded as a parent of a group, while the dam becomes the parent of single animals. When one has handled a cow every day for several years there is a very acute recognition of the little features by which it is distinguished from the rest of the herd. A daughter is certain to share some of these features, and so from generation to generation there runs this chain of recognition points which may indeed be changing as a sentence changed when it was passed by word of mouth along a line of soldiers from 'S' end up reinforcements' we are going to advance, to 'Send up three and fourpence we are going to a dance.' Though family nomenclature may be a very valuable aid in helping to establish close relationships, it has shortcomings when it becomes a restricting factor in selection based on true merit. Primrose 92nd is worth keeping because she is the daughter of the proven old breeder, Primrose 43rd; but she is a very different proposition from Primrose 93rd, who is a third cousin of the good old cow, and has nothing in herself or her immediate ancestry to identify her with her renowned but distant relative.

Objectives in Breeding Beef Cattle

It is important to have a clear-cut conception of objectives so that a breeding plan may be devised and followed. One should endeavour to restrict objectives to the minimum, for the more one is selecting for, the lower is the intensity of selection which can be practised in anyone direction. It is not just a question of doubling the number of objectives and halving the rate of progress in anyone direction, for the limitation is greater than this as reference back to our blacks and polls in Figure 6 will disclose. In every sixteen animals there were four which were true-breeding for black alone and four which were true-breeding for polled alone. For animals that are true-breeding for both characters the proportion falls to one in sixteen. Another illustration is provided by the work the author is conducting in the selection of poultry. Four cocks out of ten under progeny test in one year had daughters with a satisfactory egg production, but only one of these, the fourth on the list, had a reasonably good breed-type assessment for his progeny. Only one of the four, the second bird in order of lay, exhibited good live-ability in his offspring, but breed type was poor. No cock combined all three features in his progeny group. If this was required then it would have been necessary to have doubled or trebled the cockerels under test, so great are the odds against combining all three characteristics in the one family group.

Where there is any conflict or competition between objectives then the odds against getting desired combinations are greatly, increased. Dual-purpose cattle provide a good example of this. The supply of nutrients available for maintenance and production is limited by a cow's capacity to ingest and digest food, and nutrients required for laying down flesh will be obtained at the expense of those required for the secretion of milk. Nutrient intake can only be increased by increasing the size of the cow, and this will have its repercussions both on economy of milk production and size of joints. This must not be construed as an argument against the use of dual-purpose cattle which have such an importance in the cattle economy of Britain, but nevertheless it is true that it is a very difficult breeding problem to combine the two qualities so that there is any measure of consistency from one generation to another. The dual-purpose man has a much harder task in comparison with that of the specialist with Jerseys on the one hand, or Aberdeen Angus on the other.

Briefly the objectives of a breeder of pedigree beef cattle may be stated as follows:

1. Carcass quality
2. Early maturity
3. Adaptability
4. Longevity[1] and freedom from disease
5. Fertility

---

1 The editor questions this stressing of longevity in view of the high proportion of elderly beef which is our lot today.

6. Economy of food utilisation
7. Milking qualities
8. Breed type.

Not only does one require these qualities to be expressed in the individuals of a herd, but they must be regularly transmitted to the next generation.

The emphasis placed on each item of this formidable list varies from breed to breed and, within breeds, from herd to herd. With the Aberdeen Angus and the Scotch Shorthorn, carcass quality and early maturity are stressed, whereas in the Welsh, the West Highland and the Galloway adaptability is emphasised. Cattle of these latter breeds must be able to live on the hill, and this inevitably means some restriction on early maturity and carcass quality. Economy of gain does not compete with the other objectives, but is complementary to them. The animal that matures quickly will have the lowest food maintenance costs, and the animal with the correct proportions of fat to lean as opposed to the one which lays down excessive fat at carcass maturity will require less food per unit increase in weight. Similarly, cattle with adaptability to range conditions are economical feeders, because they can thrive on what would otherwise be wasted food, and they do not require much in the way of expensive supplementary feeding.

Longevity and fertility and freedom from disease speak for themselves, and they are of course fundamental to economical production. Milking ability may seem out of place, but it is included as a reminder that in any beef breed there are very few bulls destined to sire daughters which will have the assistance of nurse cows to cover up their deficiencies as mothers. Reasonable milking capacity is an essential where a herd is kept for the stores it produces, and this after all is their function in most beef breeds. Milking qualities may become even more important if induced twinning through the use of hormones becomes a commercial proposition. If a breed loses this function then it will only survive by virtue of its excellence in top-crossing to provide stock for fattening from cows of limited beef value, *e.g.*, colour-marking bulls used on dairy-type cows.

Breed type is a complex in selection and covers a multitude of sins. Fortunately in beef cattle type is an expression of production and not a pointer to production as it is in dairy cattle, and so there is less temptation to go astray, and length of tail or twist of the horns is not likely to compensate for a weal development of the loin or patchiness in fleshing. There have been examples in carcass animals of too much attention being paid to fancy breed points. The best instance of this, perhaps, is to be found in the Berkshire pig, where an insistence on six white points the tip of the tail, the face and four feet) very nearly ruined the breed. A realistic view must always be taken of type so that a breed is fulfilling its economic function. Superficial features such as colour markings or dishing of the face may present some evidence of breed purity, but the kind of purity the industry requires is a capacity to breed true for the characteristics which are prized when an animal is deprived of its head and hide and is hung in up the butcher's shop.

Lush (1945) quotes an instance of how an insistence on a particular point was not in the best interests of the breed concerned. Many of the original Herefords imported into America carried red spots on the face and red rings around the eyes. These markings generally appear in Hereford crosses, and so it is understandable why breeders selected away from them towards faces which were as white as possible and carried some assurance of true breeding. In the conditions of the extreme south-west of the United States, Herefords with white eyelids are more susceptible to cancer of the lid than those with the red pigmentation. Though this is a small point, it does illustrate the importance of realism in type considerations.

By and large however, an emphasis on conformity to breed type is a disability only when it weakens intensity of selection for economically important points, but such is the insistence on breed type in cattle breeding today that breed type has become one of the important economic considerations, and no man who wishes to enjoy a share of the top markets can afford to ignore the fashions of his breed. If fashions are necessary let us hope that, in the interests of more efficient beef production, they remain severely and practically masculine rather than become flamboyantly feminine. Perhaps we should be grateful that men and not women control the destinies of breed societies.

Chapter 5
Methods of Breeding

Line-breeding and Inbreeding

Hagedoorn (1939) records a distinction between these two forms of breeding made by an old breeder when talking with a young breeder. Success, according to the elder man, is attributable to line-breeding, but where there is failure the blame may be put on inbreeding. The true definition of inbreeding is that it describes matings where the animals involved are more closely related than they would be if they were selects at random from the population to which they belong, *i.e.*, it implies closer relationship than is the average relationship within the breeding group. This definition makes allowance for two important features. The first is that within most breeds there is a degree of relationship. The history of the Shorthorn breed, for instance, discloses a practice of very intense inbreeding by its founders, whose stock, and in particular the bull Favourite, are well represented in the pedigree of practically every modern Shorthorn. Over the past 150 years this relationship has been augmented at various times by the popularity of various famous animals whose descendants have been used very widely by breeders. The same story is found with breeds other than the Shorthorn.

The second point of the definition is that there is a definite purpose in the mating of related animals, namely the reduction of genetic variation. That inbreeding is effective in doing this is illustrated by the example given in Figure 8. In this case a self-fertilising plant with the alternative characters red and white has been chosen, for self-fertilisation is the most intense form of inbreeding which can be practised. Commencing with a heterozygote (Rr) the first or F1 generation gives the expected ratio of 1RR : 2Rr : 1rr, so that 50 per cent of the new generation is homozygous. If four plants are bred from each individual in this generation the homozygotes (RR and rr) will each breed true, and they will each be augmented by two further homozygotes bred from the two heterozygotes of the same generation whose offspring segregate out into a 2 : 4 : 2 ratio. The net result is that in the F2 generation the proportion becomes 6RR : 4Rr : 6rr. By the time the F4 generation is reached only 6¼ per cent of the plants are heterbzygous. If the objective in breeding had been true-breeding reds all the whites would have been eliminated by phenotypic selection, and breeding would have been confined to the pure and impure reds which would then be present in a ratio of 15RR to 2Rr in the F4 generation. After ten generations the impure reds would constitute a negligible proportion.

P1 generation	Rr	100% heterozygotes
F1 generation	1RR : 2Rr; 1rr	50% heterozygotes
F2 generation	6RR : 4Rr: 6rr	25% heterozygotes
F3 generation	28RR : 8Rr : 28rr	12½% heterozygotes
F4 generation	120RR : 16Rr : 120rr	6¼% heterozygotes

Figure 8: Decline in Heterozygosity with Self-fertilisation

In the above instance of two contrasted characters, the number of true-breeding lines is two, and if two sets of contrasted characters, say red and white and tall and dwarf, were involved there would have been 4 true-breeding lines comprising all combinations of the characteristics in question. If there were characteristics involving 20 or more pairs of genes with complete heterozygosity in the foundation plants then the number of true-breeding combinations would reach astronomic totals. With plants the sorting out of the desired combinations would be a tremendous task. With animals it would be completely impossible. We shall return to this point when we deal with the difficulties of inbreeding.

In breeding beef cattle we are denied the convenience of self-fertilisation, and so the rate of progress in reducing heterozygosity is so much slower. The closest inbreeding one can practise is the mating of full brother and full sister, or the continued mating of the youngest parent back to its off-spring, *i.e.*, the mating of son back on dam, and the mating of the resulting daughter back to its sire, and so on. With such matings it is possible to reduce heterozygosity by 25 per cent each generation. It must be recognised that in any species there is a certain minimum of homozygosity, for cattle would not produce offspring which were recognisable as cattle if this were not the case. When we speak of reducing heterozygosity, therefore, we are referring to those pairs of genes where the members are unlike. As to the number of these in any foundation stock of an inbred line one cannot even hazard a guess. If, however, we were to postulate 64 pairs, after one generation of brother-sister mating the expectation would be 48 unlike pairs. The next generation would reduce it to 36, and the next to 27. After an infinite number of matings heterozygosity would completely disappear.

Now the great problem in inbreeding is to make certain that there is no loss of desired genes. As was pointed out previously, where many genes are involved the possible number of lines is astronomic, and though continued in breeding is bound to result in genetic purity, this may be obtained at any one of many levels of genetic merit because certain genes, which are essential to optimum expression of the characteristic in question, may be lost. To clarify this point, let us imagine we are dealing with a characteristic for which there are three heterozygous pairs of genes in our foundation. We could write the genotype as (Aa Bb Cc). Inbreeding might produce any combination from (AA BB CC) represents genetic perfection to (aa bb cc), which is the very reverse. If the end-product of inbreeding is, for, instance, (AA bb CC), then we have lost the important genes BB, which have a contribution to make to the ideal. These can only be restored by an outcross, and such a drastic course may undo a great deal of what has been achieved in the way of desired uniformity. Before embarking on any programme of inbreeding, the breeder has to be certain, therefore, that he has all the factors he requires in his stock, and at every generation he has got to make certain that the parents he used are transmitting these factors. This involves selection, and selection, when characters with a multifactorial basis are involved and where there are considerable environmental influences operating to mask genetic effects, invariably means progeny testing. The plant breeder is at a tremendous advantage here. Not only is he dealing for the most part with simpler genetic situations, but he is dealing also with large numbers. Each individual is worth very little and any one can be discarded with equanimity. Furthermore, good genotypes can be quickly multiplied so that their use can become widespread in a short space of time. The unfortunate cattle breeder, however, is dealing with much more complex problems, his stock are individually valuable and his livelihood depends on them, he is faced with a very slow turnover of generations and he has only a few individuals to work with. His success in attaining genetic purity of the kind he wants is dependent to an uncomfortable degree on the element of luck.

The element of luck enters into inbreeding in another way. In America, following the success which has been obtained there with the use of inbred lines of maize to produce hybrids with greatly enhanced production, efforts have been made to develop inbred lines of pigs with a similar function. The plan of action adopted involved the development of inbred lines based on many strains at a large number of centres because of the danger that the selected foundations would not be 'able to stand up to inbreeding.' This was the advice the Americans gave to British workers when a similar scheme in Britain was undertaken. It is interesting to record that most of the original lines started in Britain had to be abandoned because of undesirable characteristics appearing as if from nowhere. At Davis, in California, Wilson commenced inbreeding with four strains of Jerseys, and only one of these now survives. No less than six undesirable recessives appeared including dwarfism, lethal spasms and eye defects. As the intensity of inbreeding increased, mortality up to four months–which is taken as the criterion of vitality–also increased (Kelley, 1946). Similar results have been reported for other inbreeding projects with dairy cattle in the United States (Robertson, 1949). In the great majority of lines unwanted recessives have appeared, or there has been some decline in functional efficiency.

Why do weaknesses appear with inbreeding? A clear answer cannot be given to this, but there are several possible explanations. One is that recessive lethal or sub-lethal factors are carried by the foundation of the inbred line. When close relatives are mated, because there are greater chances of them having the same genes in common, there is a greater likelihood of recessives appearing. In outcrosses the possibility of the gene or genes responsible for the recessive characteristic being common to the two parents is much more remote. Even so the appearance of recessives is not uncommon in some species, *e.g.*, scrotal hernia and blind gut in pigs. Another possible explanation for some of the deterioration may be due to loss of genes in the purification process. This is merely an extension of the first explanation, in that absence of genes vital to development may have an effect similar to the presence of deleterious genes. A third possibility is that homozygosity may not be consistent with optimum development and function. In the development of hybrid maize, the first step is the production of inbred lines which are characterised by lack of vigour and size. When certain of these lines are crossed astounding results are obtained, and the performance of the hybrids is greatly in advance of that of the original foundations.

Whatever the theoretical explanation may be, the reality is that intense inbreeding is fraught with many dangers. The consequence is that breeders of cattle will not normally embark on a programme of inbreeding based on the mating of closely related animals except on a very small scale. Occasionally experimental matings may be made with a few animals, perhaps a sire back to three or four of his daughters, but the adoption of an intense inbreeding plan for a whole herd involves risks which only a very wealthy man can afford to undertake. Generally breeders prefer to adopt a less intense form of inbreeding, commonly described as line-breeding, where cousins and second cousins are mated together. Here the endeavour is to preserve as high a degree of relationship as possible with some favoured ancestor without raising the intensity of inbreeding to the point where wastage is so great that the breeder is unable to maintain his herd or his sales of surplus stock. It may be completely catastrophic to a breeder dependent on sales for most of his income if 10–15 per cent of the animals he breeds are wasters and have to be discarded. The reduction of heterozygosis as a result of mating cousins together amounts to 6¼ per cent, so that it takes four generations of such mating to achieve the same result as may be obtained from mating full brother and sister. It is all a question of making haste slowly so that weaknesses may be observed and a tactical retreat made if this is considered necessary. As was pointed out previously, where there are a large number of gene pairs for which the average animal of a breed is heterozygous, then the possible number of true-breeding lines is so great that the chances of achieving everything that is required in a line compare with those of winning a first prize in an enormous lottery.

Stock-breeding has, indeed, many features of the lottery. A truly great sire, judged on his breeding ability, is a very rare animal. In the dairy world, where progeny testing is now a well-established feature, despite all the care that is taken in selection, barely one bull in a hundred can be described as outstanding when he is judged by his offspring. It is unlikely that the position is very much different with beef cattle. Consequently, when a breeder has secured such a bull he must endeavour to make the greatest use of him. His first step, of course, is one of getting the greatest number of the bull's daughters into the herd. This caters for the present, but what can he do for the future when the old bull is no longer available, and how can he concentrate the influence of the bull in the succeeding generations? If he was a Bakewell he would probably have the courage to use the bull on its own daughters. This course has a great deal to commend it, for it is in the nature of a test-mating to ascertain whether the sire carries deleterious genes, such as those that are responsible for lethal and sub-lethal characteristics. If he does then the prudent man will abandon all ideas of inbreeding, for his whole breeding plan will become subservient to the elimination of the undesired factors. One can be fairly categoric on this point that it does not pay to persevere with a line of cattle that carry undesirable recessives. The breeder has so little flexibility with a species with such a slow rate of reproduction that very little progress can be achieved within a reasonable space of time.

Another possibility is one of following the old bull with one or more of his sons. If for the sake of clarity we give the old bull the name of Royal Duke we can picture the following sort of pedigree where a son is used on his half sisters:

- **New Generation**
  - **Son of Royal Duke**
    - **Royal Duke**
    - **Cow A**
  - **Daughters of Royal Duke**
    - **Royal Duke**
    - **Cows B, C, D, etc.**

The new generation would, in breeders' language, have 50 per cent of the 'blood' of Royal Duke, and a breeder might feel that he had secured 50 per cent of the genetic superiority of the old bull by adopting such a course in breeding. This is not the case, for genes, not blood, are transmitted to offspring, and always it is a sample half of a parent's inheritance.

Alternatively because a breeder may consider it risky to adopt half-brother and half-sister matings on any scale, he may mate Royal Duke to a limited number of his daughters in order to secure a promising inbred son which would then be used on grand-daughters. We would then get this sort of pedigree:

- **New Generation**
  - **Son and grandson of Royal Duke**
    - **Royal Duke**
    - **Daughter**
      - **Royal Duke**
      - **Cow A**
  - **Grand-daughters**
    - **Black Prince (outcross)**
    - **Daughters**
      - **Royal Duke**
      - **Cows B, C, D, etc.**

Here again the breeder's aim of maintaining blood relationship would be secured because the new generation would still have 50 per cent of the 'blood' of Royal Duke, but the coefficient of inbreeding would be lower. There will somewhat slower progress in reducing genetic variation, but the breeder is safeguarded in that he retains greater flexibility in selection, and he is less likely to have to discard a large number of animals. To quote Kelley (1946) on this point: Inbreeding has been shown to be fraught with dangers, particularly when it is intense. The art of constructive breeding, therefore, is to hold high degrees of relationship, and so similarity to favoured animals, while restricting the degree and so the risks of inbreeding.

Whatever the course of action the breeder takes in endeavouring to concentrate the influence of an outstanding sire in his herd, his plan must be safeguarded by adequate progeny testing in order to make certain that desired characteristics are being retained. Royal Duke is bound to have many sorts of sons, and double grandsons, when they are judged genotypically. To be the son of a proven sire is in itself a considerable recommendation in that it increases a bull's chances of achieving the same status as his sire, but it is by no means a guarantee. No breeder can afford to judge on pedigree alone, and before he becomes too deeply involved with any bull, no matter how attractively bred it may be, he must assure himself that it is handing on the qualities which are desired. In the words of Boutflour, 'Pedigree would really be important if parents produced ancestors and not offspring.'[1] Particularly is this true with inbreeding, because of the dangers of losing important genes in the process of securing greater genetic purity. Bates was conspicuously successful in many respects with his Duchess Shorthorns, but he lost fertility within the strain. The result was that it did not survive because the introductions of drastic outcrosses destroyed its purity.

There is a danger that the breeder may be left with the impression that intense inbreeding is invariably associated with deterioration. This is not necessarily the case, for provided the breeder is fortunate enough in his foundation stock and is able to select the right parents for each successive generation, not one may merit be preserved but that goal of all breeders be attained, namely the power to breed good animals uniformly and at will. In laboratory animals there is the heartening example of the Wistar rats. In the early generations of inbreeding there were many abnormal animals which, because they were rats, were cheaply discarded and rigid selection was practised for fertility, longevity, vigour and body size. Males of the 36th–38th generation averaged 12.3 oz. at the one-year-old stage compared with 3.8 oz. for the non-inbred colony from which the inbred line originated (Kelley, 1946). After ten generations of brother-sister matings the inbred lines had a coefficient of inbreeding of 90 per cent, and so were relatively pure. In beef breeding this number of

---

1 An address to a farmers meeting in Carmarthen, January 1951.

generations involves a period of 45–50 years, which is about three times as long as the life of the average pedigree herd. Time is not the only disability with cattle. Rats have litters and so a choice may be made from the produce of every effective mating. With cattle because of single births one substantially has Hobson's choice.

To some extent attitudes to inbreeding are influenced by the success of Bakewell and the Collings. Unfortunately history has recorded the successes but little mention has been made of past failures. One wonders how many would-be Bakewells have been condemned to obscurity because they were unlucky with their parent stock. If modern experience is any criterion they must have constituted a fairly substantial body.

Outcrossing and Hybrid Vigour

The opposite of inbreeding is outcrossing, which describes matings of unrelated animals. In breeding circles it has an implication of more than just random mating, for it may involve the deliberate mating of strains which are distinctly isolated as a result of fairly intense inbreeding. Often it is adopted to correct a weakness which has arisen in an inbred line, *e.g.*, a breeder may feel that he has lost size within his strain, and he may endeavour to correct this by an infusion of new blood. A wholesale use of a sire of the new strain on the herd may produce the desired results, but these most probably will be achieved at the expense of uniformity in the succeeding generations. New gene combinations will have been created, and there is then a possibility of segregation out into a variety of new types in the way that we obtained from the mating of a Hereford and a Red Poll something completely different in the second generation, namely a pure red animal with horns. Consequently, it is usual when an outcross is made for the procedure to be controlled. By way of example we may consider a strain which has been very intensely inbred to our bull Royal Duke in the manner described in the previous section. The strain may have many excellent features, but may be lacking in substance which is a characteristic of the Black Diamond strain. The method adopted might be one of mating several potential bull mothers in the herd to a proven bull of the Black Diamond strain, and to save one or more sons for use on the herd. Such a course would cut down unwanted variation materially, but according to the urgency of the correction the breeder may prefer to restrict the use of the out-bred sons and to wait for another-generation before wholesale use is made of the new blood. This would give a pedigree of this sort for the herd sire:

Stock bull	Parents	Grandparents
Stock bull $\frac{3}{4}$ R.D./$\frac{1}{4}$ B.D.	$\frac{1}{2}$ R.D./$\frac{1}{2}$ B.D. bull	B.D. bull
		R.D. cow
	R. D. cow	R.D. line
		R.D. line

In this way the chances of avoiding unwanted variability would be greatly increased. Of course it would be necessary to ensure that the desired substance was being transmitted by the new bull, otherwise the careful planning of the above pedigree will go for naught. It is possible that the first generation outcross would be an exceptionally good bull if the two lines 'nicked', *i.e.*, the gene contributions from the two parents dovetailed in such away as to constitute a favourable genetic combination. But this does not mean that the bull will be able to transmit his own superior qualities. For this reason it is essential that each step in the above programme should be accompanied by careful progeny testing in order to make certain that the desired characteristics are being maintained. Also, in view of the chances of failure, all one's eggs should not be in one basket, and it is wise that two or three sons and grandsons of the outcross should be tried out. This means in turn that the herd must have sufficient numbers for the breeder to have the scope for such experimental matings. One sees again and again the disabilities of the small herd in planning a breeding programme.

The process described above cannot of course be completed in a short space of time. Two cattle generations accompanied by adequate progeny testing will involve the best part of eight or nine years, but this is unavoidable if variation is to be minimised and the purpose of the outcross is to be achieved. A breeder may of course short cut this process by obtaining from a fellow breeder who has also worked on the Royal Duke line young stock which correspond in their breeding to those which have been bred in the parent herd. Such a procedure was adopted by the Booth family in their periodic rejuvenations of their famous Shorthorn herds. They provide examples of what is known as the 'climatic outcross,' *i.e.*, the introduction into an otherwise closed herd of animals bred elsewhere which have similar pedigrees, *i.e.*, descended from the same foundation. Genetic differences between the herd and the introduced cattle will result from the different courses of selection which have been followed, and so union between these animals is likely to restore the flexibility of selection which the breeder requires to eliminate the weaknesses which have appeared in his herd, but at the same time variation is not likely to be so great as to constitute a grave disability.

So far we have considered only controlled outcrossing as a tool in breed improvement, but a new approach to outcrossing has been provided by American workers in a project with dairy cattle which was started at Beltsville nearly thirty years ago. The basis of this viewpoint is a contention that outstanding sires within a breed, judged for a particular characteristic or a set of characteristics, will have the same sort of genetic make-up. Such sires, provided they are adequately proved, when they are mated with each other's daughters, even though there is no relationship, are likely to give offspring which will be well above average in their breeding performance. The picture such breeding presents is that of the pedigree below:

Offspring (?)
- **Proven Sire**
  - **Proven Sire**
  - **Dam**
- **Dam**
  - **Proven Sire**
  - **Dam**

The question mark has been inserted to draw attention to the probable value of a young bull as a herd improver if it has been bred in such a way. Is there in fact a possibility of building up a superior inheritance by such a system? Can pure-breds be graded up for productive purposes by continued top crossing with proven sires in the same way as grade cattle can be raised to pure-bred status by the continued use of pedigree sires? Something of an answer is provided by the limited data which have been accumulated by Beltsville workers through co-operation with outside breeders. Production figures are summarised below for fifteen co-operating herds (Kelley, 1946).

265 foundation cows' best records average 411 lb. of butter-fat

265 1st generation daughters best records averaged 461 lb. of butter-fat

171 2nd generation daughters' best records averaged 486 lb. of butter-fat

67 3rd generation daughters' best records averaged 541 lb. of butter-fat

26 4th generation daughters best records averaged 559 lb. of butter-fat

A number of young bulls of both the Jersey and Holstein-Friesian breeds, bred according to the same plan, have been used in co-operating herds with the following results (Ward, 1946):

Jerseys (71 bulls)	
1,026 dams averaged	7,7781b. milk testing 5.19% and 4071b. fat
1,026 daughters averaged	8,215 lb. milk testing 5.32% and 427 lb. fat
Increase	437 lb. milk testing 0.13% in test and 20 lb. fat
Holstein-Friesians (85 bulls)	
1,548 dams averaged	12,365 lb. milk testing 349% and 429 lb. fat
1,548 daughters averaged	13,066 lb. milk testing 3.55% and 462 lb. fat
Increase	701 lb. milk testing 0.06% in test and 33 lb. fat

Of the 71 Jerseys used 59 (83 per cent) were herd improvers and with the Holstein-Friesians 65 out of 85 bulls (76 per cent) were in the same category. Compare this with the normal expectation of herd improvers, which is about 1 bull in 4 or 5 in the average recorded herd. To increase the chances to substantially 4 out of 5 is a breeding achievement of very considerable distinction. To complete the picture it must be pointed out, however, that Wilson at Davis has secured comparable figures with his inbred Jerseys which were selected for their producing qualities. In this instance 22 out of 29 bulls used in co-operating herds, some 76 per cent, effected improvement in the production of daughters.

The Davis bulls were bred at a very considerable expense. The average breeder could not afford to lose three strains completely or to have the wastage which was experienced at Davis. It is for this reason that the Beltsville proposition appeals so strongly. Because mates are not related there is not the same likelihood of them carrying undesirable genes in common, and so the possibilities of recessives appearing are greatly lessened. The assembled data, however, are by no means conclusive, and are restricted to dairy cattle. It is not illogical, however, to suggest that if the contention is valid for one class of stock it will have some application with others. The poultry progeny testing which has been referred to previously has been planned with the clarification of this possibility as a primary objective.

Previously it has been stated that it is quite possible that a certain amount of heterozygosity may be an important element in securing an optimum performance. The size of the Wistar rats to some extent negates this point of view, but the unexplained excellence of hybrids seems to indicate that heterozygosity may, *per se*, be important. In the development of hybrid corn (maize) in America plant breeders self-fertilised thousands of plants, but in no instance did they secure outstanding progeny. In fact, the characteristic of most inbred lines is their *low* productivity, but when inbred lines are crossed then outstanding production is obtained with certain of the combinations. 'Certain of the combinations' is a significant reservation, for in many instances it was found that inbred lines did not 'nick.'

The American's pig work, especially the evolution of the Minnesota No. 1 and the Minnesota No. 2, however, supports the Wistar rats in establishing the possibility of achieving very high merit within inbred lines, and it is noteworthy that the American Bureau of Animal Industry with its large-scale breeding projects with sheep, cattle and pigs (of which the Minnesota work is a part) accepts that outstanding breeding lines can be developed by inbreeding. In fact, with a species where individuals are valuable, it is essential that good husbandry qualities are retained in the inbred lines. It proposes, however, to combine inbred lines to take advantage of hydrid vigour. Greenwood and Blyth (1948), working at Edinburgh with poultry, have also established that strains outstanding for productivity and resistance to disease can be achieved by inbreeding accompanied by appropriate selection.

Unfortunately beef cattle do not lend themselves to the exploitation of hybrid vigour in the way that it can be done with pigs. With this latter species it is possible to combine two inbred lines to get fecundity and mothering qualities in 'incross' sows. A third 'incross' strain may then be used on these sows to get additional characteristics such as good rate and economy of gain in the second generation which is slaughtered. One has the advantage with pigs of quick multiplication, and relatively few inbred pigs are necessary to provide a fairly large number of commercial mothers in the form of the first hybrid generation. All the second hybrid generation go on to slaughter. A similar situation exists with poultry because of multiple births, but with cattle there are usually single births, and so a totally different situation is created because a much higher proportion of the total cattle population would have to be maintained as inbred lines. One cannot pre-influence sex, so one has to accept slightly more than half the calves born being bulls. As only a few of these will be required for breeding a large balance will to slaughter. With the chances there are of the straight inbreds being relatively inefficient as meat producers, their disadvantages may outweigh the advantage that would accrue from having a proportion of the fattening stock exhibiting hybrid vigour because they are the product of crossing inbred lines. There is this further point one would not expect that highly inbred females would be particularly suitable for running on the poorer breeding country which the economics of land utilisation rule shall be one of our main sources of breeding stock. In this connection it is possible that the best solution with cattle, so far as commercial breeding is concerned, is to confine inbreeding to the production of closely bred bulls for use on commercial herds, for present evidence seems to indicate that a policy of using closely bred sires of good individually, each unrelated to the females on which he is to be used, with maintain the maximum hybrid vigour and individual merit in the offspring (Lush, 1947).

CROSS-BREEDING

It seems with beef cattle that apart from some limited use of unrelated inbred sires, exploitation of hybrid vigour must substantially be confined to the crossing of one breed with another. It has already been pointed out that this is a fairly widespread practice. In parts of Scotland the West Highland breed is particularly well suited to the poorer hill country. Its cross with the Shorthorn, known as the Cross Highland, is not only able to thrive on the hills partly because of its Highland parentage, partly because of the characteristic hardiness of cross-breds, no doubt a manifestation of

Plate 6: Cross-Highland Cows with their Calves by a Shorthorn Bull

Plate 7: Welsh Blacks on Welsh Hills

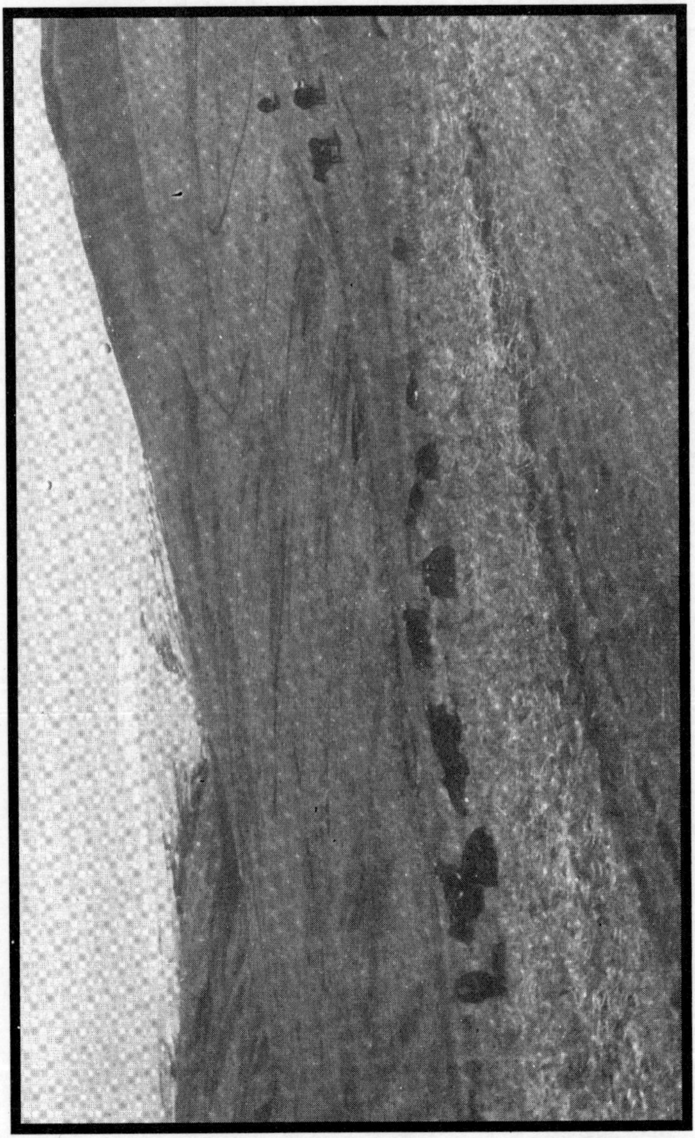

Plate 8: Plynlimmon, 2,500 Feet-Welsh Cattle Wintered on the Hill

hybrid vigour, but it also has superior carcass qualities and quicker maturity. The cross-bred females can remain on the breeding country, but the steers and stores can go down to easier country for fattening. The second generation, that is the back-cross of the Cross Highland on the Shorthorn, is so much into the Shorthorn that heifers and steers alike are usually sold as weaners.

Occasionally one encounters in cross-breeding the practice known as criss-cross breeding. In this farmers mate their cross-breds back to one parent breed, and then use the other parent breed on these three-quarter-breds to maintain the breed combination at a figure around about 50 per cent. This has the advantage that a herd can be self-contained, that whereas with continued first crossing an outside source of pure-bred cows must be tapped, unless the farm is big enough to maintain a herd of pure-breds specifically for the purpose of maintaining the herd which is used for crossing. Alternatively there must be a high-percentage crop of calves each year and a low rate of wastage from the cow herd. In criss-cross breeding it is essential that the sire used must always be a pure-bred. Otherwise there will be the violent segregation of extreme types which is a characteristic result of mating cross-breds together. There is little definite evidence of the advantage of criss-cross breeding apart from the personal observations of men who have practised it. It seems that there is a sound basis for it where there is a considerable local adaptation problem, *i.e.*, where some breed may be peculiarly well suited to the environment but may lack in carcass qualities. Such an example is that quoted above, for the West Highland is very well adapted to local conditions. Another good example is provided in some of the southern sub-tropical states of the United States, where breeders endeavour to maintain from a quarter to a half of zebu blood in the breeding herd, and use improved European breeds to produce stores for fattening. In pigs there is some definite evidence that good results are obtained from criss-cross breeding.[1]

Another variant in cross-breeding is the three-breed cross of which the best illustration in Britain is provided by sheep. The hill breeds such as the Cheviot and Scotch Blackface are remarkably hardy and are able to survive and thrive on scanty grazing. When ewes are cast for age from the high country they still have a useful

---

1 *Minnesota Agric. Expt. Stn. Bull.*, 320.

breeding life on easier farms, where they are mated to the prolific deep-milking Border Leicester. The Greyfaces and Half-breds which result are a step up the scale in carcass quality and the wethers can be fattened. The ewes are too valuable as mothers to be slaughtered, for they are characterised by good milking qualities and fecundity. When mated to down rams, the resultant lambs have an excellent carcass potential which is usually realised because their dams are such good mothers. With reasonable management the lambs from one of the bigger Down breed crosses will reach 100 lb. live weight at four months.

This stratification illustrates a very nice picture of land utilisation, using animals under each set of circumstances that are well suited to their economic function through the combination of traits of the parental breeds, and through the hybrid vigour which results from crossing. Similar possibilities exist in cattle, but there is not the clear-cut pattern or organisation we have with sheep. Partly the reason for this is that the land which corresponds to that used for Down cross-lamb production is too valuable for breeding stores and so is used for dairying. Even so one does find that Cross Highland and Hereford-Welsh cows are used for breeding, and they may be mated back to the 'improved' parent or to such a breed as the Aberdeen Angus to produce high-class stores on the better-class breeding country.

Summary and Conclusions

In the foregoing an endeavour has been made to give a simplified account of the theory of heredity and of the basis of selection and breeding systems. Necessarily this has been very sketchy and many important aspects have been neglected, while limited, space imposed such a restriction on qualifying statements that some of them may be rather bald and savour of the half-truth. Deeper reading in the subject is essential for a breeder of pedigree cattle unless he is to be a rule-of thumb mater of animals who is very much at the mercy of fortune, which may or may not provide him with just the right succession of bulls to build up a good herd. With some knowledge of the science of genetics, at least a man may have some idea of where he is going and the reasons for a certain course of action even though he may not be provided with an infallible recipe for Royal Show champions. Unfortunately genetics is not an easy subject to comprehend, but it has the redeeming feature that it is profoundly interesting to anyone for whom stock breeding is a major enterprise.

There are certain important principles[1] which emerge from the discussion, and these may be summarised as follows:

1. Decide on the sort of cattle you are going to breed and establish definite objectives. Twenty-five years constitute a big proportion of a man's working life-time, but they cover only five cattle generations. One cannot afford to dissipate time or breeding material by vacillation in a breeding policy, which must at the same time, however, be sufficiently flexible and have been planned with sufficient foresight that it will meet the changing circumstances of the industry. One thing is abundantly clear in a world which is expecting increased pressure on food supplies, namely that if we are going to continue to enjoy the luxury of roast beef then we have got to have animals which are more efficient converters of their feeding-stuffs into human food. Those attributes which contribute to economy of food utilisation and adaptation so that more efficient use can be made of farming land are bound of to become increasingly important while more attention must be paid to weight for age.
2. Collect foundation stock which conform as closely as possible to the ideals you have set yourself. Financial considerations may 1imit the quality of your females for a start, but because the succession of bulls you employ will, in a few generations, be the dominating influence in determining the quality of your herd, select your bulls with the greatest care.
3. In ascending order of importance selection should be based on (*i*) the individual merit of the animal; (*ii*) the merit of close relatives, particularly sire and dam, and of close collateral relationships such as sisters and half-sisters; (*iii*) the progeny test.
4. Because anyone sire may have such a profound influence ton a herd, even though he is of a high standard when

[1] For a fuller discussion of these points the reader is advised to consult Jay Lush, *Animal Breeding Plans.*

judged as an individual or as a member of a family group, he should be used only tentatively until such time as a sample of his offspring has been assessed. A random selection of six offspring is the minimum on which to base a progeny test, but if a greater number is feasible then the test is so much more conclusive. Necessarily one is limited in this by the size of one's herd.

5. When an outstanding parent has been obtained then the maximum number of offspring should be bred from it. Normally this applies to the bull, but of course good old cows have their contribution to make as well.
6. When an outstanding breeding animal has been distinguished, either in your own herd or in that of a fellow breeder with similar objectives and similar bloodlines, endeavour to increase the relationship of your herd to this animal.
7. Such a course will inevitably result in some inbreeding, and the prudent course here is to endeavour to maintain blood relationship without getting too high a degree of inbreeding.

   The more generations the favoured ancestor is removed from the current crop of calves, the lower the intensity of inbreeding will be. The double grandson for instance used on grand-daughters will be safer than a son, in that by reducing the rate of gene fixation there is less pressure exerted on a breeder's selection potential.

   Remember that close relationship to a notable ancestor in itself is no guarantee of breeding quality, and sparing use is still necessary until a progeny test is secured. In fact, with close breeding, progeny testing within the line becomes doubly important because of the danger of some serious defect being fixed in the whole herd.
8. If a close-breeding policy is adopted then outcrosses should be made only to correct defects which are becoming characteristic of the herd. The closer the breeding programme the more dilute the outcross must be.
9. Though recent American work has suggested promise for a diametrically opposed system of mating, namely using

proven merit and not relationship as the criterion of bull selection, on the grounds that meritorious sires within a breed with tend to carry the same sort of genes, the evidence on this is not yet so conclusive as to support such a policy unreservedly. At the same time such breeding has much to commend it early in the herd's existence, for it is a means of assembling a maximum number of the genes which are important in determining the expression of desired characteristics. This was the early policy adopted by Cruickshank. At the very best, given adequate selection of parents for each generation, close breeding will fix only the genes that are present in the foundation and which set the ceiling of excellence.

10. The foregoing remarks apply to the breeder of pedigree cattle who is responsible for supplying the industry with bulls. For the commercial producer a policy of outbreeding, using sires which are themselves closely bred, but which none the less have individual merit, is recommended. By using such closely bred sires on unrelated females, as opposed to sires which are themselves the result of outbreeding, then the maximum degree of hybrid vigour will be obtained and there will be a higher degree of uniformity in the stock they beget. Males in this instance all go to slaughter, and such females that are kept for breeding may be so much better as mothers under commercial conditions for their hybrid vigour.

Chapter 6
Adaptation of Breeds and Strains

The Nature of Adaptation

'The animal is not an isolate in a neutral environment, it is a living organism, dependent upon and responsive to the external conditions in which it finds itself, for expression of its inherent capabilities.' These words, taken from a presidential address to the New Zealand Society of Animal Production by Professor C.P. McMeekan, crystallise a fundamental concept in animal husbandry, namely the importance of having animals which are genetically attuned to their environment. The point is well illustrated by sheep which are kept under extremes of climate and soil fertility in Britain. The Scotch Blackface and similar breeds are small sheep which survive and reproduce their kind under the most stringent conditions of scant mountain grazings. They have coats which will shed heavy rain which would saturate the fleeces of close-woolled sheep such as the Downs, and they have an instinct which helps them to survive in heavy snow. The Romney Marsh, the other extreme, are large sheep which are highly adapted to intensive set-stocking on some of the richest pasture land in the world. They have the disability of low fecundity, but when Marsh farmers have attempted to replace them with the more prolific Border Leicester-Mountain crosses, without changing their system of pasture management, invariably they have had so much trouble that they have gone back to the local breed. The Romney Marsh is at home on its native pastures, but most Romneys would perish if they were transported to Scottish mountain grazings. There would be a proportion which would probably survive, however, such is the inherent variation which exists in the breed, and eventually a strain might be evolved, through the operation of natural selection, which would be very different from the original foundation.

New Zealand provides an example of the Romney being introduced to a very different habitat, for in that country, particularly in the North Island, it has virtually become a mountain sheep. Now it differs considerably from British specimens of the breed, being appreciably smaller and carrying a fleece which is better suited to high rainfall conditions. There has been more than natural selection in this change, for the directive hand of man has played a part. This situation has been described because it illustrates so effectively the considerable genetic variation which exists in our livestock despite many generations of selective breeding. It provides in part an answer to those who hold that many breeds, not only of sheep but of cattle also, are necessary if we are to make the most of a wide range of environmental conditions.

The purpose of the above discussion is not a suggestion that we should endeavour to cut down the number of breeds of cattle we use in beef production in Britain, but to explain why we find several of the breeds popular under a wide variety of farming conditions; *e.g.*, the Welsh Black has been used with considerable success on mountain grazings in Wales, while it is also found on intensive lowland farms as a dual-purpose beast. Even the so-called improved beef breeds may be used under marginal conditions. The Hereford, for instance, is recognised in many parts of the New World, where there is not a superfluity of breeds, as a first-class range animal because of its rusting ability. It has moved a very long distance from the lush pastures of its native county to the 'bad lands' of Montana.

Britain, because of her need to exploit the marginal lands if she is to improve her meat supplies, is now more conscious of the problems of adaptation in cattle than she has ever been. She is fortunate in having three breeds at least which are well suited to high hill grazing. They are the Welsh Black, which has come into prominence because of its success in Stapledon's Cahn Hill Scheme and in the pioneer work which Captain Bennett-Evans is achieving in Wales; the Galloway, which has long been renowned for its suitability for the tough conditions of south-west Scotland; and the West Highland, which is the native breed of the glens. A few years ago the Highlander was something of a curiosity, and the greatest demand for stock came from landowners who prized them as picturesque adornments of park land. Today the breed is booming and high prices are being paid for stock, not only for pure breeding, but also for crossing with the Shorthorn to produce what is known as the Cross Highland. This cross has been used by Duncan Stewart and his associates in the highly successful Ben Challum venture, which is referred to in Chapter 13. The Cross Highland cattle retain in part many of the characteristics of the Highlander, *e.g.*, the smaller size, the shaggy coat and the rustling propensities, and they have plenty of constitution–no doubt a manifestation of hybrid vigour. They have proved to be highly suitable for their job of reclaiming sheep pasturage from the dereliction of bracken and *Molinia*. From a carcass point of view the Ben Challum cattle are a very considerable improvement on the pure Highlanders, and the weaners which are the result of another top cross of good beef Shorthorn bulls, obtained from one of the best herds in Britain, are potentially first-class feeding animals. They are not kept on the hill after weaning, because these three-quarter breeds are tending too much towards the; improved breed, and it is considered safer to maintain first-cross cows only as breeding animals.

It is important to remember that these first crosses are bred under conditions which approximate to those on which they will have to survive for the rest of their lives. Adaptation is not just a function of inheritance but of early environment as well. The animal in its early stages is highly resilient, as Hammond and his fellow-workers have shown. Young animals respond to adverse conditions by developing those parts which are important for survival at the expense of less-important late-developing parts Henderson (1950), for instance, in his study of effect of plane of nutrition on wool development, kept one group of lambs on a sub-optimum plane of nutrition for twelve months, so that they were only half the size of their half-sisters who were on full feeding throughout the period. These low-plane lambs were perfectly healthy though they were undersized. A group which was switched from a high to a low plane midway through the period was characterised by thriftlessness. This, of course, is no new finding, for it is well known by sheep men that you can safely transfer sheep from bad conditions to good, if you do it gradually, but the reverse change is one to be avoided. We must recognise the importance of this point even with cattle. The Aberdeen Angus which is born on the hill is a very different proposition from its counterpart which is brought to the hill from conditions of plenty.

The Cross Highland is not the only cross-bred which is well suited to upland conditions. Hereford crosses with the, Black Welsh are very popular in parts of Wales, and here again similar results are being obtained. In New Zealand Hereford and Aberdeen Angus crosses have rendered particularly good service as breeding cows on hill country, and are preferred by many farmers to the straight breeds.

We must not think of adaptability purely in terms of suitability to hard conditions, for the ultimate function of beef cattle is to provide carcasses which are economical in terms of the labour and feeding-stuffs used in their production, and which are acceptable to the butcher. The slow-maturing beast with its lower proportion of expensive cuts may suit range conditions admirably, but it is likely to be an expensive fattener's animal producing a not very attractive carcass. The fattener's animal on the other hand may not suit the marginal farmer. Very obviously there is a conflict of ideals in the contrasted conditions of cattle production, and the question arises as to how they can best be reconciled. It cannot be done by turning the marginal breed into improved breeds by maintaining pedigree herds under quite unrealistic conditions, and selecting on standards which would be appropriate for a breeder of Aberdeen Angus or Shorthorns. The primary requirement of a breed such as the Galloway is that it shall survive and thrive under conditions where amelioration of the environment is too expensive to be attempted except in a very small degree. The most that one would suggest is that only a few of the pedigree herds, in particular the nucleus herds which supply bulls to other pedigree breeders, should be kept under reasonably good conditions where some selection can be practised for fleshing qualities. The majority of pedigree herds–those that supply bulls to ordinary run herds–should, however, be maintained under conditions where selection can be made for adaptability to the rigours which, the offspring of such bulls are likely to encounter. On husbandry grounds alone it is inadvisable to turn an over-fat, pampered bull out with range cattle, for it is more than likely that he will hang around the gate nearest the in-bye land and not get out on the hills and do his job properly.

Stratification

The more logical method of reconciliation is that adopted in the sheep industry where there is a more clear-cut definition of function, namely cross-breeding. This involves the maintenance at the top of the stratification scheme on upland grazing of appropriate pure-bred cattle in sufficient numbers to satisfy the demand for them. There is a large by-product from this level of surplus males which are steered, and these may be either sold as weaners for fattening, or else may be kept on the hills until maturity in order to serve as mowing machines. Eventually they will be fattened, but inevitably these elderly stores will produce very second-rate beef. Surplus females at this top level can be mated to beef bulls, and the resulted cross-bred females are well suited for further breeding either on the hill, as we have already noted, or on rather better land. The males, however, will all be steered, and after corresponding treatment will provide carcasses which are superior to those obtained from the pure hill breeds. The third stage corresponds to the mating of Down rams to Longwool × Mountain ewes, and, provided good sires are uses and there is no substantial check in development, really first-class beef will be the result.

The foregoing account is probably too precise and clear-cut to describe what actually happens with all the variety of conditions and methods under which cattle are kept and bred, but it conveys the principle which is involved, namely the transmutation of cattle with a primary function of improving hill country sheep pastures into good fattening stock over the course of a couple of generations by the use of bulls from the improved beef breeds. With each step there is a corresponding improvement m the plane of nutrition, so that the inherent ability of the cross-breds for flesh production may expressed.

Adaptation to Tropical Conditions[1]

The introduction of the improved breeds which have been evolved under temperate conditions into tropical agriculture has been accompanied by many disappointments and very often by disaster. This is particularly the case where high temperatures are associated with high humidity, where the level of feeding is poor and where there are insect pests. On the other hand, cattle of the zebu type are moderately thrifty and are able to withstand conditions which are highly unfavourable to the temperate breeds, *e.g.*, they appear to have a much more efficient heat regulating mechanism. In the heat of the day the respiration rate of temperate breeds in the tropics will increase and body temperatures will rise, whereas zebu cattle under the same conditions will be more or less normal. They will continue to graze during the heat of the day when European cattle spend most of their time in the shade. It is significant that the European breeds with light colours, *e.g.*, light fawn Jerseys, are superior to dark fawns or black cattle in their ability to resist high temperatures because there is more reflection of the sun's rays (Rhoad, 1940). A pigmented skin beneath the light-coloured hair, however, affords protection against burning. The greater relative skin area of the zebu is undoubtedly an important contributing factor in heat regulation.

The zebu has considerable advantages in respect of resistance to disease. This may be in part a reflection of its greater thrift under these conditions, for thriftless cattle the world over are more subject to infections, *e.g.*, a well-fed calf seldom suffers ill effects from worms. The zebu with its short sleek hair has some mechanical advantage against tick infestation as compared with the longer-haired temperate breeds.

Amalgams with the Zebu

A great deal of work is being done in various tropical and sub-tropical areas to combine the best qualities of Zebu and European cattle. This work varies from crossing and criss-crossing to maintain 25–50 per cent of Zebu blood to the development of new breeds such as the Santa Gertrudis, which contains sufficient Zebu blood to

---

[1] For a full account of this read F.A.O. publication, *Breeding Livestock Adapted to Unfavourable Environments.*

ensure adaptability to the conditions of southern Texas. The King Ranch[1], where the breed was evolved is in the coastal plain region of southern Texas, where temperatures are high and stock are affected by internal and external parasites. Because of isolation from corn-growing areas stock must be fattened off range grass. The first cattle used on the ranch were the Spanish-derived Longhorns, which were induced from Mexico. They were small prolific animals whose greatest virtue was hardiness, but they were not even passable carcass animals. The first step was grading up of these Longhorns with pedigree Hereford and Shorthorn sires until the whole ranch was stocked with high grades or pure-breds of the two breeds–approximately 25,000 of each. The two breeds were kept separately on the land to which each was best adapted. On the stronger and better country the Herefords, though lighter, were the more prolific, better foragers and produced a better finished carcass. They lost substance and deteriorated on the light sandy lands, and suffered more than the heavier Shorthorns from a variety of affections. Neither of these breeds was particularly happy under these conditions, and though the shorthorns were easier to maintain on open range they suffered from protracted drought and often produced very poor crops of calves–as low as 40 per cent in some seasons. Both breeds suffered greatly from flies, ticks and mosquitoes, and in wet seasons from the attentions of screw worms.

Some preliminary crosses were made with zebus, and then it was decided that an attempt should be made to fix a new type combining the desired characteristics of Zebu and British beef cattle. The bull Monkey, an outstanding sire, resulted from the mating of a Zebu to a high-grade Shorthorn cow. Mated to a Zebu × Shorthorn dam he produced another good bull, Santa Gertrudis, so that these two bulls upon which the breed was based were approximately 50 per cent of each of the two parent types. In the evolution of the range herd many bulls of 3/8 Zebu and 5/8 Shorthorn blood were used on cows of similar breeding so that substantially the breed is more Shorthorn than zebu.

The success of the venture is indicated by details reported by Kleburg (quoted by Phillips, 1948). Steers of the new breed have

---

[1] This description is based on that given by R.W. Phillips in the F.A.O. publication, *Breeding Livestock Adapted to Unfavourable Conditions.*

averaged 75–100 lb. heavier at a year and 150 lb. heavier at two years than British breeds kept under similar conditions. Four-years-old Santa Gertrudis steers have averaged approximately 1,400 lb. live weight when grass fat and have dressed out 3 per cent better than the British breeds, while breeding stock maintain themselves in better condition on range feeding.

The Santa Gertrudis venture is notable example of what man can do to improve his economic circumstances by planned breeding and selection with the objective of securing animals which are better suited to natural conditions over which he has little control. It is the reverse process of what normally happens where animal production is developed, for usually it is the environment which is changed to suit the stock, and not the stock to suit the environment. It points a finger to what can be done in Africa and Northern Australia and other tropical areas to augment world supplies of beef. Work with Zebu hybrids is going on in many parts of the world, and Kelley (1943) has reported very encouraging results from North Queensland from stock carrying 25–50 per cent Zebu blood, which yielded greater returns than British cattle under comparable conditions and produced good carcasses with a fine texture of muscle. Once again the ingredients have been put in the melting-pot, and new combinations are being secured to enlarge the productivity of cattle.

Chapter 7

Growth, Development and Body Form in Cattle

PRENATAL DEVELOPMENT

The starting point in the sequence which has as its climax the fattened beast, is the union of the egg, produced by the dam, with the sperm which is produced by the sire. Each parent contributes substantially one-half to the inheritance of the calf which will develop. These microscopically small germ cells contain the vital hereditary units which determine the *potential* size, shape and usefulness of the mature beast. The *actual* development, as we have seen, is determined by environment which operates on the basic inheritance of the animal.

The fertilised egg divides and redivides, gradually increasing in size and complexity. Over the first half of pregnancy, which most usually lasts 282-283 days, the tissues and organs are laid down, but there is a priority in the development of the various parts, *e.g.*, the brain and nervous system and the circulatory system are early developing, while the reproductive system is late developing. Nature has a well-defined sense of first things coming first, and ensures that there is adequate development of organs and tissues which are essential for survival at any given stage of development. In the early stages of pregnancy most of the obvious growth and development is made by the tissues and fluids which surround and nourish the developing foetus. At four months, for instance, the foetus proper is only about ten inches long, and superficially does not appear to be very different from the foetus of any other mammal at a corresponding stage of development. In the latter half of pregnancy growth of the foetus is very rapid, and pregnant animals should be well fed over this stage, as Wallace (1948) has shown by his work with sheep. Lambs from ewes which were poorly fed over the last eight weeks of pregnancy were not only substantially lighter than those from ewes which were well fed over a corresponding period, but also they were physiologically younger. Large lambs have a better chance of survival because they are able to suckle strongly, and the ewe, through being well nurtured prior to lambing, has an enhanced milk flow. The same principles of feeding prior to parturition apply to cattle, and particularly is this likely to be important with breeding cattle run on poor pastures.

Size of the calf at birth is controlled by factors other than the level of the nutrition during pregnancy. The more important of these are sex of calf, whether the dam is a heifer or a mature cow, and breed. The following figures illustrate these points:

Birth Weight of Calves
(From McMeekan, 1943)

Breed	*Calves from Mature Cows*		*Calves from 2-years Heifers*	
	Bulls	*Heifers*	*Bulls*	*Heifers*
Jersey	61	56	57	50
Friesian	88	84	85	78

Though the data presented relate to dairy breeds, they apply equally to the specialised beef breeds. The bigger breeds such as the

Shorthorn have larger calves than smaller breeds such as the Galloway. Pure beef breeds tend to have lighter calves at birth than pure dairy breeds of corresponding mature weight. Cross-bred calves tend to conform to the birth weights which are typical of the dams' breed. To some extent this may be due to the plane of nutrition supplied by the dam, in that bigger dams which are able to supply more nourishment to their calves *in utero* will have correspondingly bigger calves than those from smaller dams. The classic example of the influence of the dam on the size of the new-born is furnished by reciprocal crosses between the Shetland and Shire (Walton and Hammond, 1938). A Shire mare mated to a Shetland stallion had a foal which was three times the weight of the foal produced by a Shetland mare mated to a Shire stallion. Hammond (1941) postulates a growth-controlling substance in the blood of the dam that limits the size of the young to permit normal parturition. In practice, the farmer who is thinking of mating some of his low-producing dairy cows belonging to one of the smaller breeds, *e.g.*, the Ayrshire to a larger beef breed such as the Hereford to produce cross-bred calves for fattening, need not expect an unduly high proportion of difficult calvings because of this limitation of size of calf at birth in conformity with the size of the dam.

Twin calves, individually, are smaller than singles. Rate of twinning in cattle is normally very low in beef herds, and so this is not a very important consideration. However, the perfection of a technique of hormone treatment to induce multiple births may change this. One of the main factors operating against specialist beef production is the high cost of a rearing calf, which can be borne only in herds where stock have a pedigree value, or where cattle are an adjunct of some other line of farming such as dairying or sheep production, which provides the bulk of the farm income. A calf per cow per year provides insufficient income from land which has alternative and more profitable avenues of utilisation, but two calves per cow annually would alter the whole position, for though gross income per acre would not be very high, in outgoings, particularly labour costs, would be low to is not envisaged that multiple twinning would be a proposition on it hill grazings where a cow is doing all that can be asked of her if she rears one good calf, but on farms where rather better environmental conditions can be provided its development may be a very worth-while proposition.

Growth and Development Following Birth

The calf at birth is all head and legs, and in this respect it resembles all farm animals, because in order to ensure survival nature has provided for the essential parts being adequately developed. Gradually, in response to an adequate plane of nutrition, the calf increases in size (this we call growth), and it changes in body proportions until the mature shape is achieved. This latter series of changes is known as development.

Rate of growth is by no means steady throughout the period of immaturity, and in its first few weeks the calf grows he fairly slowly, but as it becomes accustomed to its new environment rate of growth accelerates until it becomes relatively stable, and each increment of increase per unit of time bears a fairly steady relationship to the previously observed weight. As maturity is approached rate of

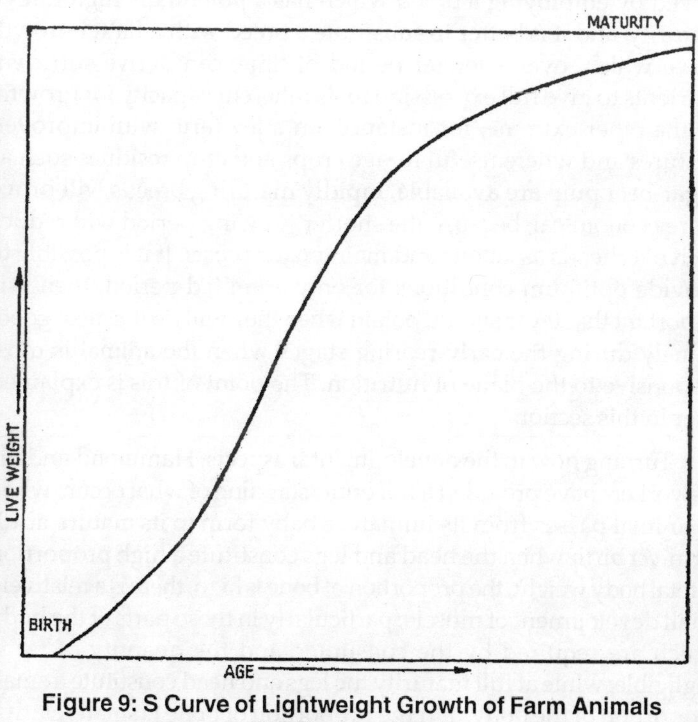

Figure 9: S Curve of Lightweight Growth of Farm Animals (McMeekan 1943)

growth declines, so that if we plot live weight against age we get the characteristic S curve which is illustrated in Figure 9. The steepness of the curve and age at which maturity is reached will vary, not only between breeds but between individuals of a given breed. Characteristically the Aberdeen Angus which is earlier maturing will have a much steeper curve of growth than the Galloway or West Highland, which reach mature size slowly.

The above curve of growth is derived under good conditions feeding and management. It will be greatly modified if conditions are not optimal. Though the economic circumstances may necessitate underfeeding at certain periods, generally speaking, it is unwise to restrict an animal's development when it is capable of making maximum growth, for at such times it will be making the most profitable gains in terms of food consumed. If it is not economically feasible to provide ideal conditions for growth and development, as is the case on hill country farms, then no point is served by employing a breed which has a potentially high rate of maturity, and it is better to substitute a breed with a flatter growth curve which, over a longer period of time, can derive sufficient nutrients to give full expression to its inherent capacity for growth. At the other extreme, for instance, on a ley farm with improved pastures and where useful forage crops and crop residues such as sugar-beet pulp are available, rapidly maturing breeds will prove more economical, because the shorter growing period will reduce such overheads as labour and maintenance costs. If it is possible to provide optimum conditions for only a limited period, then it is important that these should obtain when they will do the most good, namely during the early-rearing stages when the animal is most responsive to the plane of nutrition. The point of this is explained later in this section.

Turning now to the developmental aspects, Hammond and his co-workers have provided a full understanding of what occurs when an animal passes from its immature baby form to its mature adult form. At birth when the head and legs constitute a high proportion of total body weight, the proportion of bone is high, there is a relatively small development of muscle, particularly in those parts of the body which are required by the consumer, and the quantity of fat is negligible; while at full maturity the legs and head constitute a small proportion of the body, and the proportion of bone is small relative

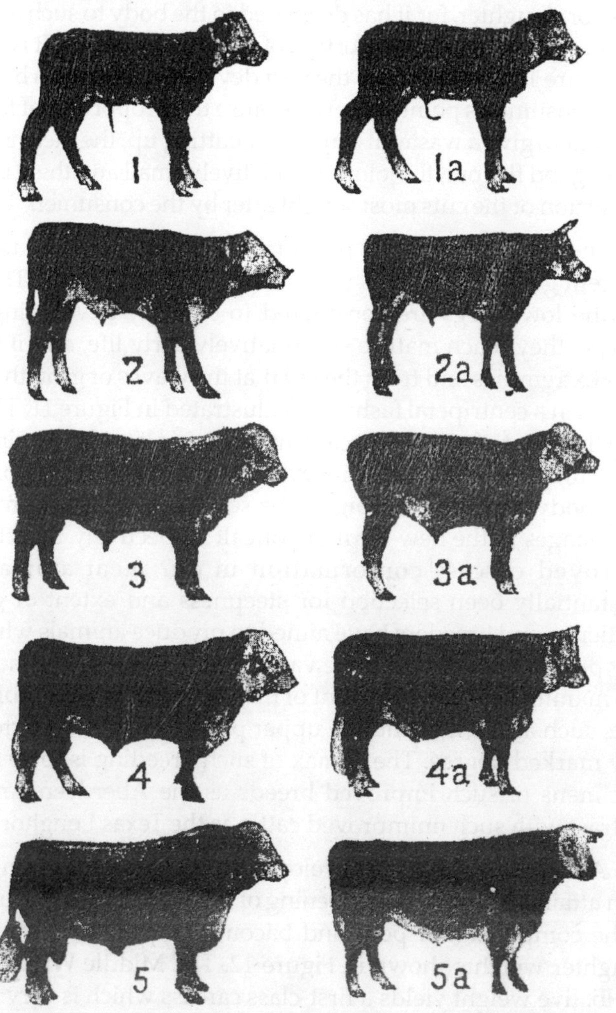

Figure 10: Hereford Cattle: Changes in Body Proportions with Age and Nutrition. All animals reduced to the same shoulder height (Hammond 1941)

1: bull, 2 days; 1a: bull,2 days 2: bull, 5 weeks; 2a: steer, 30 months, badly reared; 3: bull, 13 months; 3a steer, 11 months, well reared; 4: bull, 22 months; 4a: steer, 22 months, well reared; 5: bull, 5 years; 5a: bull of 100 years ago.

to muscle and fat. At this stage the animal has passed the optimum stage for slaughter, for it has deepened in the body to such an extent that there is too high a proportion of the cheaper joints. It is at stage 4 of Figure 10 that one finds the best development from a butcher's and a consumer's point of view, because the proportion of fat is not too great to give a wasteful carcass for cutting up, the meat is tender but of- good flavour, the joints are relatively small and there is a high proportion of the cuts most sought after by the consumer.

The changes of body proportion are explained in terms of different growth gradients within the developing body. The head and the lower legs are considered to be early-developing parts because they reach mature size relatively early life, and it is from these extremities and from the tail that the waves of growth pass to the loin in a centripetal fashion, as illustrated in Figure 11. The loin, from the point of view of carcass maturity, is a late-developing part, and in unimproved animals it never attains a high proportion of the adult body, *e.g.*, the wild pig or the scrub bullock conforms in its adult stages to the new-born pig or calf respectively. Selection for improved carcass conformation in our meat animals has substantially been selection for steepness and extent of growth gradients, and breeders have aimed to produce animals which not only pass rapidly through the various stages of development, but also manifest this development of the late-maturing valuable body parts such as the loin and the upper part of the hind quarters to a very marked degree. The climax of such breeding is to be seen in specimens of such improved breeds as the Aberdeen Angus in contrast with such unimproved cattle as the Texas Longhorn.

A secondary phase of development occurs after full length has been attained. This is the deepening of the body, which is illustrated in the comparison of pork and bacon type pigs at characteristic slaughter weights shown in Figure 12. The Middle White at 100–120 lb. live weight yields a first-class carcass which is very similar in proportions to that of the Large White at 200–220 lb. live weight. If the Middle White, however, is maintained on full feeding until it has reached this latter weight range it grows little in length, for it has substantially exhausted its potential for growth in this direction. Increased weight is mainly obtained through a deepening of the body–the development of a middle-aged spread.

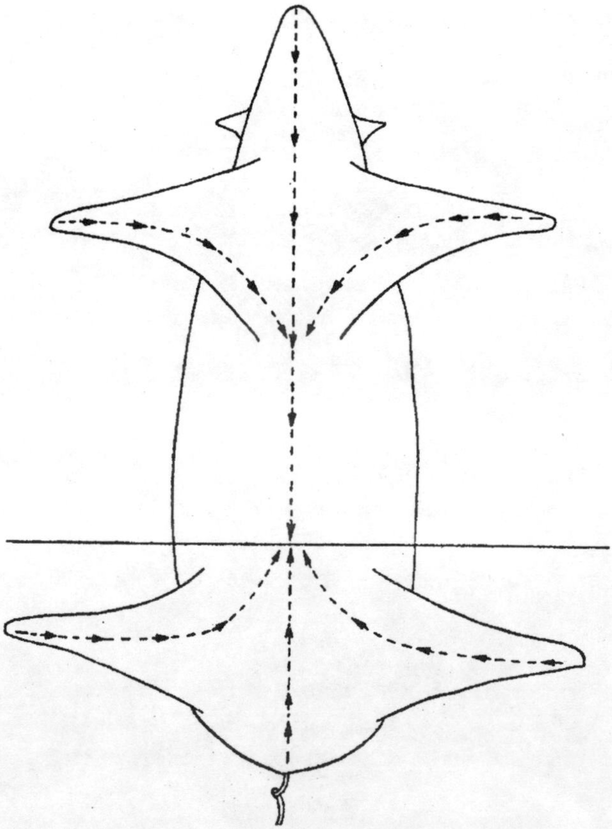

Figure 11: Plan of Animal with Legs, 'Spread-eagled' to Show 'Waves of Growth' from the Six Extremes (head-tail-legs) to the Latest Developing Part (loin) (McMeekan, 1939)

To a large extent this deepening is due to the laying down of a deep layer of subcutaneous fat, the development of adipose tissue being a climax in tissue development that also manifests differential growth. The brain, the nervous system and bone are early-developing tissues, while muscle is intermediate and fat is late-developing tissue. Here again the primitive animals similar in its proportions to the new born of the same improved species. The scrub bullock, even at full maturity, has a high proportion of bone, limited muscular

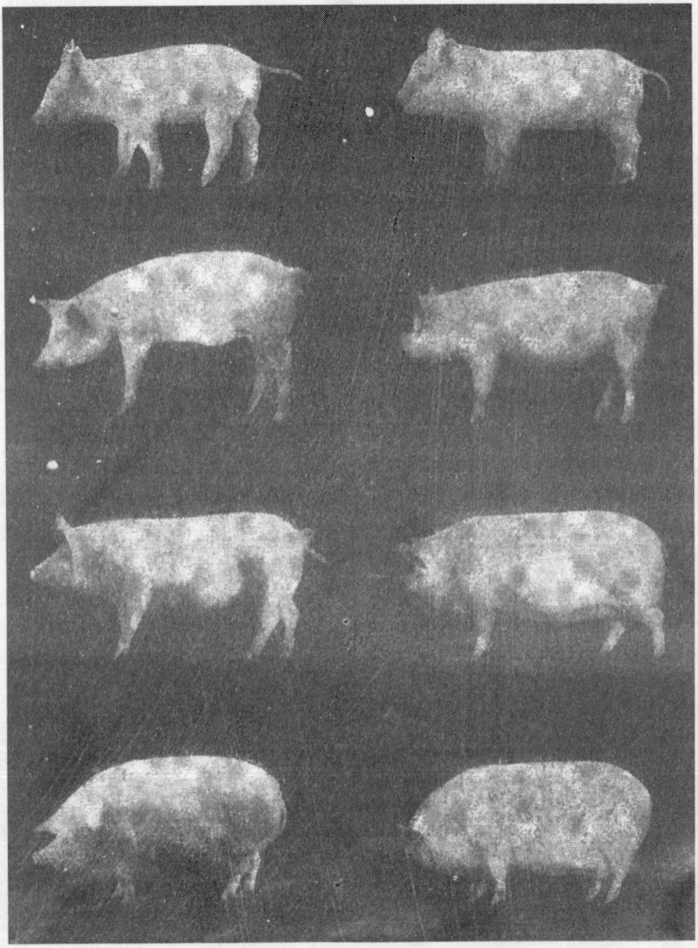

Figure 12: Changes in Body Proportions of Pork and Bacon Type Pigs with Advancing Maturity. All animals reduced to the same shoulder height (Hammond 1941)

***Left*: Bacon Type, Large White; *Right*: Pork Type, Middle White.**

development, particularly in the valuable joints, and insufficient fat to satisfy the consumer. Selection by breeders in their evolution of the improved strains has been directed also to an attainment of maximum muscular development and a desirable degree of fat development. Over the past forty years there has been a tendency to reduce proportion of fat in the carcass, because with the increased supplies of other edible fats, combined with an increase of workers in sedentary occupations, the emphasis in demand has been for joints with just that sufficiency of fat which prevents drying-out in cooking and which safeguards tenderness, consumer demand has also changed in respect of size of joint, since the modern family in contrast with that of Victorian days is small in number and is accustomed to a variety in diet. The Victorian father carved for a large table on Sundays, and the cold joint which remained was served subsequently in the week, but the modern housewife with a small electric or gas oven prefers a small joint which will provide for no more than one cold meal. Breeders of beef cattle have had to modify their breeding objectives to suit in these changes in demand. The two ton bullock which aroused such admiration in the early Victorian days is in the nature of an interesting curiosity today. From both the butcher's and the housewife's points of view the practical ideal is a beast; of about 1,150–1,200 lb. live weight which kills out at 600–700 lb. and yields a high proportion of edible carcass. The proportion of bone in this carcass must be low, and muscular development, particularly in the loin region, along the ribs and over the buttocks must be high and the fat development adequate but not excessive. From the farmer's viewpoint the to beast must attain this size and these proportions quickly, so he demands animals that come to such a market maturity at an early age.

Early maturity, *i.e.*, the capacity to pass quickly through the developmental changes, which have been described in terms of growth waves, so that ideal carcass proportions are attained at an early age and a light weight, has been a primary consideration until meat rationing was imposed. Throughout the war years and until 1949 quality aspects were neglected because of the urgency of getting greater supplies of meat, but in that year the rate of payment was changed, to discourage the marketing of animals over 14 cwt. live weight. This action had evoked protests from graziers who had been forced to pay high prices for stores, and who had been able to justify this high initial outlay by carrying beasts to heavy weights, but from the viewpoint of the butcher and the consuming public the return to smaller carcasses was very welcome. Apart from the drawback of the overfat carcasses which result when early-maturing cattle are carried to very high weights, rationing has accentuated the demand for very small joints. The unfortunate butcher, presented with the problem of cutting up a very large carcass into very small joints is forced to abandon the standard cuts which fit the arrangement of bone and muscles. He can do no more than hack off a portion of meat, disregarding grain of muscle or the balance of tissues.

On another score overfat carcasses are wasteful. An animal makes most rapid and economical gains early in its growing stages, *i.e.* when it is passing along the straight shaft of the S in the normal curve of growth (*see* Figure 9). When the curve flattens most of the live-weight gain is due mainly to fat deposition, whereas earlier live-weight gains are mainly increases in bone and muscle. The energy content of fat is high, and because nutrient intake is limited by an animal's power to ingest and digest food, rate of gain, when a concentrated energy tissue such as fat is laid down, will necessarily be slow, and food requirements per lb. live-weight increase will be high. If fat is required then the higher food requirements may be justified, but when the majority of the consuming public requires less fat than is obtained normally from a heavy-weight carcass, then this over-fattening is wasteful and should be discouraged.

Another factor, apart from increasing rate of fat deposition, contributing to less economical gains with advancing age is the lower moisture content of meat from older animals. All this points to the advantage of rapid growing and fattening from birth to slaughter. Provided food costs permit, such a practice would be ideal, but the economic conditions of beef production are such that farmers cannot generally afford to feed heavily throughout life. For instance, on hill country three-years-old bullocks are the most effective controllers of rough grazing, and the upland farmer of necessity must punish his stock if he is to improve his pastures for sheep grazing. Again, winter feeding based mainly on concentrates does not pay at present prices, and unless a farmer is prepared to accept a loss on bullock fattening as a fair charge for producing farmyard manure, the alternative is one of keeping bullocks going over the winter months until pasture growth commences on whatever there is available in the form of cheap bulk foods, *e.g.*, oat and barley straw, hay, silage, foggage and sugar-beet residues.

Influence of Nutrition on Body Form

Added weight to the above arguments in favour of good feeding over the early-rearing stages is given by the findings of McMeekan (1940), who subjected pigs to controlled planes of nutrition. He found that over the early-growing period good feeding accelerated, and bad feeding retarded, the development of the late-maturing parts. If nutrients were limited then the early-developing parts exercised a priority in drawing on them. If bad feeding is continued for too long a period no amount of subsequent good feeding will repay the damage which is done. The growing animal has considerable resiliency and will recover from the effects of short periods of malnutrition, but if the underfeeding is over a long period the capacity for full development may be lost by those parts of the body or those tissues which have been grossly penalised by such underfeeding. Such effects may be observed in the large heads and stunted bodies of stock which have been 'badly done', and their form at maturity resembles strongly that of unimproved cattle–the proportion of bone is high, the shoulder is heavy and the loin and hind-quarters poorly developed. When brought on to good feed such animals will fatten, but their carcasses are not attractive to the butcher because of the predominance of cheaper cuts. Bad feeding over this early critical formative period will undo all the good of generations of careful breeding and selection, and a potential winner at Smithfield can be reduced to the level of a scrub, *e.g.*, No. 2a in Figure 10.

The Contrast of Beef and Dairy Types

Figure 13 illustrates the changes which have been effected in cattle types as a result of selective breeding. From the original foundation stock which was the raw material of men like the Collings, two distinct types of Shorthorn have been evolved. One is the massive Scotch-type Shorthorn, which is both a farmer's and butcher's beast, quick to mature and endowed with a high proportion of the cuts that the public require. The other is the lean, flat-boned, triple-wedge type which we have come to associate with heavy milk production. The development of these two distinct Shorthorn types is one of the best examples we have of divergent evolution. On the one hand, breeders whose main concern was meat production have concentrated the genetic factors which are responsible for depth of flesh and early maturity. They have selected in an environment which has permitted of full expression of such qualities, and they have

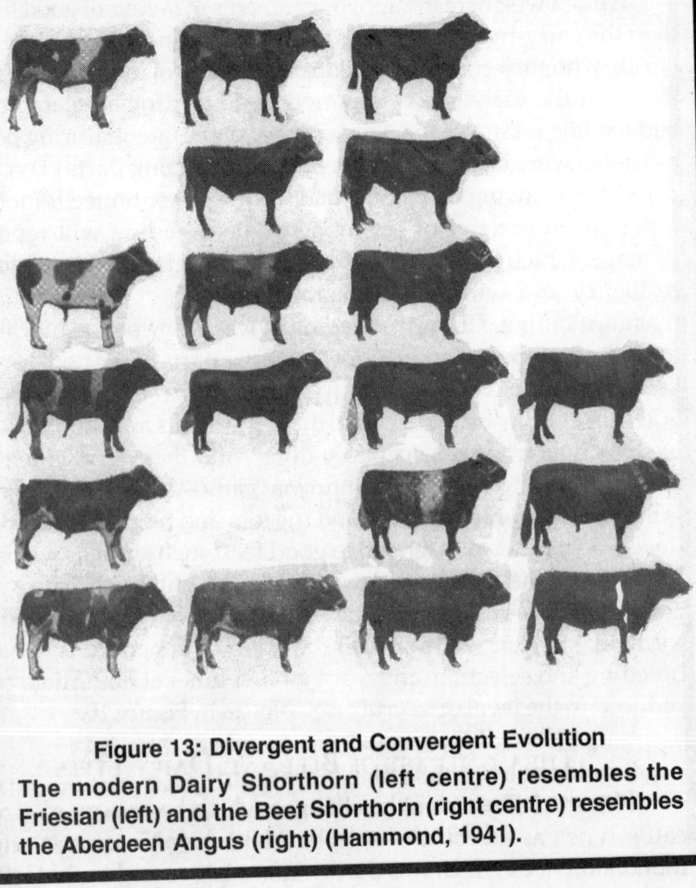

Figure 13: Divergent and Convergent Evolution
The modern Dairy Shorthorn (left centre) resembles the Friesian (left) and the Beef Shorthorn (right centre) resembles the Aberdeen Angus (right) (Hammond, 1941).

exploited the outstanding breeding animals which have arisen through fortuitous and favourable gene combinations. Breeders of Aberdeen Angus, Herefords and other specialised beef breeds worked on parallel lines but with different foundation material, and they all achieved a similar functional objective. If we disregard the superficial breed characters of coat colour, horns and colour pattern and look at typical representatives of each breed in silhouette, their similarity is unmistakable. The Dairy Shorthorn on the other hand, regarded in the same manner, shows a striking resemblance to the Friesian, which has been bred for the same economic function.

The distinct cattle types should be regarded more as the result rather than the cause of their differing functions. The metabolism of the dairy cow is directed towards the production of milk rather than meat. She has a greater capacity to ingest and digest nutrients than a beef cow, and her circulatory system is so developed that large quantities of blood are directed to an actively functioning mammary gland, which is very much larger than that of the beef cow. The latter's gland has very much less secretory tissue, and its substance is composed largely of adipose and connective tissue. This is very strikingly illustrated in Figure 14, which gives cross-sections of glands from Sophie 19th of Hood Farm, a very high-producing Jersey and Blackbird of Dallas, a notable Aberdeen Angus cow (Swett *et al.*, 1937). The typical dairy cow differs from the typical cow in another important respect, in that the anterior pitutary gland of the former has a greater concentration of lactogen, the hormone which initiates and maintains milk secretion (Espe, 1946). The inherent qualities of the dairy cow are such that her physiological processes are organised for milk production, while there is a very finely adjusted endocrine balance that determines that the nutrients she digests will mainly go to the production of milk. A high-producing cow may eat 25 lb. of starch equivalent in a day, enough for her own maintenance and for the production of 7–8 gallons of milk, while a beef animal of corresponding weight gaining at the rate of 2½ lb. live weight per day, a very good rate of increase, needs only about two-thirds this amount of energy for maintenance and production. Skeletally the dairy cow does not differ greatly from a beef cow to the degree that one might expect (*see* Figure 15). There are some differences in that the bones of the beef animal tend to be shorter and thicker, a quality which is associated with depth of fleshing, and the spring of the rib tends to be higher, so that in cross-section it appears round in comparison with the wedge-shaped dairy beast. Such a conformation favours depth of fleshing long the back in the case of the beef animal and the converse ill the case of the dairy animal. Mainly, however, the angularity of the dairy cow must be regarded as a result of its production going into the bucket, whereas in the case of the beef animal production becomes part of the animal body, and manifests itself in depth of flesh over the hind-quarters, the back and fore-quarters. When we see a blocky rectangular beast, which is thick through whichever way we look at it, we are seeing its production, but its identical twin which has been on store feeding will exhibit many of the qualities we associate with the dairy type.

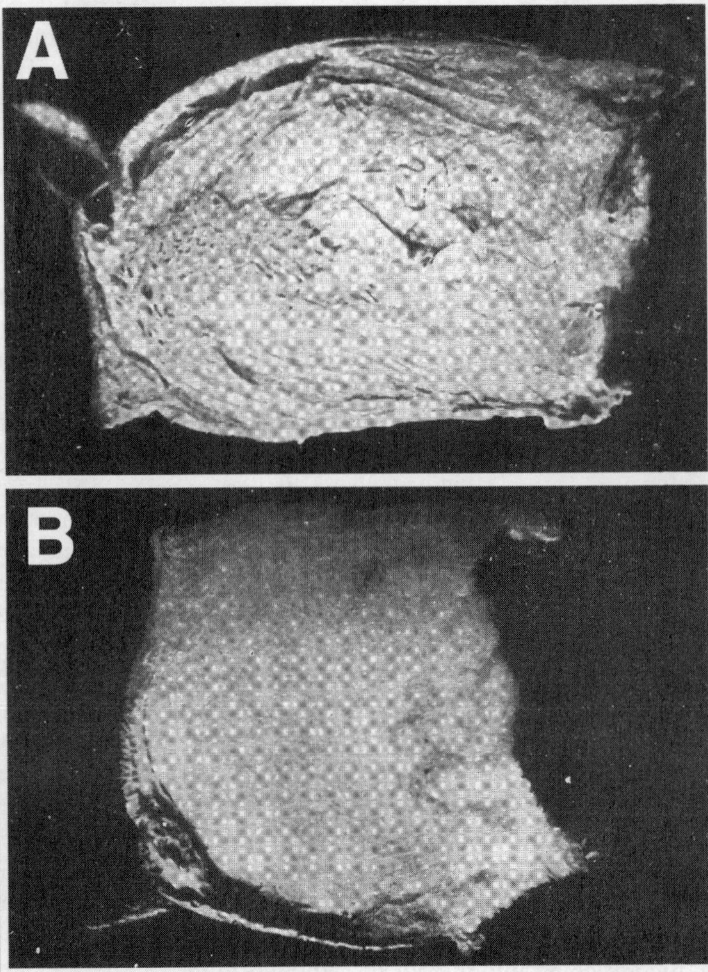

Figure 14a: Vertical Transverse Sections through the Udder of a Specialised Beef Cow (Blackbird). A: Near quarter; B: Front quarter (Swett, 1928).

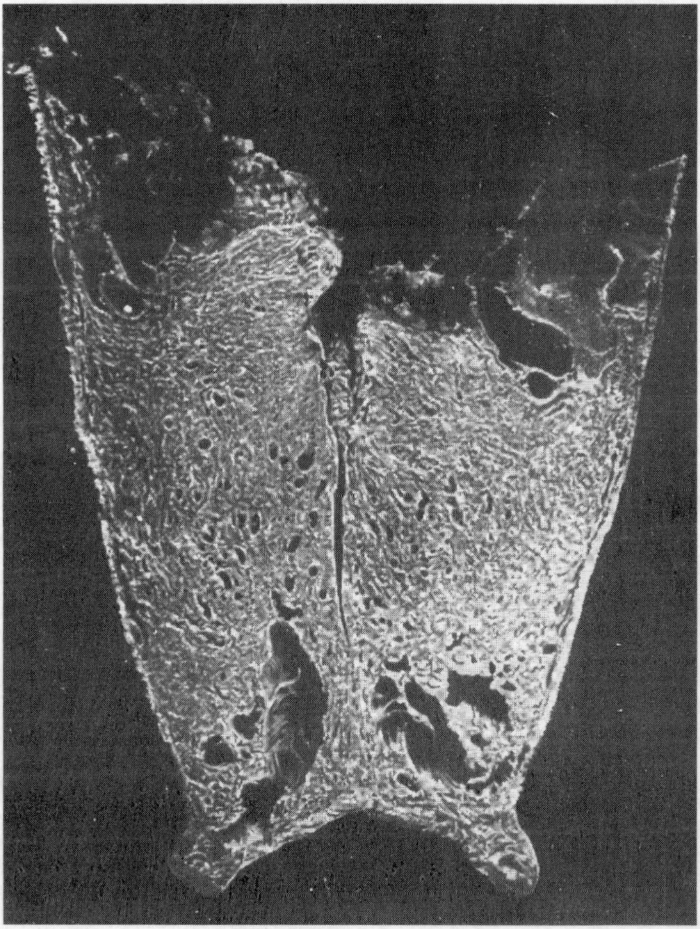

Figure 14b: A Vertical Transverse Section through the Near Quarters of a Specialised Dairy Cow (Sophie) (Swett, 1928)

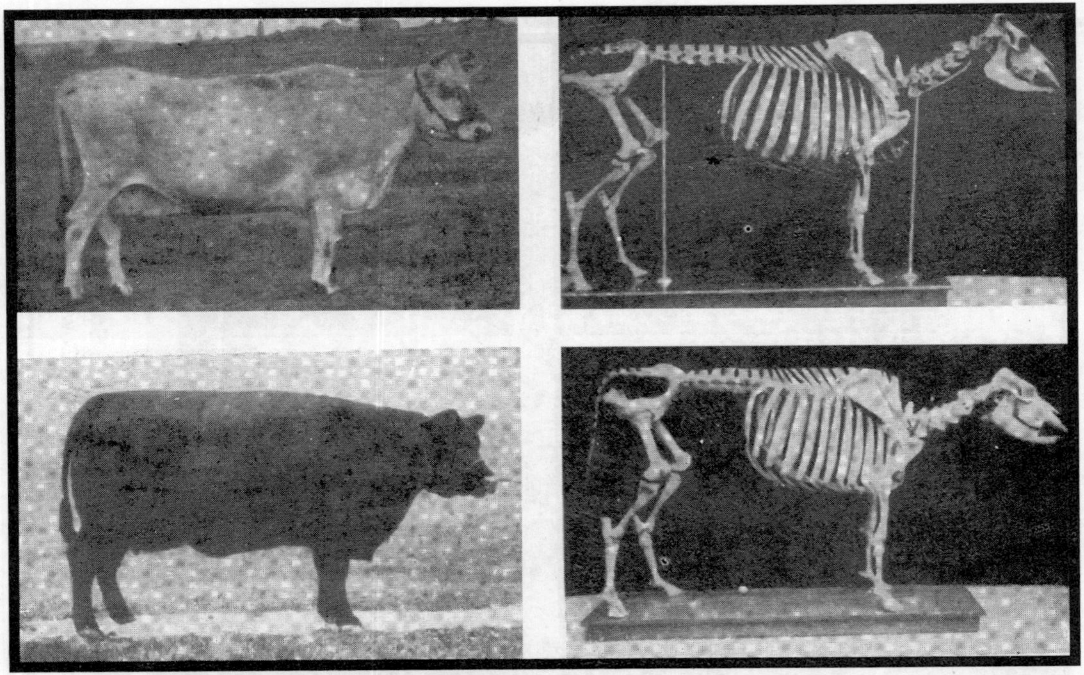

Figure 15: Body and Skeletal Differences Between a Specified a Beef Cow and a Specialised Dairy Cow (Swett, 1928)

It cannot be inferred from his that if such a specialised dairy animal as the Jersey is fed on a high plane of nutrition throughout life it will exhibit good beef qualities. The objective in evolving this breed has not been depth of flesh, and it lacks factors for the expression of this character in a high degree. However, it is interesting to note that pedigree Jersey breeders who are concerned in preserving the fine Island types tend to limit the nutrition of their calves, quantitatively, in order to avoid coarseness.

Generally, however, the extreme dairy type, when fattened, tends to give an undesirable carcass such as that illustrated in Figure 16. The leg is in proportion to its depth, the ribs are flat, the loin is deficient, the rib of beef has a shallow eye muscle and there is a high proportion of bone. On the other hand a good beef animal will have a well-developed eye muscle which is the substance of a rib roast or a sirloin (see Figure 17). Furthermore, when killed in prime condition the muscles will be well marbled with fat. In the early stages of fattening, fat is deposited first in the gut and kidney regions. Next comes the subcutaneous fat, which forms a layer over the muscles to give the smooth rounded appearance of the finished bullock. Finally in the fattening process, fat penetrates; within the muscle bundles to break the uniform colour of the muscles, to promote a condition known as 'marbling.' In unimproved and in specialised dairy cattle one finds that the process of fattening does not generally proceed as far as the final marbling stage. There is a heavy deposition of fat around the kidney and around the viscera, and there will be some fat deposited on the muscles but not to the same degree as in the specialised beef breeds.

It is seen that there are very considerable differences between beef and dairy types that are the outcome of years of deliberate breeding and selection. Though breeders of dairy cattle may have often tended to dissipate their powers to select intensively for sustained high milk production because they have paid too much attention to conventional dairy-type characteristics which are not really important, they have selected away from the attributes which the beef men have considered important. The two sets of breeders have created populations which differ strikingly, notably in respect of the genetic factors which control glandular activity.

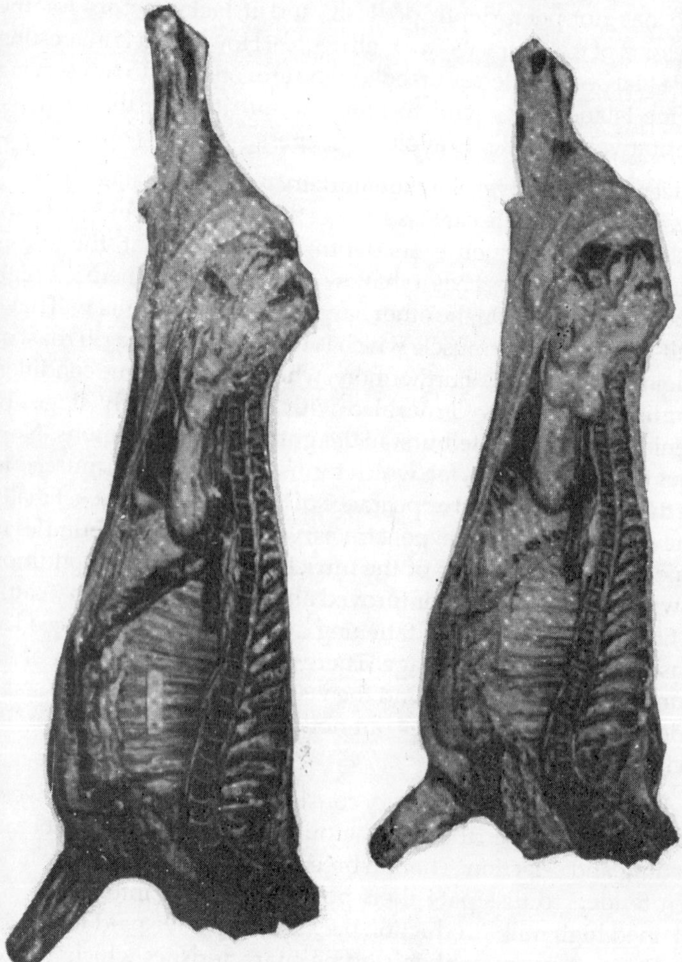

Figure 16: A Poor Side of Beef (Left) Compared with a Good One (Hammond, 1941)

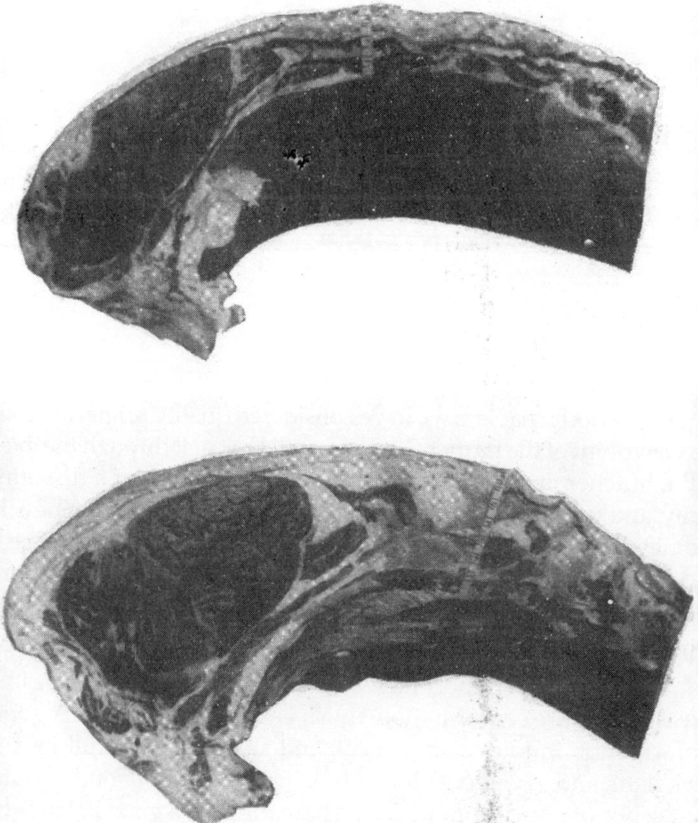

Figure 17: A Contrast in Ribs of Beef (Hammond, 1941)

Chapter 8
Beef Quality

In previous chapters we have considered quality primarily from the viewpoint of the farmer. Now we will look at it through the eyes of the butcher and the consumer. Though quality is at a discount today, and the annual spectacle of the Smithfield Fat Stock Show is a somewhat tantalising reminder of the past, quality may come back into its own once more if supplies improve and something more than weight range, age and estimated killing-out percentage will be taken into account when fat stock are marketed.

There are three important features which define excellence in a carcass. They are conformation, finish and quality of meat. A good conformation implies a short neck and shank, a thick full loin, a thick flank and a well-developed hind end with depth of flesh and an absence of bony prominences. There must be a good balance of side so that a high proportion by weight consists of the more attractive cuts such as the loin, ribs and hind-quarters. Excessive depth of chest, relative to length and hind-quarter development, is not wanted, for the shoulder and brisket provide some of the cheaper cuts. Normally a butcher could always find a market for these cheap cuts, but at a price substantially below that paid for rump steak or sirloin of beef. When he assessed the value of a beast in the sale ring he had to make some estimate of the yield of the various cuts of meat in order to get a proper appreciation of its value to him. Herein lay the great art of fat stock purchase, which is rapidly being lost thanks to the operation of the Ministry of Food, who have failed to supply any substitute for the discriminating eye of the master butcher, who now has to take pot luck with his allocations.

Correct finish on a carcass implies a smooth but not an excessive covering of fat which is evenly distributed. Patchiness or excessive deposition over particular regions is not wanted either by butcher or consumer. The housewife wants muscle and only that amount of fat which will prevent drying-out during cooking. The modem family normally is able to obtain a sufficiency of edible fat in the form of butter, lard or cooking fat, and does not need the dripping which was once such a feature of cheaper dietaries. Judgment of finish in the living animal calls for very considerable experience. Apart from visual examination, it is determined by feeling with the tips of the fingers the amount and the texture of flesh over the rectangle formed by the hook and pin bones, over the loin and along the ribs. The flesh should be moderately firm without any hint of what is appropriately described as 'blubber,' *i.e.* soft patches of fat which are most commonly encountered over the hind end.

Quality of meat is controlled by a complex of factors, including colour and flavour of meat, the size of the muscle fibres and muscle bundles, the amount of connective tissue, and the amount and distribution of fat, particularly the intramuscular fat on which is dependent the characteristic marbling of good-quality meat. Not only does quality vary from animal to animal but from region to region within the same animal.

The principal factors influencing the quality of a carcass as a whole are: breed or type, condition, age, sex, feeding and management, exercise, methods of slaughter and methods of storage (Hirzel, 1939). We will not deal at any length with the breed factor, for in the absence of precise data which describe the normal breed characteristics one is able to do little more than provoke a pointless breed controversy. However, one can safely point out that the Aberdeen Angus and its crosses have dominated the championship awards at Smithfield, and that the breed is pre-eminent for the production of early-maturing carcasses with a high proportion of edible meat and a low proportion of bone. All beef, however, is not produced under the favourable conditions to which Smithfield winners are subjected, and it must be remembered that the several British breeds of beef cattle have been evolved to do a job of work under a variety of conditions. Furthermore, within the breeds, despite nearly two centuries of deliberate breeding and selection there is still a great measure of inherent variation, and at the risk of being platitudinous it is stressed that it is the individual rather than the breed which is important.

Condition at slaughter, which is closely related to age and the system of feeding and management to which a beast is subjected, influences not only the proportion of the various tissues but the yield of dressed carcass relative to live weight. A lean store will have a yield of 50 per cent or less, while a fully prime mature beast will kill out at 65 per cent. The influence of age and condition on carcass composition is shown in Table 1, which gives details of dissections carried out on nineteen Shorthorn steers (Wood and Newman, 1928).

Table 1: Percentage Composition of Dressed Carcasses (Wood & Newman, 1928)

Class	*Protein* %	*Fat* %	*Water* %	*Bone Waste & Loss* %	*Marbling Fat* %
Baby Beef Store	12.6	12.4	47.4	27.6	3.2
Baby Beef Half-fat	12.5	12.2	48.0	27.3	4.8
Baby Beef Fat	12.3	20.0	44.5	23.2	8.0
2 yr. old Store	12.5	14.3	49.7	23.5	5.4
2 yr. Fattened 1 mth.	12.3	20.7	45.3	21.7	5.2
2 yr. Fattened 2 mth.	10.8	21.7	44.4	23.1	6.8
2 yr. Fattened 3 mth.	11.6	21.0	45.7	21.07	6.1
2 yr. Fattened 4. mth.	10.9	19.9	46.8	22.4	7.2
2 yr. Fattened 5 mth.	11.2	29.7	39.8	19.3	9.1
2 yr. Fattened 6 mth.	12.6	29.2	35.9	22.3	9.4
3 yr. old Store	11.8	20.0	49.0	19.2	4.6
3 yr. old Store	11.6	22.4	46.6	19.4	5.2
3 yr. old Store	10.5	28.2	44.3	17.0	7.0
3 yr. Fattened 1 mth.	12.4	20.7	46.6	20.3	5.2

Table 1–Contd...

Class	Protein %	Fat %	Water %	Bone Waste & Loss %	Marbling Fat %
3 yr. Fattened 2 mth.	11.6	27.7	43.4	17.3	10.3
3 yr. Fattened 3 mth.	11.0	29.9	45.0	14.1	7.9
3 yr. Fattened 4. mth.	11.4	36.1	35.2	17.3	9.4
3 yr. Fattened 5 mth.	10.8	28.7	43.5	17.0	8.9
3 yr. Fattened 6 mth.	10.7	31.4	43.1	14.8	9.3

The percentage of edible protein multiplied by four gives the approximate percentage of lean meat. This, generally speaking, is the most stable of the tissues over the range of ages and stages of fattening, but there is a tendency, however, for the proportion of muscle to fall as a beast gets older and fatter. The figures given for bone also include waste, but they may be taken as generally indicative of the relative importance of bone, which declines with advancing age and condition. Fat, on the other hand, being a late-developing tissue, increases with advancing age and condition. The increases and decreases of the various tissues are by no means uniform, and they exhibit the very considerable individual variation one finds in stock. This variation does not invalidate the general conclusions given above.

The amount of marbling fat increases fairly steadily with age and fattening. It also appears that the muscle of the baby beef is slightly less marbled than that of older animals which are in prime condition. This result is in keeping with the conclusions of other workers, who have found that marbling increases with age (Hammond, 1932). Marbling, however, is not so important in the muscle of a young animal as it is in an old one. Tenderness of meat is believed to be closely associated with the size and development of muscle fibres and muscle bundles, though the amount of connective tissue present is very important, *e.g.* the foreleg cuts are notoriously tough and contain much more connective tissue than the loin. Hammond (1932) has established a close correlation between tenderness and smallness of muscle fibre ($r = 0.71$), and tenderness and size of muscle bundle ($r = 0.33$). Fibre size increases with age and with exercise, while this latter factor reduces the amount of marbling fat and thereby aggravates toughness. The male has larger muscle fibres than the female; and the castrate male is intermediate between the two. The meat of fattened animals is tenderer than that of lean animals despite the fact that there is an increase in connective tissue and possibly in size of muscle fibres with fattening. It is probable that with the laying down of fat in the connective tissue the connective fibres are split up on cooking. Tenderness, as is well known, is increased by storage, and it is usual to hang meat until such time as *rigor mortis* has completely disappeared. This increase in tenderness is due to chemical changes in the actual muscles and the connective tissue of the muscles.

Colour of meat, both of fat and muscle, is a fairly reliable guide to quality. Beef, such as that obtained from old bulls and dairy cows is very dark in colour, due to the presence of considerable concentrations of haemoglobin, and this is true of cuts derived from the muscles of a young animal which are actively used, *e.g.* those of the lower leg as opposed to the *longissimus dorsi* or eye muscle, that large muscle along the back which gives the substance to a rib roast or a sirloin. Veal, by way of contrast, is practically colourless. Beef normally attains its optimum colour at about two years of age, *i.e.* a light purplish red. The age effect is often obscured by the amount of exercise the animal takes, for exercise appears to increase the amount of haemoglobin in muscle.

Excessive exercise immediately before slaughter leads to darker-coloured muscles. When animals are killed in a feverish condition the capillaries are dilated and the carcass is more difficult to bleed. Apart from the colour factor, proper bleeding is important because a badly bled carcass does not keep well.

Frequently one sees on a butcher's counter joints in which the muscular tissue is quite a bright pink. This is due to exposure to the air, for freshly cut meat has a dull-red colour with a purplish tinge. This colour intensity increases up to about three hours from cutting, but progressively, according to temperature and humidity, the surface does out and meat takes on a blackish tinge. Meat which is stored over long periods tends to change in colour from the normal red to brown.

Colour of fat is derived from carotin pigments in the food, but the intensity of this colouring is controlled by a variety of factors including breed, nutritional circumstances, age and exercise. The colour of body fat appears to be closely linked to that of milk fat. Jerseys which have a yellow milk fat are notorious for the bright colour of their body fat, which is not attractive to the consumer, who prefers a creamy white fat such as that obtained from most of the beef breeds when they are fattened without check. This last point is important, for animals which have ups and downs in condition–such as a dairy cow which has had a long life in the byre or a mature range bullock for whom summer plenty has, several times, been followed by winter scarcity–are characterised by deeply pigmented fat. It appears that the carotin pigments which are normally laid down with fat remain behind when the fat is utilised through the animal 'living on its condition.' When fresh fat is formed the residual pigment in the adipose tissue intensifies colour. The greater likelihood of their having been subjected to falls in condition probably accounts to some extent for the deeper coloured fat of older animals, and naturally they will by virtue of their age have ingested more pigment.

Feeding is probably the most important single factor accounting for colour of body fat. When cattle are fed on carotin-rich fodders such as pasture and other green feed, the intensity of fat colour will increase, while those fed on concentrates, straw, hay and roots, which are deficient in carotin, will produce a white fat. It must not be assumed that grass-fed bullocks will necessarily have an undesirable colour of fat. On the contrary, animals of the recognised beef breeds which appear to have an inherent capacity to eliminate food pigments will have an attractively coloured fat if they are not subjected to severe checks and are killed at a reasonably early age.

It may be taken, therefore, that fat colour is a fairly good guide to meat quality. If one is offered a joint with deep coloured fat, one can be fairly certain that it has Channel Island antecedents, or else it is derived from an animal of some age, such as a displaced dairy cow. Examination of the muscle colour and texture will generally confirm the suspicions that have been aroused. It is a fairly safe rule when offered a choice of joints, if other things are equal, to select the one with the whitest and crispest fat.

Optimum flavour in meat is very difficult to define, for one person's preference may not be another's. The average person now prefers the mild-flavoured meat derived from young animals. Good, flavour is generally associated with good marbling, but this may to some extent be due to the physical effects of marbling on promoting smoothness of eating (Hammond, 1932). Intensity of flavour is usually associated with colour. Veal, for instance, is comparatively tasteless, while bull beef has too much flavour for the average palate. Normal storage for limited periods appears to improve flavour.

Characteristics of the more Important Cuts

There is a very considerable variation in quality of meat according to the anatomical region from which it is obtained (Hiner and Hankins, 1950), and some attention will now be given to the more important cuts of beef and their uses in the trade. The system of cutting and nomenclature followed is that used by Wood and Newmen (1928), namely the 'London cuts,' which are fourteen in number. These are illustrated in Figure 18. It must be stressed that there is considerable local variation in the systems of cutting and naming of joints, while the wholesale joints may be sub-divided in the retail trade into component parts, *e.g.* the round becomes the silverside and topside.

The following notes on the various wholesale cuts are based on information from Wood and Newman. The weights given are the range for 3-year-old bullocks in prime or approaching prime condition.

Leg (hind shin or hock) (14–16 lb.)

This is one of the lowest-priced joints due to the high proportion of bone and waste (about 50 per cent by weight) and the inferior quality of the muscles which, as they pass down the leg, become more fibrous and are sheathed in tough coverings which at the ends become tendons. The meat is mainly used as gravy meat, for making soup or for stewing beef.

Round (60–66 lb.)

This joint contains the femur, which is the largest long bone in the body. Bone and waste amount to only 10 per cent of the total cut, while the proportion of muscle is high, constituting rather more than half of the total weight. The meat is of good quality and comes into the high-grade category. The silverside portion, so named because of the colouring of muscle sheaths, is usually boiled either fresh or pickled. Corned or pickled beef (which is not to be confused with tinned beef) is usually silverside. Silverside does not make a

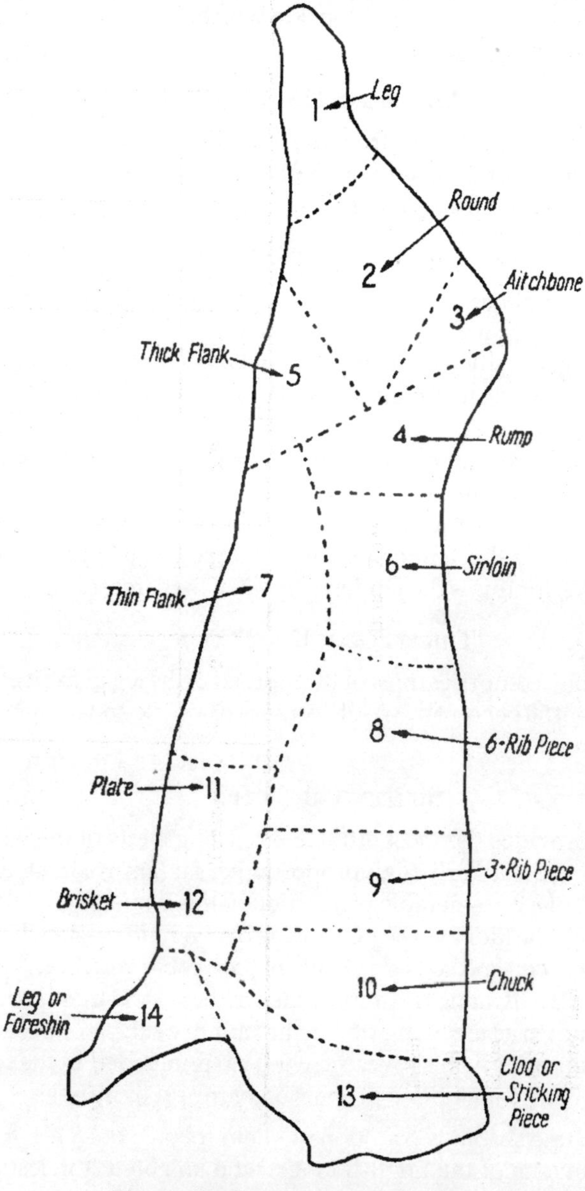

Figure 18: Cuts from a Beef Carcass (after Wood and Newman, 1928)

good roasting joint, for it is fairly low in fat, and dries out in cooking. This applies to some extent to topside which, however, is sold for roasting.

Aitchbone (13–15 lb.)

This is a triangular cut from the top of the round with a fairly high proportion of bone (about 25 per cent). The meat is of good quality and is used for roasting.

The Rump (27–32 lb.)

The percentage of bone is moderate at about 14–15 per cent, while muscle normally comprises at least half the weight of the joint. Fat is generally well distributed between the muscles of a fat animal. The muscle texture is particularly good, and it is one of the tenderest parts of the carcass. The flesh, which is of very good flavour, is particularly well suited for grilling or frying, and is the highest-priced part of the carcass. The fillet steak is cut from this joint and consists of the psoas muscle lying below the sacral vertebrae. This is the cut known as the 'tender-loin' in the United States. The name is appropriate, for this is the tenderest meat of the carcass.

Thick Flank (25–27 lb.)

This joint comprises most of the muscles of the leg in front of the femur. About 50 per cent by weight consists of muscle and the amount of bone is negligible.

Sirloin (50–56 lb.)

This provides the most attractive roasting joints of the whole carcass. There is a fairly high proportion of fat (approximately 40 per cent), but a considerable proportion of this is suet, the hard fat surrounding the kidney. The percentage of bone and waste is low at about 11 per cent, and consists mainly of the lumbar vertebrae. Quite often one or two floating ribs are included in the cut and these provide the joint known as the 'wing rib.' In the 'country cut,' as opposed to the 'London cut' given above, the wing rib is included in the fore-ribs. The cut also includes a proportion of the psoas muscle.

The name sirloin is traditionally held to have been accorded this joint by one of the English kings, who knighted it in jest at a lunch, as a mark of his esteem for the quality of meat it provides. A 'baron of beef' consists of both halves of the sirloin unseparated, together with the rumps. It corresponds to a saddle of mutton. This is not a trade joint, but one specially cut for traditional feasts and dinners.

Thin Flank (16 lb.)

It is composed of layers of fat and muscle which form the abdominal wall. It is low quality meat which finds its best use in sausages.

6-Rib Piece (45–50 lb.)

This includes the last six ribs of the thorax. Normally on cutting the pieces are boned and rolled to form the conventional rib roast. From a young carcass one gets very good quality meat from this region, but with older animals there is a tendency for the muscle to be coarse, and the joints are too big for household trade. The proportion of bone is fairly high in the rib cuts (about 16 per cent), and this makes them fairly expensive.

3-Rib Piece (30–40 lb.)

This cut is very similar to the last in quality and uses. It comprises the fourth to the sixth ribs of the thorax. It may be included with the chuck to form the pony of beef.

Chuck or Leg of Mutton Piece (60–70 lb.)

This joint contains the shoulder blade and the first three ribs, so that there is a fairly high proportion of bone (about 14 per cent). There is a considerable amount of tendon and cartilage, and the muscle tends to be fairly coarse and stringy. It provides second-grade roasts, but blade steaks cut from the lower part of the shoulder blade provide the best stewing steak.

Plate (25–33 lb.)

This cut includes the posterior half of the breast bone and rib ends. There is, however, a surprisingly low percentage of bone (10–12 per cent). The bulk of its weight in a prime animal is made up by fat which is layered between flat muscles. Pre-war in the retail trade it was often boned and cooked for sale as cold pressed beef. Today it is sold either for boiling or roasting.

Brisket (25–30 lb.)

This cut which is very similar to the plate in use and in value consists of the forepart of the breast bone, rib ends and the lower part of the dewlap. It is sold, fresh or pickled, for boiling.

Clod or Sticking Piece (35–45 lb.)

This comprises the forepart of the fore-limb and the neck. The latter part is the sticking piece and the former the clod. The clod contains the humerus (the upper bone of the forelimb which is not free as it is in man, but enclosed in the body proper), while the sticking piece contains the bones of the neck. There is a very high proportion of bone and waste (about 25 per cent), and the muscle is of poor quality. Its main use is for stewing.

Leg or Fore-shin (12 lb.)

This corresponds to the forearm in man, and contains the ulna and radius. The muscles are small, and there is a high proportion of tendons. Approximately 45 per cent is bone or waste. The meat which can be cut off it is used for stewing or for making soups. It is even less valuable than the corresponding part of the hind leg.

Chapter 9

Nutrition-Scientific Principles

INTRODUCTORY

The foundations of the science of animal nutrition were laid by the researches of men such as Kellner and Armsby, who used the ox as their main experimental animal, and yet, paradoxically, scientific principles are applied less to the feeding of beef cattle than they are to any other class of farm animal with the exception of the sheep. The reason for this is that the special role of sheep and beef cattle in the complex of land utilisation is the conversion of the low-quality foods such as rough pastures and bulky forage crops into valuable products such as meat, hides and wool. Though the pig, the hen and the dairy cow are much more efficient converters of to their food into human food (see Figure 19), they require much more concentrated and valuable feeding-stuffs than either sheep or beef cattle, and often this food may be directly useful for human consumption. Feeders normally operate on fairly narrow margins, and they cannot afford to waste food through unbalanced rations, and so they have come to

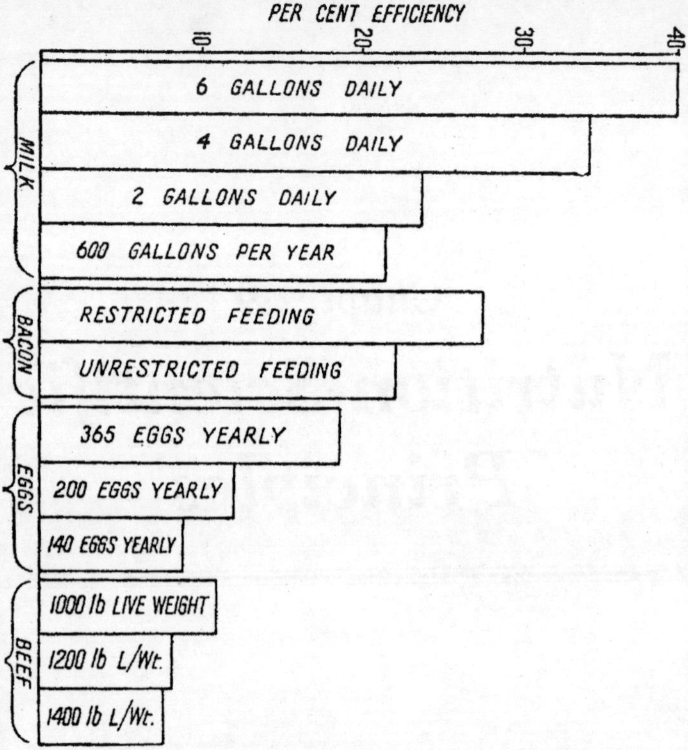

Figure 19: Relative Efficiency of Food Utilisation (McMeekan 1943)

rely on the appropriate feeding standards which have been devised through careful experimentation.

Because the feed of beef cattle and sheep is generally of fairly low quality there is not the same pressure as there is for cows, pigs and poultry, and, in practice, judgment based on experience is more important than any feeding standard. This does not mean, however, that scientific principles are wasted on the practical feeder. On the contrary, for only by having a knowledge of the particular virtues and shortcomings of the various feeding-stuffs at his disposal in relation to the differing needs of his livestock at different stages of development can a farmer hope to obtain the best results from his stock and his feed supplies. It is not implied by this that there should be rigid rationing or balancing of dietaries, for this is impractical under the extensive husbandry systems which usually characterise beef production, but that the system of feeding should generally conform, within the limits of what is economically feasible, to the physiological needs of the stock. This point is particularly well illustrated in grass feeding of cattle. Pasture is notoriously variable both in quality and quantity. At its best it is a very valuable food for cattle, but at its worst it can be either a sappy food which will cause scouring and digestive upsets or a coarse fibrous food with little better than a maintenance value. The farmer can greatly extend the availability of pasture at its optimum stage by fertilising, by the use of special strains and species and by judicious grazing, mowing and resting, but eventually his efforts are limited by climate and season, and supplementary feeding has to be adopted. It is important that these supplements should be selected in relation to the particular needs of the stock and the deficiencies of the pasture on which they are grazing, and the over-riding consideration of whether the course adopted is a profitable one. It is for reasons such as this that a somewhat fundamental approach has been made to the problem of feeding cattle. In the absence of this the only substitute is an empirical approach, which is not conducive to progress.

Composition of Food

An animal's food consists of a variety of complex chemical compounds, built up by plants and animals, that provide the energy required for maintaining body temperatures and all forms of muscular activity, as well as the raw materials for building bone, fat and muscle. The undigested fraction, which is not broken down by mastication and the action of the digestive juices, is excreted from the body in the form of dung. Other waste products, not of digestion but of metabolism, are excreted in the breath, from the skin and in the urine.

Food may be divided into six main fractions as follows:

1. Water
2. Carbohydrates
3. Fats and oils
4. Proteins
5. Minerals
6. Vitamins

Water

A very high proportion of the animal body consists of water, and particularly is this the case with young animals, 80 per cent of whose muscle tissue consists of water. In addition water is essential for normal physiological processes, and though an animal may live for some time when it is denied solid food, it will quickly succumb if it is deprived of water or of foods containing a high proportion of water. It is, for instance, an important component of blood in which nutrients are carried in solution or emulsion to the cells of the body, and which carries the waste products of cell activity to the lungs or kidneys, which are organs of excretion. It is a constituent of digestive juices, and of the glandular secretions which play such an important part in normal body function. It goes without saying that animals should always be supplied with adequate water.

Carbohydrates

Carbohydrates include a highly complex series of substances which contain carbon, hydrogen and oxygen in the constant proportion of 1 : 2 : 1. They range from the simple water-soluble sugars to more complex insoluble substances such as fibres. Those carbohydrates such as starch and fibre which are not water-soluble are not available to the animal until they are broken down by digestion to sugars which are soluble. Some of the more complex carbohydrates are so resistant to the action of digestive juices and bacterial action in the digestive tract that they pass from the animal body without yielding up their quota of energy. Particularly is this the case with the fibre from very mature herbage, such as the straw of a crop ripened for grain. Cattle have digestive tracts which are specially adapted to the handling of fibrous foods, and indeed a certain minimum of fibre is essential to preserve tone in the tract. Pigs on the other hand need feeding-stuffs with a small amount of fibre and a high proportion of the more readily digestible carbohydrate starch which is quickly broken down to sugar and absorbed by the blood stream.

Carbohydrates are oxidised in the animal body to produce energy just as wood is oxidised in a fire to produce heat, which is one form of energy. The gaseous end-products in each case are the same, namely carbon dioxide and water vapour. Carbohydrates surplus to the immediate needs of providing energy for muscular movement or for keeping the animal warm are stored in a concentrated form as body fat, which is a reserve of energy to be used in times of shortage.

Fats and Oils

Fats and oils also contain the elements carbon, hydrogen and oxygen, but the proportion of carbon is much higher than it is in the case of carbohydrates, and so fats have a correspondingly greater energy value, varying from 1.9 to 2.4 times that of an equivalent dry weight of carbohydrate, according to the source of the fat. As in the case of carbohydrates, food fats are used to provide energy or are stored as animal fat. The process of fat digestion is rather different from that of the other nutrients in that the broken-down fats are emulsified, and do not into solution in the way that sugars and starches do. They are maintained in their original form to a greater degree, and if an animal is fattened slowly, *i.e.* a very small proportion of the body fat laid down is derived from carbohydrates and the greater proportion comes from food fats, and if these have low melting points, a rather soft and undesirable fat which is liable to go rancid will result. In contrast, when an animal is fattened quickly, and most of the fat is built up by the animal from sugars, a firm crisp fat typical of the species will result.

It is important that the proportion of fat in any ration should not be too high, as it will tend to depress digestibility of other constituents by forming a film which protects food particles from the action of specific digestive juices. Furthermore, a very oily diet may cause scouring.

Proteins

Proteins differ from fats and carbohydrates because in addition to carbon, hydrogen and oxygen they contain nitrogen and sometimes other elements such as sulphur and phosphorus. The muscular tissue of the animal body as well as gland secretions and the contents of body cells contain protein, and this must be derived from the food for, unlike plants, animals are unable to supply their protein needs to any appreciable extent from nitrogenous substances other than proteins. It is this exclusive function of protein which renders it so important as a component of animal food, and feeding standards for livestock invariably include a statement of minimum protein needs.

Proteins are by no means simple substances from a chemical point of view, and there are many different kinds of protein. They are composed of compounds known as amino acids, which are linked together to form the protein proper. Proteins from different sources will contain different proportions of the various amino acids, and according the relative abundance of particular amino acids, so then will the feeding value of a protein vary for a specific purpose, *e.g.*, lysine is one of the amino acids which is important in milk production, and the value of a particular protein for dairy cows is partly determined by lysine content. This gives rise to a concept known as *biological value of proteins,* and though it is outside the scope of this book to pursue this topic further, it is important to understand that there is a very considerable variation in the value of proteins for different feeding purposes. In practice this is covered by using more than one source of protein in compounding a ration. One protein-rich food may be deficient in some essential amino acids which an animal cannot synthesise, but the shortcoming may be made good by another protein, which though by itself is inadequate, fortunately contains the deficient amino acids in such quantities that there is a dovetailing effect. Particularly when dealing with vegetable proteins the use of a mixture appears to be important, but protein from animal sources is invariably good for both growth and lactation. Fortunately the quality of protein from spring and summer grass and the fodders derived from such material is very suitable for cattle.

If protein is fed in excess of an animal's needs it can be broken down to provide energy, or it can be used for the deposition of fat. In this event the surplus nitrogen is excreted in the form of urea. It is interesting to note that the kidneys of pigs which are largely fed on such a protein-rich food as separated milk are much larger than normal because of this extra functional burden. Protein is invariably an expensive item, and its net energy value, pound for pound, compares unfavourably with that of carbohydrates, so it is nutritionally and economically wasteful to feed excessive protein. It has been suggested (Sjollema, 1950) that grass with a protein content greatly in excess of the animal's needs will increase the rate of metabolism and, in consequence, maintenance requirements. Though this may be the case, and though in theory it is wasteful to feed twice as much protein as a bullock needs, in practice grass is one of the cheapest foods, and it does not pay to feed a balancing carbohydrate with existing price relationships.

MINERALS

Minerals are required by the animal for a variety of purposes, including the formation of the skeleton, for the secretion of various glands of the body and as a constituent of blood. In all there are thirteen mineral elements which have been established as essential– namely calcium, phosphorus, chlorine, sodium, magnesium, copper, cobalt, manganese, iodine, iron, sulphur, potassium and zinc. Some of these elements are required in relatively large quantities, for instance calcium and phosphorus which are important constituents of bone, while others are required in such minute quantities that for many years their importance was not detected. The best example of these so-called trace elements is cobalt, which was established by Filmer and Underwood (1936) to be essential to animal health. How very small the requirements of cobalt are for a sheep will be appreciated when it is stated that the difference between normal health and a wasting death on pasture is one of eight as opposed to three parts of cobalt in every ten million parts of dry matter ingested. Another trace element of some importance, particularly with young cattle, is copper, which is quite often deficient in the herbage produced by peat soils (Cunningham, 1944). The symptoms of copper deficiency are emaciation and very characteristic 'peat scours.'

Much has been written about mineral deficiencies, and many ailments in stock have been ascribed to them. This unquestionably has been a great boon to vendors of stock licks, and a great deal of money has been spent quite unnecessarily on mineral supplements. To some extent this has been brought about by our ignorance of normal mineral, requirements of livestock, not only quantitatively but in respect of mineral balance as well. It must be admitted that there is a great deal yet to be learned about minerals, but there is, however, little positive evidence to show that cattle require mineral supplements with the normal run of feeding one encounters in beef production. Generally speaking a farmer is better advised to follow the advice of his veterinary surgeon in this connection than the glib words of a vendor of mineral licks.

VITAMINS

Vitamins are highly complex substances which are essential to normal health, and, like trace elements, knowledge of their existence and function is comparatively recent and is rapidly expanding. With beef cattle which are fed on green feeds and which have access to sunlight there is apparently no need to take steps to provide them specially as one has to with pig and poultry production by intensive methods.

Classification of Feeding Stuffs

A convenient though somewhat arbitrary classification of feeding-stuffs is as follows:

1. Roughages
2. Succulents (including green feed)
3. Concentrates

Roughages

The roughages are bulky foods characterised by a high fibre and a low protein content. Generally their digestibility is low and their main function in cattle feeding is one of satisfying appetite. Included in this group are the various classes of hay and straw and the lowest grades of dried grass. It is important, however, to realise that there is wide variation in the quality of roughages. Hay made from leafy pasture, cut before it has passed the flowering stage and conserved with a minimum of weather or mechanical damage, will have more than double the feeding value of poorly made hay from pasture which has passed to the full seeding stage. Later we shall see the importance of producing the concentrate-sparing roughages when we consider the urgent problem of self sufficiency in feeding-stuffs.

Succulents

Succulent foods may be divided into two categories, the green feeds such as young cereals, grass, kale, lucerne and so on, the silage made from such feeds, and root crops such as mangolds, turnips and fodder beet. Both groups are characterised by a fairly low dry-matter content ranging from 8 per cent in white turnips to 30 per cent or higher for silage made from very mature material which has been allowed to get overheated. The dry matter of roots contains a fairly high proportion of sugar, and they are very digestible. The protein content is low and fibre is negligible, so when they are fed to cattle some fibrous food and a protein supplement is required in addition. The green feed group, on the other hand, is relatively rich in protein, though the percentage of digestible protein falls with advancing maturity with a corresponding rise in the proportion of fibre. Pasture, for instance, cut at the early flag stage and lucerne cut at the early bud stage, will yield on drying a protein-rich food which will compare quite favourably in this respect with some of the oil-seed cakes, and will have a considerable value for balancing starchy foods. The green feeds have a high carotene content, and this is important because carotene is the precursor of vitamin A, which is formed in the liver of animals to give them protection against vitamin A deficiency diseases.

Succulent feeds are laxative and so over-feeding, particularly with inmature grass, young cereals and rape, will cause severe scouring. This can be countered by allowing the feed to mature or by providing some additional fibrous food.

Concentrates

The concentrates as a group are characterised by a low moisture content, a high energy value and good digestibility. The fibre content is low, but the protein content may vary so widely that it is customary to divide concentrates into three main categories on the basis of their protein content. The cereals constitute a protein-deficient group and normally are used with feeds which will supply the necessary protein. Peas and beans, most of the grades of dried grass and some of the oil-seed residues come in a medium-protein group ranging from 12–25 per cent of digestible protein. In the high-protein group we get animal residues such as meat and liver meal, fish meal and dried separated milk, which have little place in beef production because they are expensive and more suited to intensive animal production such as pig and poultry keeping. Because of high biological values and possibly because of additional unidentified factors, animal proteins have a particular efficiency in the feeding of young stock during their phase of rapid growth. Though considerable quantities of vegetable proteins are necessarily used for the feeding of British livestock, it is very usual to include a small proportion of animal protein in the ration of pigs and poultry because experience shows that this is beneficial. With cattle, however, animal protein is reserved mainly for the early-rearing stages and generally a milk product is used.

There are some vegetable feeds in the high-protein group. The most important of these in Britain is decorticated groundnut cake, which contains over 40 per cent of digestible protein.

The food values of some of the more important feeding-stuffs in cattle feeding are given in Appendix 1, and these would be used if one were compounding feed rations along the lines which will be described later. However, the foregoing classification is of some value practically because of the part the eye of the experienced feeder plays in cattle feeding. Because he recognises the importance of a firm dung, of thrift and bloom, and of continued progress he probably pays more attention to the quality of feeding-stuffs, as defined in the above very general terms, than he perhaps realises. He combines suitable proportions of succulents, roughages and concentrates according to his experience and the reactions of his stock. He recognises that within each category there are certain foods with particular virtues, *e.g.* linseed cake will put a bloom on stock as no other feeding-stuff will. He is knows that bran is an ideal mild laxative for animals which are off colour, while undercorticated cottonseed cake is an excellent counter to scouring in stock turned out to fresh grass. No chemical analysis will give these estimates of worth of a particular food or combination of foods. The traditional diet of winter-fattened bullocks in Aberdeenshire is based largely on freshly threshed oat straw and large quantities of turnips possibly with only very small additions of crushed oats and cake. The progress of these bullocks and the quality of the carcasses they yield exceed any expectations based on analysis of feeding-stuffs used.

Expression of Food Values

Digestible Protein Equivalent

In analyses of feeding-stuffs one often encounters the term 'crude protein,' which is found by determining the amount of nitrogen and multiplying it by the of factor 6.25. This figure includes not only the true protein but also a proportion of simpler nitrogenous substances such as ammonium compounds, nitrates and amino acids. They are assigned a feeding value of only half that of a digestible true protein, and this must be taken into account when one is dealing with foods which are much higher in digestible crude protein than they are in digestible true protein if we are to derive a worth-while measure of protein worth. A good example is provided by a sample of dried lucerne meal with the following analysis: crude protein 22.3 per cent; digestible crude protein 15.9 per cent; and digestible true protein 11.2 per cent.

On a straight chemical analysis the lucerne meal has an impressive crude protein content, but it is only 71 per cent digestible, and this reduces the figure as far as the animal is concerned to 15.9 per cent. This latter figure includes 11.2 per cent of true digestible protein, so there is a balance of 4.7 per cent of non-protein nitrogenous substances to which only a half value is attributed. This means that the digestible protein equivalent of the lucerne meal is 13.5 per cent, which is a substantial reduction from the original crude protein figure to which buyers and sellers of dried lucerne attach such importance. The usual equation for determining digestible protein equivalent is as follows:

$$\text{D.P.E} = \frac{\text{Digestible Crude Protein} + \text{Digestible True Protein}}{2}$$

In our example:

$$\text{D.P.E} = \frac{15.9 + 11.2}{2} = \frac{27.1}{2} = 13.55 \text{ lb. per 100 lb. of lucerne meal}$$

Examples of feeding-stuffs with relatively high digestible crude protein in comparison with digestible true protein are green cruciferous crops (kale and cabbage), young pasture, green legumes and the silage made from them.

With grains and other feeds derived from mature plants digestible crude protein and digestible true protein approximate much more closely. In Appendix 1 protein values have been expressed in terms of digestible protein equivalents which have been computed from analyses given in standard tables of feeding values such as that included in Woodman's *Rations for Livestock,* which should be consulted for feeding-stuffs not included in Appendix 1.

Starch Equivalents

A variety of methods have been adopted in various parts of the world to describe the comparative values of the different classes of feeding-stuffs. The most popular method in Britain which is especially applicable to cattle is the *starch equivalent* system, which was established by the German nutritionist, Kellner. He adjusted the ration of a mature store bullock so that it was neither gaining nor losing weight. A known quantity of digestible starch was then added to the maintenance ration, and the resulting amount of fat stored by the bullock was calculated. It was found that for every 100 lb. of starch which was assimilated 25 lb. of body fat was formed. This gave a basis for comparison, and other foods were substituted for the starch and the necessary calculations were made. For instance, 100 lb. of linseed cake produced 18.4 lb. of fat. A little simple arithmetic will show that this result would have been achieved by 74 lb. of starch. In other words, 100 lb. of linseed cake has a starch equivalent value of 74. This figure refers to the production or fattening value of linseed cake when it is fed in conjunction with a maintenance ration which is suitably balanced for minerals, vitamins and protein.

The starch equivalent values for feeding-stuffs which are listed in tables have not all been derived by such a laborious method. Kellner determined the productive value of pure digestible nutrients contained in feeding-stuffs, and was able to establish an equation by which the starch equivalent values of any feeding-stuff can be derived from analysis and a knowledge of the digestibility of the various components. It is beyond the scope of this book tc discuss this point further. From the practical feeder's viewpoint the important consideration is that for feeding cattle or sheep starch equivalent is a simple numerical index of productive value, and if this and the digestible protein equivalent are known then it is possible to compare one food with another, in respect of the two most important attributes.

Chapter 10
Nutrition-Feeding Standards and their Application

EXPRESSING FOOD REQUIREMENTS

Our next consideration is a statement of the food requirements of an animal according to its particular needs. In this we are concerned with three main items–appetite, digestible protein equivalent and starch equivalent. Minerals and vitamins are not normally included in feeding standards for beef cattle, the assumption being that these will be satisfied in the normal ration.

It is customary in Britain to think of an animal's requirements in two parts–the maintenance ration and the production ration. The former covers the proportion which is required to maintain an animal's vital functions such as blood circulation, respiration and so on. More simply it can be defined as that proportion of the ration which is required to keep an animal healthy without gain or loss of body weight or of particular tissues. The second portion of the ration over and above that required for maintenance of that which is available for production which may be in the form of milk, eggs, live-weight increase or work. The size of the production ration is more or less independent of the maintenance ration in that it is proportional to the volume of production, *e.g.* two animals of the same weight but with one producing twice as much milk as the other will have the same maintenance requirement, but the higher producer will have twice the production requirements of her lower-producing mate. When the rations for the two animals are computed these differences have to be allowed for if each is to produce efficiently.

Though such a division of the total ration is somewhat arbitrary, nevertheless it is valuable in several respects. It is recognises, for instance, that in any form of animal production there is a food overhead in maintaining normal health. The amount of food required for this purpose varies according to a number of circumstances of which the most important is the size of the animal, which is most conveniently expressed in terms of live weight. It is seen in Table 2 how maintenance requirements rise steadily but not proportionately

Table 2: Appetite, Maintenance Starch Equivalent and Total Protein Requirements of Bullocks (From Woodman, 1948)

Live Weight cwt.	*Appetite, Dry Matter Daily* lb.	*Starch Equivalent for Maintenance* lb.	*Total Digestible Protein* lb.
5	14½	4	1¼
6	17	4½	1¼
7	19	5	1½
8	20½	5½	1½
9	22	6	1½
10	23½	6½	1½
11	25	7	1½
12	26½	7½	1½
13	28	7¾	1½
14	29½	8¼	1½
15	31	8½	1½
16	32½	8¾	1½

as live weight increases. In beef cattle, where we are interested in slaughtering within certain live-weight ranges, this rise in maintenance with size does not concern a farmer as much as it does in dairy production, for, other things being equal, with two cows giving the same volume and quality of milk, the lighter cow will be the more efficient producer in terms of food utilisation. However, with carcass animals we are concerned that an animal reaches carcass weight and proportions in the shortest possible time. The beast which requires 3 years to reach 1,300 lb. live weight is very much less efficient than one which attains the same weight in 2½ years, because there is 6 months more of daily maintenance in the total food bill, to say nothing of extra labour and accommodation costs. A prolongation of a fattening period is only justified when cattle are wintered cheaply in order to take advantage of cheap seasonal food such as pasture.

Maintenance requirements are also influenced by the circumstances under which animals are kept. The figures are given in Table 2 relate to stall-fed animals, but if they are out at pasture they are appreciably higher. Sjollema (1950) gives a figure for dairy cows on good pasture which is about 25–30 per cent higher than that for stall-fed animals. Where pasture is scant, as it is very often on upland grazings, where cattle have to take more exercise in search of food, maintenance requirements are much higher than they are on good grazing. Though cattle, as opposed to pigs, have a considerable capacity to withstand low temperatures, they are not happy under cold, wet or draughty conditions, and experience shows that cattle come through a winter very much better if they have shelter of some sort. This does not mean that they should necessarily be housed or yarded all the time, but that they should have the benefit of some sort of wind break and a reasonably dry place for lying down.

The amount of food required per lb. live weight is not constant over the course of growth and fattening because there is a steady change in the composition of live-weight gain as an animal matures. Wood and Newman (1928) state that a 3-Year-old bullock consumes 22½ lb. of dry matter per lb. of salable meat as compared with 11¾ lb. for an 18-month-old bullock. In a young animal there is a higher proportion of water and a lower proportion of fat in the carcass than there are at maturity. The calorific value of fat is very much higher than that of muscle, and so an animal during the last stages of feeding, when it is laying down almost exclusively pure dry body fat, will require practically twice as much food per lb. live weight gain as it did when it was a young store. The changes in production food requirements with advancing age and condition are given in Table 3.

Table 3: Changes in Food Requirements per lb. Live-weight Increase with Maturity (Woodman)

Stage of Maturity cwt.		*Starch Equivalent lb.*	*Digestible Protein lb.*
1–3	gaining about 1 lb. live weight per day	1.1–1.5	0.25–0.20
3–5		1.5–1.8	0.20
5–6½		1.8–2.0	0.18
6½–8½		2.0–2.25	0.16
7½–8½	gaining about 2 lb. live weight per day	2.25–2.5	0.15
9–10		2.5–4	0.15–0.05

The figures in Table 3 relate to a fairly normal set of conditions in cattle raising. In the early stages, up to about 2 years old, young stock are not generally grown at their maximum rate, which may be as high as 2–2½ lb. daily but are kept going, developing flesh and frame. As sizable stores they are brought on to heavier feeding, and these are allowed to give full expression to their capacity to put on weight to reach the required degree of fatness in the shortest possible time consistent with the quality of food available and the cost of this food. Once prime condition is reached there is no point in going any further, for apart from the fact that each increment of weight obtained is expensive in terms of food required, an over-fat carcass which is not wanted in the meat trade will result. Unfortunately the system of grading and payment at present adopted in the marketing of fat stock does not penalise the over-fat animal, and as a result there is a needless waste of feeding-stuffs which is not being checked. The marketing of over-fat animals is to a large extent a hangover from the war and immediate post-war period of expensive stores, when farmers were forced to recoup their high initial outlay by taking them to the heavy weights which the existing system of payment encouraged.

The satisfaction of appetite is as important as a sufficiency of nutrients in a complete ration. It is not enough that we supply in a ration sufficient protein and energy foods to satisfy maintenance and production requirements, but there must be sufficient bulk as well. Otherwise cattle are likely to develop depraved appetites, and they will eat their bedding or wooden fittings in their yards. Normally with beef cattle sufficient bulk to satisfy appetite is not a problem, for invariably they are fed on a high proportion of fibrous foods such as hay. In fact the danger is the opposite one of their not being able to obtain sufficient nutrients from the bulk they are forced to consume. A 9-cwt. bullock, for instance, will eat about 22 lb. of dry matter in a day, which will be contained in about 25 lb. of hay. If the hay is of poor quality with a starch equivalent of about 30 and a digestible protein equivalent of 3, then the bullock would be getting barely enough nutrients for maintenance. In practice it is improbable that a bullock would eat such a quantity of poor quality hay, for a feeding-stuff, which is the sole item in the diet, has to be of high palatability if an animal is going to eat it to the full extent of its appetite. It is unlikely that poor quality hay would have such a palatability. If the hay in question were cut down to 17–18 lb., and 7–8 lb. of a good concentrate mixture were fed, the starch-equivalent intake would be in the vicinity of 10–11 lb. per day, and a store bullock would grow at the rate of about 1½ lb. per day. It is seen therefore that one of the essentials in computing a ration for fattening stock is to make certain that the food offered will allow animals to obtain, within the physical limitation of their appetites, the nutrients they require for the full expression of their growth potential.

Normally it is reckoned that the daily dry-matter intake of a bullock amounts to about 2¼–2½ per cent of its body weight. This is a somewhat lower figure than is attributed to high-producing dairy cows whose dry-matter intake may rise to 3½ per cent of body weight and more, so it appears that appetite is to some extent conditioned by function. Other factors affecting appetite apart from size are stage of development, palatability, physical state of food and exercise. Young animals with a proportionally larger digestive tract tend to have proportionally larger appetites than older animals. With foods such as pasture the intake is at a higher level partly on account of palatability and partly because of the quick passage of such food through the alimentary tract. The higher dry-matter intake of bullocks on pasture as compared with stall-fed animals is to some extent offset by their greater maintenance requirements due to the energy expended in foraging. At the same time a certain minimum of exercise appears to be important, for without moderate exercise appetites may become jaded and nutrient intake will suffer in consequence. The physical state of food may be associated with palatability, *e.g.* cattle are not particularly fond of very finely ground and dusty foods.

Johnston Wallace and Kennedy (1944) have shown that length and condition of pasture will affect intake. With dense leafy grass about 4–5 in. long intake by beef cows was estimated to amount to about 32 lb. of dry matter daily, whereas when the grass was short it amounted to only 10 lb. Cattle have fairly characteristic and limited grazing habits, and it appears they will not extend their grazing time in the course of the day to such an extent that it will compensate for the lower rate of intake under sparse conditions. With long mature grass intake is also depressed. Johnston Wallace records that with beef cows on 10-in. pasture it fell to 20 lb. of dry matter per day. The dry-matter content of this grass was high, and no doubt a palatability factor was operating.

Reference has already been made to the importance of variety. The writer has had experience of dairy cows on a sole diet of grass silage which were initially eating up to 120 lb. daily, but whose consumption fell to three-quarters of this figure after several days. They maintained this consumption of silage when they had hay in addition. Particularly with bulk foods, where high intake of nutrients is secured only through exploiting the dry-matter intake to the full, is it important to secure a variety in the diet. Good hay, good silage and some green forage together will secure better results than feeding anyone alone.

Of course there are times, particularly with winter feeding of stock intended for grass fattening, where cattle are not required to grow at their maximum rate, and here it is a matter of maintaining the animals in a forward store condition. The question of satisfying full nutrient requirements within the limits of appetite does not arise here, and the stock will be fed of reasonable food that is available, perhaps oat straw to appetite in addition to some succulent food such as silage, preferably, if the soil type allows, with a run out on to pasture.

It will be noticed in Tables 2 and 3 that the protein requirements of the younger animals are proportionately higher than they are for the more mature. This is because muscle which is built up from food protein is an early-maturing tissue relative to fat. Apart from maintenance requirements the protein needs of the fattening bullocks are very small. Generally it is agreed that a total daily intake of 1½ lb. of digestible protein will cover all needs, and with the usual run of feeding-stuffs protein is seldom a limiting factor. It is only when the diet consists of straw and roots that there is likely to be any deficiency. The position is very different from that of the dairy cow which is producing a considerable amount of protein in milk, *e.g.* a cow giving 5 gallons daily requires over 3 lb. of digestible protein equivalent, and though in the spring and summer she will obtain this from good leafy pasture, in the winter months some form of protein supplement will be necessary. With beef cattle out at grass there is invariably an intake of protein well above the animals' needs, and the surplus is used as an energy food and the nitrogen being excreted in the urine in the form of urea. The urine of bullocks or of any dry cattle, eating high-protein foods is, in consequence, very much richer in manurial value than the urine of dairy cows fed on a similar diet. In practice this is recognised in the building up of soil fertility. One of the best instances of this is provided by the reclamation of light volcanic soils in New Zealand which were deficient in phosphate and nitrogen. Phosphate applied at seeding encourages the growth of a clovery sward which is preferably grazed by store bullocks. The stock nitrogen derived from the nitrogen-fixing clove encourages grass as opposed to clover growth, and under appropriate management a high-producing balanced sward will be established on what was virtually unproductive land.

This situation has its parallel in the old system of feeding practised in East Anglia when bullocks were wintered in yards to provide dung for the arable land. It was customary to feed 10–14 lb. of oil-seed cake to these bullocks to get a rich nitrogenous manure, and no doubt it was considered an economical way of getting nitrogen back on to the land at a time when the use of artificial nitrogen was very limited. Furthermore, linseed cake puts a bloom on cattle which is not generally secured with other foods, and this was an additional consideration when cattle were sold by auction. Today, however, with relatively cheap artificial nitrogen and very expensive protein foods there is no point in exceeding the minimum protein requirements, which can be provided by 50–60 lb. of good leafy silage produced cheaply by the clamp and buck rake method.

The preceding discussion is away from our primary consideration of protein requirements for full production, but it has been introduced at this point to emphasise the importance of using feeding standards to secure economical production. It is one thing feeding excess protein when the cheapest food available is protein rich grass or silage but it is bad business to use a protein-rich supplement costing £40 a ton or more when the supplement could be home-produced oats costing no more than £16 or £17 per ton. It has to be a very good muck to compensate for this disparity in prices. Unfortunately there are still many traditional feeders who cling in part to the practices of another economic era. It is not suggested that there are farmers who still feed 10 lb. of linseed cake daily, but there are many who still use some cake which could be replaced by protein-sufficient bulks which can be produced cheaply on the farm.

The Use of Feeding Standards

The following example shows how feeding standards and tables of food values can be used to compute a ration for bullocks which are being taken in yards from a forward store condition at about 8 cwt. to slaughter weight at about 11 cwt. They should achieve this weight with suitable feeding in about 170 days, for such bullocks should grow at the rate of 2 lb. per day. The feeding-stuffs available are good grass silage, meadow hay of above-average quality and crushed oats. The initial dry-matter intake of the bullocks will be about 21 lb. daily, rising to 25 lb. at the end of the period (see Table 2). The initial requirement for production would be 2½ lb. of starch equivalent per lb. live-weight increase, but this would rise to 3½–4 lb. by the end of the period. Similarly maintenance requirements would increase over the fattening period from 5½ to 7 lb. of starch equivalent. Total starch equivalent intake would commence at 10½ lb., and would rise to 14–15 lb. daily at the end. Their increase in nutrient requirements (35 per cent) is proportionately higher than the increase in appetite (20 per cent), and so the ration has to be improved progressively as the animals approach slaughter weight. The bulk of the crushed oats, or any alternative food such as dried beet pulp, should therefore be reserved for the later stages of feeding. Protein requirements will be stable at 1½ lb. digestible protein equivalent over the whole period. Initially the ration could consist of hay and silage as follows:

55 lb. of very good silage gives	11 lb. D.M.	1½ lb. D.P.E.	7 lb. S.E.
10 lb. of good hay gives	8½ lb. D.M.	½ lb. D.P.E.	4 lb. S.E.
Total	19½ lb. D.M.	2 lb. D.P.E.	11 lb. S.E.

Reference to the standards would show that while appetite is not satisfied there is more protein than necessary and enough starch equivalent for growth. It would not be necessary for any adjustment to be made in protein, for silage should be a very cheaply made feeding-stuff, and any modification here may tend to make the ration more expensive. In practice the ration would be about ½ cwt. of silage daily plus hay to appetite as the last feed of the day. If hay was in short supply no more than 5–6 lb. daily need be fed, and long oat straw could be provided for the bullocks to pick over. Though oat straw has a low starch equivalent value (20 S.E.), if cattle are able to pick out the leafy portions they will secure quite an appreciable proportion of their nutrients from this feed.

Towards the end of the fattening period when appetite has risen to 25 lb. of D. M. daily the silage could be increased to 60 lb., but the hay could remain at 10 lb. Together these would provide nutrients as follows:

65 lb. very good silage gives	13 lb. D.M.	1¾ lb. D.P.E.	7½ lb. S.E.
10 lb. good hay gives	8½ lb. D.M.	½ lb. D.P.E.	4 lb. S.E.
Total	21½ lb. D.M.	2¼ lb. D.P.E.	11½ lb. S.E.

If the silage was of really high quality and very palatable it could be increased to 75–80 lb. daily, but usually at the last stages of fattening the need is for a more concentrated ration as well as some variety in the diet to stimulate appetite. This would involve the feeding of about 4 lb. of oats, providing a further 2½ lb. of starch equivalent daily, or 14 lb. in all. With the pickings from oat straw the bullocks would be getting sufficient nutrients for about the calculated live-weight increase.

The estimation of feed value of the hay and silage used presents something of a difficulty in that the farmer cannot obtain any precise

Plate 9: Pioneer Cropping on Dalfur Hill (1,700–1,800 feet), Montgomeryshire

Plate 10: Labour is no Longer Cheap

Plate 11: Bulk Feeding to Bullocks should be Streamlined in Dairying

Plate 12: Outwintered Stores Thrive in the Spring

figures for the material he has available. Here he can only go by experience assessing his hay and silage as good, very good or just average. He must realise, however, that if he wishes to secure reasonable gains from his cattle with the minimum of expensive concentrates, that only the best grades of hay and silage made from leafy herbage under good conditions will secure such a saving. If lower grades of hay and silage are fed then the corn ration must be increased proportionally.

Because many farmers are finding that yard fattening is unprofitable if it is based to a large extent on expensively to produced roots and corn, they prefer to winter bullocks cheaply so that they are available as forward stores for finishing on grass. The type of feeding adopted would of course be determined by the availability of feeding-stuffs according to the system of farming adopted. Such residues as oat and barley straw will be important on most arable farms, while kale, silage, hay, sugar-beet residues and possibly some roots may be used. The aim in this case is to keep cattle in a forward store condition, so that over a winter-feeding period of about 150 days they have gained at the rate of about 1 lb. per day. The problem of providing sufficient nutrients for full growth within the limits of appetite does not arise here, and so poorer grades of hay and silage can be used. Starting with 8 cwt. stores we would have the same appetite of about 21 lb. of dry matter daily and a protein requirement of 1¼ lb. Because only 1 lb. live-weight increase is required, the following ration would be adequate:

10 lb. seeds hay giving	8½ lb. D.M.	½ lb. D.P.E.	3 lb. S.E.
40 lb. grass silage (2nd quality) giving	10 lb. D.M.	¾ lb. D.P.E.	4 lb. S.E.
Total	18½ lb. D.M.	1¼ lb. D.P.E.	7 lb. S.E.

This will be slightly below appetite in respect of dry matter but this can be satisfied, and there will be adequate starch equivalent and protein for both maintenance and growth at the rate of 1 lb. live-weight increase daily, if the cattle are allowed to pick over oat straw.

If it was desired to economise in the use of hay the following ration could be fed:

50 lb. grass silage (2nd quality) giving	12½ lb. D.M.	1 lb. D.P.E.	5 lb. S.E.
30 lb. mangolds giving	4 lb. D.M.	1/8 lb. D.P.E.	2½ lb. S.E.
Total	16½ lb. D.M.	1 1/8 lb. D.P.E.	7½ lb. S.E.

Balance of appetite would be made good by feeding oat straw.

Marrow stem kale or any other green succulent could be used to replace silage to supply the bulk of the protein and starch equivalent, *e.g.*

60 lb. M.S. kale gives	9½ lb. D.M.	¾ lb. D.P.E.	5½ lb. S.E.
10 lb. seeds hay gives	8½ lb. D.M.	½ lb. D.P.E.	3 lb. S.E.
Total	18 lb. D.M.	1¼ lb. D.P.E.	8½ lb. S.E.

Balance of appetite would again be made good by *ad lib* feeding of oat or barley straw, which has preferably been derived from a spring seeding.

If the animals are intended for grass fattening, and soil type and accommodation permit such a course being adopted, it is preferable to give these cattle a run-out on pasture at least during the day. Yarded cattle when they are turned out to grass in the early spring tend to scour badly and lose flesh until either the feed hardens up or the stock get used to their changed diet. Cattle wintered on grass, on the other hand, will start to put on flesh almost immediately grass becomes plentiful. It is important to avoid this spring check if possible, for good stores of about 9½ cwt. in April, on reasonable fatting pastures, will grade out at 12–12½ cwt. before the end of July, when pasture starts to get short and before prices fall to their lowest level.

When wintered cattle have access to such grazing the extra exercise will increase maintenance requirements, and there will be some increase in appetite. There will probably be no saving in other foods or any appreciable increase in live-weight gains unless the pastures are particularly good. The only gain to be expected is an obviation of the early spring check, which may be equivalent to a month or more of feeding on grass.

When one comes to the computation of rations for cattle on pasture, one is immediately up against the difficulty of not knowing precisely either the total intake of dry matter or the nutrient value of that intake except in very general and rather empirical terms. Successful feeding on pasture is much more dependent on judgment and experience than it is on yard fattening, but there are certain very well established features which are basically important.

If pasture is sparse and stemmy one need not expect bullocks to fatten on it. In the first place maintenance requirements may be 50 per cent higher than they are on really good pasture. Secondly, the best grass species for fattening are not found in such pastures but in dense swards on high-fertility soils with an adequate moisture supply. Thirdly, intake of dry matter is low under such conditions of grazing, and even if the material was nutritious, intake of nutrients would be insufficient for normal growth. Only when really high-quality pasture, consisting dominantly of such leafy species as rye grass, timothy and white clover, which are not allowed to run to top, is provided for fattening cattle will a maximum intake of nutrients and a maximum rate of growth be obtained. It is the farmer's business to supply such pasture if he is going to make economic gains. If he cannot do this he is better employed growing stores for someone else to fatten.

The best quality of grass is that obtained from rotationally grazed pastures which are rested for a sufficient period to give the animals a good 'bite,' and which are utilised quickly so that the animals are not subjected to ups and downs in nutrition. By this it is meant that as soon as the best of the grass is eaten the fattening stock should be moved to a fresh field, and stores should be used to clean up the residues.

With a good rotationally grazed pasture the starch-equivalent value will range from 55–65 lb. per 100 lb. of dry matter, and the digestible protein will run at 15–20 per cent over a fairly long season, varying according to climatic conditions and the dominant species of grasses. A 9-cwt. bullock going on to such pastures, when it settles down, will be eating at least 25 lb. of dry matter daily, or about 125 lb. of grass. This will contain at least 14 lb. of starch equivalent and 4 lb. of protein equivalent. There is protein to burn, and even after allowing extra energy requirements for maintenance because of the energy used in grazing, there will be enough starch equivalent for

2–2½ lb. live-weight increase per day. As the animals approach slaughter weight their appetites will increase appreciably, and extra energy for increased fat deposition will be very largely met and so growth will be maintained. At 11½ cwt. a bullock will be eating about 30–32 lb. of dry matter daily containing 16–17 lb. of starch equivalent. With maintenance assessed at 8 lb. of starch equivalent daily there is still plenty of energy remaining for a 2 lb. rate of gain daily. Comparable figures of live-weight gains will be obtained from high-class fatting pastures managed on traditional lines, *i.e.*, where the stock numbers are adjusted to keep pastures under control to preserve leafy growth.

The difficulty arises with grass fattening that with the onset of an early summer drought feed may fail both quantitatively and qualitatively faster than cattle can be drafted off to equate food supplies with stock requirements. One may be faced in the mid-summer period or else just before the winter with 11-cwt. cattle which are not quite finished and are going back or standing still. Here it is necessary to feed some supplements, either silage or concentrates. It may be argued that it does not pay to feed concentrates at this point, but it may be equally true that it will be much more of a losing proposition to let the animals fall away in condition or to market them in a half-finished condition. A couple of hundredweight of concentrates may make a very real difference to them as a financial proposition. It is important, however, not to feed unnecessarily expensive concentrates. If the pasture has any leaf to it at all, and the deficiency is mainly quantitative, then it is unlikely that supplementary protein will have to be provided. Let us assume that the dry-matter intake of a 11-cwt. bullock has fallen to 20 lb. a day, and the protein equivalent of this is as low as 8 per cent. Even here the intake will be at least 1½ lb. of protein daily, and this will more than suffice. There is no point in feeding cake at £35 a ton when crushed oats at two-thirds the price will do the job. If feed is so poor that some protein should be fed, the silage clamp would prove to be a more economical answer.

Preparation of Feed

Apart from crushing and grinding of cereals and perhaps chaffing of straw and hay, one is not very much concerned with food preparation with beef-cattle feeding. Pulping of roots used to be important, but labour costs rule this out on most farms, and one does not encounter it very frequently on English farms except where pedigree cattle are being prepared for shows or sales.

There is a mistaken impression that if one puts roughages through a course of fine grinding (as in a hammer mill) or chaffing there is a big improvement in food value. This is not markedly true. For instance, there is no improvement in digestibility, and in fact this may be slightly reduced because the feeding of dusty meals may impair the efficiency of the digestive juices (Woodman, 1948). There is, however, some increase in starch-equivalent value food is chaffed, because, less energy is required in mastication. It is questionable, however, whether the energy and time expended in mechanical chaffing or grinding compensates for the gain by the animal, and there are good grounds for letting the animal handle long roughage. It is then able to pick out the leafiest bits which are valuable, and to refuse the practically worthless stems, which are trodden into muck where they will make their best contribution. Grinding beyond the chaff stage, which for instance is sometimes done with chaff produced in threshing, does not enhance feed value and represents so much wasted effort.

When preparing grains for feeding to cattle there is no advantage in grinding them very finely. In fact this may be a detriment, because they become pasty in the mouth and unpalatable. Furthermore, if fed out of doors there is a greater danger of loss by wind. Oats which are the most important cereal fed to cattle are best prepared by rolling. Cattle have very efficient digestive systems, and there is no question of crushed oats being passed out in the dung in only a partly digested form.

Though this is not strictly a question of food preparation it is convenient at this point to stress that mangolds should not be fed unless they have been stored for at least 6 weeks. The fresh roots contain a high proportion of amides, and these may cause digestive upsets. Normally mangolds are reserved till after Christmas and so this danger is avoided. Fodder beet need not be stored before feeding, but if beet is fed, either fresh or clamped, it is advisable to limit intake to 40 lb. daily for 8–11 cwt. stores after the cattle have had a gradual introduction to the roots. Fodder and sugar-beet tops should be wilted for at least a week and intake should be limited to about ½ cwt. daily.

Chapter 11

Beef from the Dairy Industry

Dual-Purpose Cattle

Over the past fifteen years there has been a revolution in the relative importance of the various types of cattle in Britain. In common with most European countries with long-established and highly organised agricultural systems dual-purpose cattle had been favoured because they fitted in so well with the conditions of mixed husbandry. Between the wars, however, beef prices were relatively unfavourable in comparison with those obtaining for milk (Price, 1949), which, since 1933, has had the protection of organised marketing while beef, in competition with imported supplies and receiving only a small subsidy, was subject to market fluctuations until the Ministry of Food commenced its operations at the beginning of the war. During the war years a deliberate policy of encouraging milk at the expense of beef was followed by the Government who, very wisely, were concerned that supplies of this essential protective food were maintained. The great volume of imported feeding-stuffs which had formerly been available for all classes of cattle was reduced to a very low level,[1] while pasture lands which had been available for beef cattle were ploughed to produce crops for direct human consumption. Something of the extent of the change of emphasis in cattle production is indicated by the figures given in Table 4, which compares the relative importance of the leading breeds under the Ministry's Bull Licensing Scheme, and again in 1949. The spectacular rise of the specialised dairy breeds at the expense of the dual-purpose breeds emphasises how great the revolution has been. Forty years ago the Friesian was a curiosity and the Ayrshire a breed with only local importance in the south-west of Scotland. In 1950 the two breeds accounted for 42 per cent of the bull licences in England and Wales as compared with 8 per cent in 1937. Meanwhile the Shorthorn proportion fell from 65 to 30 per cent.

Table 4: Bulls Licensed in England and Wales (For the year ending 31 March)

Type	*Breed*	*1937*		*1950*	
		No.	*Per cent*	*No.*	*Per cent*
Beef	Aberdeen Angus	760	2.02	408	1.43
	Devon	1,031	2.74	495	1.73
	Galloway	308	0.82	93	0.32
	Hereford	2,194	5.83	1,722	6.03
	Highland	4	0.01	4	0.01
	Sussex	189	0.50	120	0.42
Dual-purpose	Shorthorn*	24,600	65.38	8,836	30.92
	Dexter	35	0.09	29	0.10
	Lincoln Red	1,604	4.26	927	3.24
	Red Poll	623	1.66	473	1.66
	South Devon	423	1.12	435	1.52
	Welsh	393	1.04	292	1.02
Dairy	Ayrshire	445	1.18	3,159	11.05
	Guernsey	1,882	5.00	1,639	5.73
	Jersey	613	1.63	994	3.48
	Friesian	2,502	6.65	8,944	31.30
	Kerry	19	0.05	9	0.03
		37,625	**100**	**28,579**	**100**

* Includes beef-type Shorthorns

1 In 1938 there were 8.6 million tons of purchased feeding-stuffs as compared with 4.5 million tons in 1948 and 3.3 million tons in 1949 (figures given to Farmers' Club by Sir James Turner, December 1950)

This is not the whole picture. Over the period of comparison artificial insemination has moved from an experimental stage to a commercial proposition, and today about 30 per cent of the national herd (England and Wales) is inseminated artificially. Unquestionably this has been a factor in speeding up the rate of breed change, and it is significant that the Friesian breed in 1951–52 accounted for 36 per cent of all inseminations as compared with 21 per cent for the Shorthorn.

As one travels through the countryside one notices how the colour and character of British cattle have changed. Fifteen years ago reds and roans and whites were dominant along the Thames Valley through the East Midlands and in the northern counties. Today one sees very nearly as many black- and-whites. Only, in the south-west do we find farmers stubbornly loyal to their local breeds, and even there foreign interlopers which have been bred to serve the pail rather than the butcher are gaining in popularity.

The change of breeds has been accompanied by a change of emphasis on function within the dual-purpose breeds. There are many Shorthorn herds today where the cows are as characteristically dairy in their conformation as Friesians. More and more, bull breeders have found if they are going to sell their stock to advantage they must have the backing of milk records which have become an increasingly important criterion in selection at the expense of fleshing ability. The old-fashioned Shorthorn may hold her own at the Royal, but at the London Dairy Show she gives ground to the cow which manifests the triple-wedge conformation.

If this trend continues it may have unfortunate consequences so far as domestic beef production is concerned. In the first place it will mean a curtailment of supplies, for however sanguine one may be of ultimately achieving an appreciable level of store-cattle production from the hills, the reality is that it is going to take many years before this land can be developed and stocked to constitute a compensatory source of cattle for fattening. Secondly, there is a prospect of a considerable deterioration in the quality of domestic beef, as an increasing proportion of total supplies is accounted for by specialised dairy cows which are discarded from the milking herds. A lean dairy type which has had several seasons of heavy milk production can yield nothing better than manufacturing meat, and yet necessity may demand that it will be cut up for Sunday joints.

It may be suggested that as the needs of the liquid milk market are satisfied and a greater proportion of the milk is diverted to the cheaper manufacturing outlets, prices will fall to such a point that farmers will find it profitable to turn to beef. Unquestionably this will be true for farmers on the margin of dairying, but the more probable reaction of men with farms organised for dairying and a considerable amount of money invested in dairy stock and equipment, will be an intensification of efforts to increase efficiency of milk production, and thereby preserve the margin of profit. An important factor in reducing costs is an increase in the average level of production, and in this objective the specialised dairy breeds have considerable advantages. Unfortunately we have no precise yardstick to measure milk-producing efficiency, but figures for the more important dairy and dual-purpose breeds given in Table 5 give some indication of the strength of the argument in favour of specialisation in dairy production.

Table 5: Production and Live Weight of the More Important Breeds (Based on M.M.B. recording figures for 1949)

Breed	*Estimated Live Weight lb.*	*Recorded Yield lb.*	*Butter-fat Test %*	*Yield Milk Per lb. Live Weight lb.*
Ayrshire	1,050	8,088	3.81	7.7
Friesian	1,300	9,141	3.45	7.0
Guernsey	975	7,473	4.49	7.7
Jersey	850	7,051	5.05	8.3
Red Poll	1,150	7,476	3.59	6.5
Shorthorn	1,250	7,365	3.57	5.9
South Devon	1,400	6,738	4.26	4.8

On a straight production per cow basis the Friesian leads the Shorthorn and the Red Poll by about 1,600 lb., and it takes a lot of by-product beef to compensate for this extra milk which is not produced at any appreciable extra cost so far as plant and equipment are concerned, though extra food will of course be required for its production.

When production is expressed in terms of live weight the advantages of the small specialised dairy cow are manifest. To this must be added the very considerable advantages which small breeds have in their adaptation to grazing conditions. It is a maxim of pastoral farming that the more mouths one has to the acre, the more efficient will be the utilisation of pasture and, in consequence, the greater will be the production per acre (Fawcett, 1929).

One reaction to increased supplies of milk may be that there will be greater premiums paid for quality as expressed by percentage butter-fat test. In this respect the Red Poll and the Shorthorn are at a considerable disadvantage when compared with the two Channel Island breeds. These are the most extreme dairy breeds we have, and if they increase in popularity they will have a very small contribution to make to beef supplies. Fortunately for those who require meat as well as milk in their diet the closed herd book policy of the Jersey Breed Society is operating against this serious potential threat to our beef ration. If the Jersey Society had a grading-up policy comparable with that of some of the other dairy breeds there would probably be a very widespread increase in the numerical importance of the breed.

What are the possibilities of improvement of the dual-purpose breeds so that they can compete more favourably, so far as milk production is concerned, with the specialised dairy herds? From the discussion in Chapter 7 on the contrast of beef and dairy types it will be seen that with the lactating cow there is competition for nutrients between milk and meat. The proponent of dual-purpose cattle does not suggest, however, that during lactation his cows should be capable of dressing out A+ or better. On the contrary, he wants a cow which will put on condition when she is dry, but which will milk it off when she is in production. He wants his animals to have fleshing propensities so that discards from the herd through accidents or disease will have a reasonable salvage value as compared with a specialised dairy cow of similar age. In view of the very high wastage from dairy herds which probably approaches an average figure of 25 per cent per annum, this salvage figure has been a very important consideration with dairymen, particularly those owning flying herds. The residual beef value of a purchase, should she become diseased or be of inferior quality as a milker, is in the nature of a hostage to fortune. It is interesting in this connection to conjecture whether the popularity of dual-purpose cattle has not been a factor contributing to short herd life, for when residual beef value is small, as it is with breeds such as the Jersey and Ayrshire, a dairy farmer is bound to take all the precautions he can to avoid the practically dead loss of wastage.

But to return to our point, the main requirement of a dual-purpose breed, of course, is that the surplus males appropriately reared will make reasonably good carcasses of beef. The emphasis here is on the phrase 'appropriately reared,' for more and more evidence is accumulating to show that ultimate type is very materially influenced by plane of nutrition over the early developmental stages. Heavy feeding during the first nine months will lay the foundations of a blocky deep-fleshed animal. Even a Jersey calf which is suckled over a considerable period will retain beefy attributes right throughout its milking life, while a heifer calf of a specialised beef breed will achieve something of a dairy conformation if it is reared as the majority of dairy heifers are reared. Type is not a strongly inherited characteristic, because it is so considerably modified by environment, and provided a farmer has stock with reasonable fleshing propensities he can mould them to a considerable extent to suit his needs.

The breeding of cattle which combine to a satisfactory degree the capacity to produce milk or meat upon demand, when suitable treatment is given, is one of the most difficult objectives in breeding though by no means an insuperable one. We have too many examples of dual-purpose herds averaging 900 gallons or more where steers are raised as satisfactory beef animals at 2½ to 3 years of age for an opposite view to be held. But with our existing techniques and philosophies in breeding it is hard enough to achieve consistency even with specialised dairy cattle where the objectives are much simpler. The more objectives one has, even though they are not in conflict as they are to an appreciable extent with milk and beef, the slower will be the rate of progress in any given direction. This is very well illustrated by Rae (1947) in a study of the effectiveness of selection in sheep. In the flocks he studied where 40 per cent of the yearlings could be culled he derived the following figures for improvement in wool production:

fleece weight alone	0.64 lb. per generation
fleece weight + one character	0.41 lb. per generation
fleece weight + two characters	0.39 lb. per generation
fleece weight + three characters	0.23 lb. per generation
fleece weight + four characters	0.20 lb. per generation

A breeder of cattle would be very fortunate with existing rates of wastage, if he could afford to discard as many as 40 per cent of the annual crop of heifers. In most herds about 75 per cent of the heifers born are required to maintain herd numbers so that potential gains by heifer selections, based on all available criteria, are not very great. Rendel and Robertson (1949) have suggested that in a herd where a 25 per cent discard of heifers for replacement can be effected the improvement in yield will be about 1 per cent per generation. This amounts to about 1½–2 gallons per year[1] in a herd averaging 900 gallons as the extent of the gain which may be expected from saving heifers from the highest producing dams. Small as this figure is, it is of great magnitude in comparison with what would be obtained if it were stipulated further that the heifers being selected had to exhibit a propensity for fleshing and in addition had to be reasonable specimens of a breed.

Progress in this connection would not of course be confined to selection of daughters from the highest available dams, for other means of improvement would be attempted, but multiplicity of aims would affect each in a similar manner. The achievement of truly dual-purpose cattle calls for the most precise selection techniques. Because milk- and meat-producing abilities are so masked by environment, and because we are dealing with animals with a low rate of reproduction, this means an efficient system of progeny testing. We must be able to distinguish the living sires which are most capable of transmitting the desired characters so that their influence can be extended as widely as possible. Fortunately we have a tool in artificial insemination, which will greatly increase the contribution these rare outstanding sires can make.

A dual-purpose breed cannot be obtained by compensatory matings, though dual-purpose individuals may be obtained by this method which has been one of the main contributing factors to the decline of the Shorthorn. Unfortunately there is a common herd book for both dairy- and beef-type Shorthorns, and breeders have been free to switch their types according to fancy and market trends. If a breeder considered that he was losing flesh in his cattle there was no bar against him putting a Scotch Shorthorn over his dairy herd. An outcross like this may produce a desired result in the first

---

1 Five years is allowed for a cow generation.

generation, and the breeder will be well satisfied with his immediate results. In. the long run, however, he destroys a large measure of the strain purity that has been achieved, and in the subsequent generations there is a danger of segregations into the extreme parental types and worse.

New Zealand affords us with a very good example of the evils of this sort of breeding. Before the days of refrigeration the majority of the cattle there were dual-purpose Shorthorns–Bates type rather than Booth. When refrigerated ocean transport became practicable the first emphasis was on beef, and Scotch Shorthorns were widely used. When dairying became established as a substantial export industry twenty years or so later, it was found that the Shorthorn had practically been ruined as a dairy breed and had to give way to specialised breeds, notably the Jersey. Shorthorn breeders who wished to preserve the milking qualities of their breed thereupon formed a distinct breed society with a separate herd book. By this time the damage had been done and the Shorthorn became a secondary dairy breed. Despite the fact that the Dairy Shorthorn has been segregated for forty years, and though it has one of the widest ratio of bull-heifer registrations of any of the dairy breeds, thus indicating very severe selection of male stock, it has a very poor record as a breed under sire survey (Ward, 1949). Whereas 31 per cent of all Friesian bulls and 17 per cent of all Jersey bulls submitted to sire survey have achieved 'Merit' status (*i.e.* a high grade of proven sire), only 12 per cent of the Shorthorn bulls have a similar rating.

The greatest misfortune the Shorthorn breed has had to suffer is the absence of colour labels to distinguish beef and milking strains. The Red Poll breed has been very fortunate that the Aberdeen Angus is black. The tragedy of all this is that the Shorthorn is fast losing its place in the national herd at a time when we have a greater need than ever before for good Shorthorns which combine the best of both worlds. Whether the breed can be saved from a further severe numerical decline or not will depend on the rapidity and the effectiveness of the action that can be taken.

Every year more than a million calves are slaughtered for baby veal in Great Britain. These are mainly bull calves of dairy breeding, though there will be a small proportion of undersized or thriftless heifers which are not considered to be worth rearing. With our shortage of cattle for feeding it is interesting to consider the possibilities of a proportion of this huge tally being diverted to beef production. If dual-purpose cattle were in their old ascendancy the answer would be simple, for incentives to rear these calves for beef would soon divert a big proportion of them to the desired end, but now that many of them are extreme dairy-type calves it would be false economy to endeavour to turn them into feeding cattle.

The most positive measure that can be taken to reduce their numbers would be a reduction in the annual toll of disease in our dairy herds which is responsible for an average herd life of about four years. If the average life of a dairy cow could be increased to five years, not an unreasonable figure under conditions of good management, not only would dairy production rise through there being a greater proportion of mature cows in production, but also more intensive selection could be increased in respect of heifers for replacement. These could be bred from the top producers, and it would not be necessary to mate low producers to dairy bulls. Instead they could be mated to bulls of extreme beef type to produce calves, bulls and heifers alike, which would be worth rearing for beef production. In this the specialised beef bulls would be achieving a function akin to that of Down rams which are used on mountain and mountain-cross ewes to produce rapid-maturing lambs of good carcass conformation. Breeds like the Hereford would impart a substance to calves derived from specialised dairy breeds such as the Ayrshire to produce a very valuable carcass beast.

The possibilities of this course of action prompted the development of a scheme for free artificial insemination from colour-marking bulls. Farmers have been encouraged to mate their poorest cows in this way with two ends in view. The first is to increase the supply of cattle for fattening, and the second is to eliminate low producers as dams of replacement stock. Such cross-breeding is being further encouraged by a calf-rearing subsidy paid on weaker steers which are judged to be suitable for fattening. In the year ending 31 March 1950, no less than 11 per cent of all inseminations were accounted for by beef bulls (Edwards, 1950). The free insemination scheme has now been discontinued–the very good prices realised by bull calves suitable for rearing, generally by a system of multiple suckling, have provided all the incentive which is necessary.

The main factors limiting the rate of expansion of crossing with beef bulls are the characteristically small size of British herds and the high rate of wastage. The greater proportion of our dairy herds has less than twenty cows, and with very small numbers there is a danger that abnormal sex ratios may upset the herd replacement programme. Farmers in these circumstances might be tempted to keep heifers of part-beef breeding for dairying, but such a course would be to the detriment of milk production. Alternatively, farmers who have had an unduly heavy proportion of bull calves from cows mated to dairy bulls might buy surplus stock from more fortunate neighbours. Unless heifers are bought, however, buying of replacements is a practice which needs no encouragement, for unfortunately when one buys older animals one buys more than cattle. It has been characteristic of several wastage surveys made in Britain that losses from disease are much lighter in herds which are self-contained than they are in those where replacements are purchased. The position of course will be very much better when the attestation scheme achieves something of a national significance.

Very wisely the Government stipulated that the free insemination scheme would apply to only colour-marking beef breeds. The Aberdeen Angus, the Galloway and the Hereford are able to leave a trade mark on their stock which informs the discriminating purchaser that he is being offered stock with a beef ancestry. If he wants to fatten then the colour-marked stock will suit his purpose, but he can leave them well alone if his requirement is stock for a dairy herd. If, for instance, beef Shorthorns were used confusion would result and there would be a danger of beef-bred heifers going into dairy herds to perpetuate the problem of wastage because of low production.

Looking at the problem from a national point of view, if effective average production per cow could be raised to 750 gallons per annum by a combination of factors including breeding, better management and feeding and by control of disease, we would require only 3 million cows to produce 2,200 million gallons of milk, which would more than suffice for liquid-milk needs, for the higher-priced manufacturing categories and for calf rearing. If the average life of cows in a stabilised national herd was 5–6 years, then the annual requirement of dairy heifers would be about 700,000, after making some allowance for heifer wastage. This would mean that over a million dairy cows could be mated each year to beef bulls to give us the raw material for producing 6 million hundredweights of first-class beef annually. Add to this the steers from dual-purpose breeds and from those dairy breeds where calves may reasonably be reared for beef production and the stores which can be reared from cattle kept on the hills, and we have such an impressive total that the Ministry of Food, if it still exists, will be able to cock a snook at exporting countries who demand, not always without justification, a higher price for their beef.

The foregoing may be criticised as a piece of wishful thinking, and that a national average of 750 gallons and a herd life of 5–6 years is well beyond our powers of attainment. Not very far away from us there is a country, the Netherlands, where annual production is in the vicinity of 770 gallons as compared with our own average of just over 600 gallons, and there are thousands of our own farmers working with a variety of breeds who have herd averages of 800 gallons and more. So far as disease is concerned the success which has followed the use of 'Strain 19' in the control of contagious abortion and the effectiveness of penicillin in controlling certain forms of mastitis is very encouraging. Perhaps the most serious bar to our goal is the depressing frequency of herd sires, fashionably bred and with full pedigree qualifications, which lower the average level of production in the herds in which they are used. The American geneticist Gowen spoke very true words when he said our objective in breeding is not the production of better stock than we have today, but the production of the best we have uniformly and at will. We have got to lower our wastage due to low production by *not* breeding the cow that has to be discarded on this score.

In this connection the breed societies have a tremendous responsibility. When we compare the structure of British herd books with those of a country such as Denmark, where pure-bred stock are segregated according to their breeding worth into an élite register, we cannot but conclude that our aims in breeding for the commercial needs of our dairymen lag far behind. Fortunately the Ayrshire Society has now established a list of Approved Bulls which is based on a realistic progeny test, and it has also instituted a register of cows with high life-time production to constitute the basis of a system of selective registration. Breeders are being given an objective, and purchasers of bulls are being given a standard, and this cannot but react to the good of all concerned. In their own interests other breed societies will have to follow suit and abandon a system of preferment which is based on a highly selected and unrepresentative sample of offspring. It is significant in this connection that through the rapid development of artificial insemination the responsibility of bull purchase for 25 per cent of our dairy cows is the hands of an authority, the Milk Marketing Board, which will demand stock with reasonable prospects of breeding daughters better than their dams. Gradually as artificial insemination gathers momentum, the inferior bull will become more and more of a drug on the market, and it will end up as it deserves, a castrate candidate for the butcher's shop.

This departure from the main theme of providing beef stores from dairy herds into the realm of dairy herd improvement has not been made merely to ride a hobby horse. Better dairy stock and a lower rate of wastage are inseparable from our problem of producing more beef from our limited land resources. Two cows producing 1,600 gallons of milk require less food than 3 cows with a similar total production, while a herd with a life of 5 years requires proportionately less keep for rearing replacements than a herd that turns over every 4 years. The food that is saved is more food for the beef stores than can be produced by the proportion of dairy cows which are mated to beef bulls because they are no longer required to breed herd replacements.

Beef Stores from Dairy Breeds

Reference has been made previously to this source of cattle, and the breed which has been in mind in this connection is the Friesian. In its native country breeders have endeavoured to retain some propensity for fleshing, and the typical Dutch Friesian conforms much more closely to the dual-purpose ideal than the British Friesian or the American Holstein-Friesian. Even the British Friesian is being used quite widely for beef production, and there is now quite a considerable movement of Friesian and Friesian-cross calves to traditional rearing areas such as Aberdeenshire from the south. In the farming press one sees, quite frequently, reports of farmers with good herd averages who are retaining their Friesian steers and rearing them for beef. The following example[1] is typical: An East Anglian dairy farmer with a recording average of 1,300 gallons per cow marketed over the course of three years 183 Friesian bullocks

[1] *Farmers' Weekly*, 20 May, 1949.

approximately 3½ years old. They averaged over 15 cwt. apiece, and 86 per cent were graded A+ or better. Possibly they did not compare in carcass conformation with a line of Blue Greys, but they would be a vast improvement on what would be obtained from discarded dairy cows which now account for at least 40 per cent of our home-produced beef.

At the present time some very interesting work is in progress at Cambridge, where Mansfield and Brooks are rearing Hereford, Dairy Shorthorn and Friesian calves on various planes of nutrition. Their work has not progressed sufficiently to give conclusive results, but it is already abundantly clear that it is possible to obtain reasonably good beef animals from Friesian calves which have been reared on a good plane of nutrition. Hammond (1943) and his co-workers, notably McMeekan (1940), have shown how critical planes of nutrition, over the early stages of life, are in determining form and carcass composition in sheep and pigs. Mansfield and Brooks are apparently repeating this result with cattle. Mansfield (1949) advocates from his experience in this and other work with cattle that the time to feed quality food is over the first nine months. He adopts a system of multiple suckling (which will be described later) with liberal concentrate feeding and free access to good bulk foods. Frame and substance are laid down in this way, and the resulting beast at nine months is substantially the beefing at a corresponding age that used to be produced, mainly from dual-purpose breeds, in the years before the war when concentrates were cheap and there was an adequate premium for quality. With this foundation it can be wintered cheaply on bulks such as hay, straw, silage, green forage and roots, and it can be summered on grass which also supplies the final nutrients for fattening when the beasts, are about two and a half years old. So far the Cambridge work indicates that it is uneconomic to feed expensive concentrates over the final fattening period. These are reserved for the juvenile stage when the most efficient use can be made of them.

The final results of this work will be awaited with considerable interest, though already preliminary results and the experience of farmers is placing the Friesian in a new light, and it is quite probable that the movement of black-and-white calves from the bobby calf trade will gather momentum. In November 1950 there was a large importation of Dutch Friesians, and judging by the prices that were paid for them the new blood is going to be very fashionable. It may well be that the greatest contribution these Dutch cattle will make to the British Friesian will not be the raising of butter-fat tests but an increase in the fleshing propensities of Friesian steers. In so far as any cow has some flesh to keep her bones together she is dual-purpose in function, and a bit more flesh than that may make a world of difference to the usefulness of the Friesian breed in the mixed husbandry of Great Britain.

Of the beefing qualities of the other dairy breeds little will be said. The Channel Island breeds have a much too extreme dairy type for steers to have any real value for beef. Furthermore their fat is characteristically yellow and unattractive. There are, however, some Scotsmen who are rearing Ayrshire steers for feeding, but this is not very general. One suspects that it is an expression of misplaced loyalty for a local breed whose reputation is secure in the byre but is doubtful in the fattening court.

Multiple Suckling

The rearing of calves on foster mothers, under the system known as multiple suckling, is gaining rapidly in popularity. The aim is to provide a calf which is being reared for beef with about 90–100 gallons of whole milk over its first three months to lay the foundations of a good carcass. The number of calves suckled per cow varies naturally according to the level of milk production. A cow giving approximately 2½ gallons a day will cater for 2 calves averaging about 6–8 weeks old. From a labour-demand point of view the system is very good. Once the calves are trained it is just a question of securing the cows and letting the calves in. One's greatest concern is not to be caught in the stampede of hungry calves racing to their foster mothers. The whole operation night and morning can be covered in a very short space of time. From a milk-cost point of view the system need not be very expensive providing depreciation on nurse cows can be eliminated, *e.g.* by the use of heifers which after one season of suckling are sold as cow-heifers. During the spring and summer nurse cows can be run on pasture and concentrate feeding can be eliminated. Over the course of a year a cow giving 700 gallons can rear up to 7 calves, and though this milk if sold in churns might have a value of £100 this is not a true estimate of its cost for calf rearing. Apart from the low labour demands referred to above, there are no expensive building and equipment costs to be borne. The milk could be costed in the cow's udder at no more than 1s 8d a gallon over the year and much less in the spring, so the total value of milk consumed per calf would be well under £10.

Calves under this system are introduced to concentrates just as soon as possible, normally at about 3 weeks of age. By the time they are 3 months old, when they will be progressively weaned by once-a-day suckling, for a period they will be eating at least 2½ lb. of concentrates daily in addition to good clovery hay which should be offered them *ad lib.* from 3 week onwards. As milk is discontinued the protein intake must be adjusted as the demands at this stage are very considerable. Calves over the summer months of course can go out to pasture once they can be conveniently driven, *i.e.* normally 8 weeks. They will derive a great deal of their protein and other needs from good pasture, and the small allowance of concentrates can be based on grains such as crushed oats. If calves are run on pasture they must either have a great deals of range or else they should be rotated at frequent intervals if they are run on small fields. Figure 20 illustrates the importance on this point. It is based on information obtained by workers at Ruakura Animal Research Station in New Zealand, who contrasted the growth rates of Jersey calves which were set stocked (*i.e.* were kept for long periods in the one pasture) with those that were rotationally grazed on dairy pastures *in front* of the milking herd (McMeekan, 1947). The figures are not as impressive as the calves themselves. A difference of 80 lb. in weight at 9 months of age in a Jersey is the difference between a normally developed calf and one that is a bag of bones which will have difficulty in surviving its first winter. Calves must have clean grazing and good grazing, and in this respect leys have much to commend them. Unless a farmer is prepared to provide this he is much better advised to keep his calves indoors and feed them on expensive concentrates. Though he will deny himself the reduction in rearing costs which will result from a main reliance on grass, at least he will have worth-while calves. If they are kept on the one field week after week parasitic infections will be built up and the quality of grass will deteriorate also. Calves are highly selective in their grazing habits, and very quickly with calves alone on a pasture a high proportion of it will run to stem. Progressively the calves will get poorer grazing, and deficiencies in their nutritive status will aggravate the conditions of worm infection. Another precaution to be taken in the grazing management of young calves is to prevent scouring. If they are

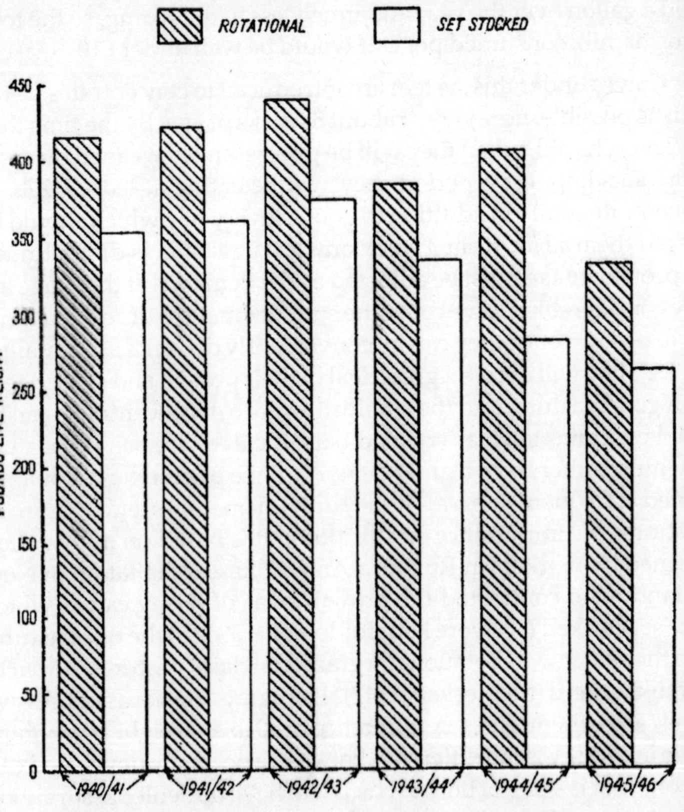

Figure 20: Rotational Grazing of Dairy Heifers, Ruakura Animal Research Station, New Zealand

brought in at night, which will be the normal course of action in the spring when grass is sappy, they can be fed on hay to correct any tendency to scour.

Some emphasis is placed on the use of grass in the above manner, for concentrates at present prices cost the best part of 4d per lb. by the time they are fed to calves. With the costs of labour and of milk consumed and the initial purchase price of suitable calves which has been substantial, the margin of profit will be greatly reduced if heavy concentrate feeding has to be resorted to. Nine months of

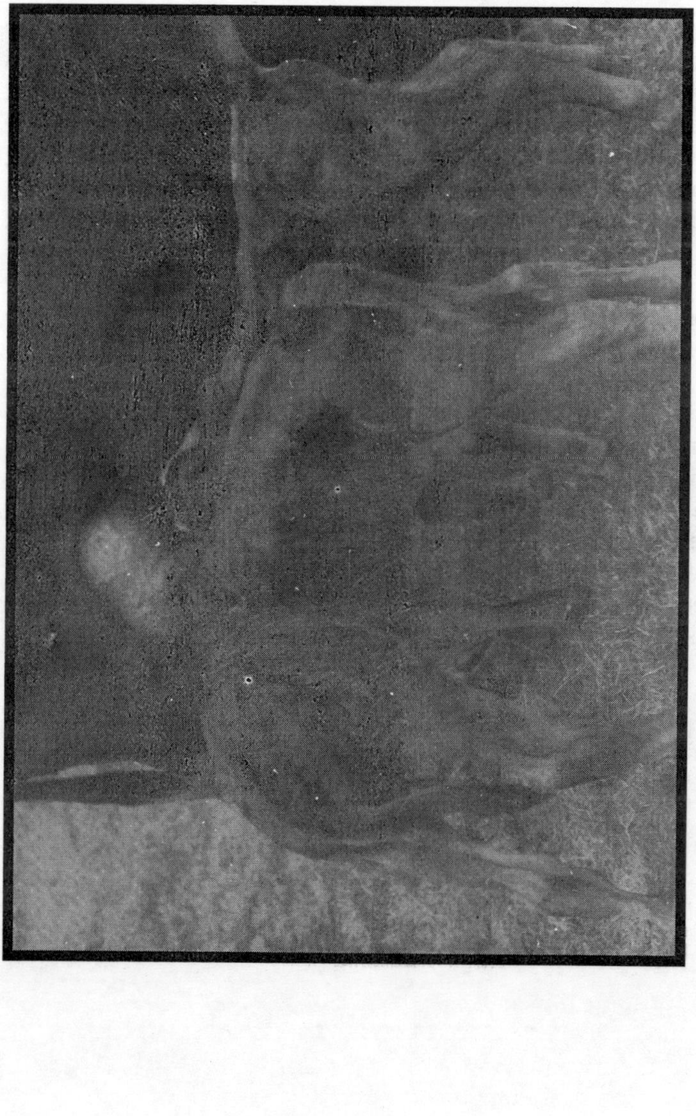

Plate 13: Multiple Suckling will Lower the Cost of Producing Stores

concentrates at an average rate of 3 lb. per day amounts to about £13 per calf. Over the winter months calves can be fed good silage instead of grass to effect an appreciable saving in concentrates in this period. Silage puts a bloom on young stock not unlike that associated with the feeding of linseed cake.

One important feature about multiple suckling is that it can be adopted on farms which are not laid out for dairying. The only fixed equipment required is satisfactory accommodation for the calves, which must be kept warm and away from draughts, some place where the nurse cows can be secured so that they don't take avoiding action against their foster children, and yarding accommodation for the winter should soil and other conditions demand that stock be kept off pastures. Existing buildings can often be modified for this purpose without the interference of some outside authority whose responsibility it is to safeguard quality of milk. For the man whose interest is in fattening stock rather than dairy cows it is a system of livestock farming which has much to commend it, and properly organised under present conditions, it can be a not unprofitable undertaking. It is probable that with the enforcement of the new regulations governing the production of milk for sale multiple suckling will become a profitable alternative on farms which have hitherto relied on milk. A factor limiting its expansion is the extremely high price which calves suitable for rearing command, especially in the early spring. It is not exceptional for good calves a week old to realise half their weaner value.

Chapter 12
Fattening of Cattle

Before World War II meat production could be divided into three main categories–veal, baby beef and mature beef. An intermediate classification could be introduced between the last two, namely the beefling which was a reflection of the popular demand for small joints from young animals. During and since the war, however, the character of production has changed vastly. Veal production even in pre-war days catered for a luxury trade, and milk-fed veal has now practically disappeared, while baby beef is a memory in this country, though it is still very important in the United States. The main emphasis has gone over to the fattening of mature beef, *i.e.*, of animals at least two and up to four years old.

Veal Production

Veal was normally a by-product of dairying, especially, where dual-purpose cows were kept. The Red Poll, the Dairy Shorthorn and South Devon were ideal for the purpose, while very good veal was obtained from Friesians. The starting-point was a heavy calf, 80–100 lb. live weight at birth, and the aim was to take it without check up to 225–75 lb. live weight in about 90–120 days, when it was slaughtered. The very finest veal, where the cooked flesh is not dissimilar to the breast of chicken, was obtained from milk-fed calves which were kept in small pens to reduce movement to a minimum. Exercise of course leads to a darker-coloured muscle, while the use of feeds other than milk has a similar effect. Sometimes on cream-selling farms separated milk was substituted for whole milk after a month, and cereals were used to supplement the milk. This of course cheapens the cost of production materially, and is the only form of veal production worth considering today.

The extreme dairy breeds were not used for veal, as they are too sparsely fleshed and have too high a proportion of bone. Calves of this type surplus to breeding needs are usually slaughtered within a few days of birth and are used in the 'bobby veal' trade. Very small qualities of flesh are obtained, and this is so characterless it is best used in the manufacture of meat pastes.

Baby Beef

Baby beef is derived from prime cattle of about 15 months which weigh in the vicinity of 7–8 cwt. at slaughter. The meat is of very high quality in that it is extremely tender, but it is inclined to shrink in cooking (an unforgivable sin in these days of rigid rationing), and it is relatively flavourless. Again dual-purpose cattle were important in the production (as in it the case of veal it is better to write in the past tense), and the Red Poll, in particular, and the Dairy Shorthorn were the most important breeds. Cattle were grown without check from birth to slaughter. As calves they were given a good start with whole milk–either bucket fed or multiple suckled–and at an early age they were given as much concentrates and hay as they wanted. After three months they were weaned from milk, but the quality of feed was still maintained. Silage and succulents such as roots, kale or green-feed might be introduced, but always the level of concentrate feeding was such that the cattle made rapid gains, and as much as 6–7 lb. of concentrates were fed over the final fattening stages. Cattle were kept yarded throughout, for rate of growth, it was considered, would be retarded if the young cattle went out to grass.

Such a level of feeding would be completely uneconomic in these days. The system was only possible when concentrates and labour were cheap and cattle could be prepared to meet a premium market in May and June. Today the only cattle which are fed on such a scale are show beasts, where cost of feeding is no object, and young pedigree bulls, both dairy and beef, which have to be reared on an extravagant plane of nutrition so that bull licensing officers may be assured that they have the right genetic make-up for the purpose for which they are intended, whether it be dairying or beef production. The cost of such feeding and management up to 15 months of age may exceed £100 per beast with present day labour and food costs, so it is not surprising that baby beef production is now a memory of more expansive days.

BEEFLINGS

Beeflings were normally killed between 18 and 24 months of age over a weight range of 8–11 cwt. Very often they were animals which had been intended for baby beef production, which had grown rather than fattened. Alternatively, stores intended for more mature beef which had developed very well could be preferentially treated to give a similar result. In the present-day price schedules there is still something of a premium for the animal which on a weight basis would qualify for the beefling grade. There is a premium of 3s per live cwt. for cattle estimated to kill out at 55 per cent or better as follows: for steers over the range 9–13 cwt. live weight and for heifers and cow heifers over the range 7½–11¾ cwt. Live weight. Because of the high cost of stores the tendency now is to market at the upper limits of these weight ranges. This, combined with the fact that cattle may be well over 2 years old despite their fairly low weights, really takes them out of the beefling class.

MATURE BEEF PRODUCTION

Today this is by far the most important category, for the emphasis is now on quantity rather than quality. Age of slaughter varies from 2½ years up to 4 according to the history of the store, and live weights normally range from 10 cwt. to 16 cwt. live weight and more. Even though there is this emphasis on quantity some deductions are made on the heavier beasts because it was found that farmers, in order to spread the high initial cost of stores, were getting their stock over-fat. Butchers complained that such carcasses were very wasteful in cutting and not at all suited for rationing. Over 13¾ cwt. and up to 15¾ cwt. (inclusive) there is a deduction from the basic price of 5s per live cwt., and this penalty is increased to 10s for animals 16 cwt. and over. One cannot but feel that weight classification is too inflexible as a basis for down-grading cattle. There are some breeds which are very large framed and late maturing, notably the Lincoln Red, the South Devon and the Friesian, and it is just as wasteful to market such beasts before they are properly finished as it is to carry small early-maturing beasts past their optimum condition to the point where they are laying down unwanted fat, very extravagantly in terms of nutrients required per lb. live-weight increase.

The production of this mature beef may be divided rather arbitrarily into the two categories, summer and winter fattening. The arbitrary nature of the classification comes about in this way. Very often bullocks may be partly fattened on grass in autumn and finished in yards over the early part of the winter to avoid the expense of five months of store feeding before grass is available once more. Alternatively cattle may be carried through the winter in a forward store condition, either in yards or on suitable pasture for out-wintering, for fattening in the early summer while premium prices still obtain. This is a practice which is growing in importance because it is relatively profitable.

Winter Fattening

The classical method of winter fattening is that associated with the Norfolk four-course rotation, where yarded bullocks were fed liberally on straw, roots and oil-cakes, partly for the profit they yielded but mainly for the dung which was then indispensible for maintaining heart in arable land. The system was by no means confined to the Eastern Counties, but was characteristic of an the arable districts of Britain, especially in Aberdeenshire and in the East Lothians, where winter fattening in a revised form is still important. The rate of root feeding used to be exceptionally heavy, and 112 lb. daily, pulped to assist in maintaining this high level of intake, was not uncommon in East Anglia, while cake feeding at the rate of 6 lb. of linseed and 6 lb. of cottonseed was customary over the final fattening stages. In addition the beasts received seeds hay and feeding straw to pick over. Mangolds were the popular root in East Anglia, but in Scotland swedes and turnips were and still are very popular. The Scots were not such heavy root feeders, and placed a great deal of emphasis on oat straw of good quality. It is customary in Scotland to cut oats before they are dead ripe, while there is still some green in the straw, and even today it is usual to provide freshly threshed straw, and as a result a feeding-stuff of relatively high quality is obtained. Certainly the gains made by bullocks are much greater than one would expect from the analyses of the feeding-stuffs.

The great decline in this system of fattening has been due to a number of contributing causes, notably the high cost of food in relation to the feeder's margin, the development of ley farming to restore fertility and structure to arable land and the greater availability of artificial fertilisers, especially nitrogenous fertilisers. Certainly the old system of lavish cake feeding to produce good dung was an expensive and inefficient way of administering nitrogen to the land, because much of the nitrogen was lost by leaching or as ammonia in the muck-making process, especially if animals were kept in open or partly covered yards. There have been modifications in feeding practice, as subsequent discussion will show, but there is still room for very considerable improvements in methods of feeding, because foodstuffs account for by far the greatest proportion of the feeder's margin. A highly seasonal character too is developing in the marketing of beef as a result of an increased emphasis on grass fattening, and this is not in the interests of the industry or the consumer. The implications of this will be discussed in Chapter 14.

Methods of accommodating cattle vary now from improvised yards constructed from straw bales on the field where the F.Y.M. will be ultimately applied, through to permanent open yards, semi-covered yards and fully covered yards or courts. The extreme type of accommodation is a long shed, in almost all respects like a standard milking shed, where the cattle are tied. This method still has support in Scotland especially for final finishing. Cattle which have reached a forward store condition in the courts are transferred to the feeding shed, where they can receive individual attention. Though farmers may have preferences in regard to accommodation, in most instances they have to make do with what they have. Returns have been too low and building costs are too high to permit of much more than slight modifications. In fact, most modifications which have been made to bullock fattening yards have been conversions to dairying.

Apparently only substantial business men who have acquired farm properties, or well-to-do market gardeners and hop-growers who value F.Y.M. can afford to erect new accommodation today. Generally such accommodation takes the form of a properly oriented shelter with an open yard attached. This is a system which has a lot of support among feeders who believe that the stock benefit from having direct sunlight when the days start to lengthen, and certainly it is very much cheaper than fully covered yards, though naturally the quality of F.Y.M. is not so good when it is subjected to leaching.

It is unfortunate that winter fattening cannot justify new accommodation, for feeders are thereby forced to use facilities which were designed for nineteenth-century conditions when labour was cheap. In the United States where winter feeding is a very important feature, especially on mid-west farms, suitable accommodation permits a man to make the tending of a hundred or more cattle a part-time job. Removal of F.Y.M. can be performed very much more efficiently by mechanical means when layout permits of full movement of machines. Most layouts in Britain are ill-suited to this purpose.

It is important that yarded bullocks are not run in very large lots unless individual ties such as those used in many modern yard dairy units are adopted in order to ensure that each beast gets a fair share. In the absence of these, fifteen per yard is a maximum, and even with this number adequate trough and rack room must be provided to reduce bullying to a minimum. Stock should also be evenly graded for size. Store cattle are much too expensive, and the feeder's margin is much too slight to allow unnecessary passengers to be carried. Stock subject to bullying are best put in a loose-box where they can be given individual attention. There is a great deal to be said for polled cattle in yard feeding, and this is where the polled breeds and their crosses score. It is significant that in America the polled character has been bred into the Hereford and the Shorthorn. Where polled cattle are kept 80–90 sq. ft. per beast is adequate space in a covered yard, and 120 sq. ft. in a partly covered yard which requires about 35 sq. ft. per beast to be sheltered. If horned cattle are kept a much larger allowance must be made, and even the increased space will not prevent horn damage.

Formerly it was common to fatten two lots of stock over the winter. Forward stores about 2 years old, sometimes younger, weighing 8–10 cwt. were brought into the yards in the late summer and fattened to take advantage of the high prices prevailing at Christmas-time. Their places were taken by another set of stores, which were brought in from permanent grass, which had enough of a turf to withstand poaching. These would be finished to meet the good market prevailing over the spring/early summer period. Now it is more usual to fatten only one lot of beasts, and rather heavier stores are yarded in the autumn and fattened over a longer period to be marketed in the spring. The idea is to produce as much F.Y.M. as possible with the few stores that are available. Something of the changes which have occurred in fattening over the past twenty-five years are illustrated by the figures given in Table 6, which is based on records kept at the Norfolk Agricultural Station at Sprowston.

Table 6: Bullock Fattening at Sprowston, 1927–49 (Rayns and Owers, 1950)

	1927–28	*1935–36*	*1944–45*	*1946–47*	*1948–49*
Initial weight (lb.)	812	994	1,183	1,078	1,064
Weight increase (lb.)	319	364	259	293	294
Final weight (lb.)	1,131	1,358	1,442	1,371	1,358
Fattening period (days)	128	140	177	178	181
Daily gain (lb.)	2.5	2.5	1.6	1.7	1.6

Apart from the lower rate of gain and the slower turn-over of capital much heavier stores have been used in recent years, and they have been carried to much heavier weights. Back in 1927–28 the emphasis was on the beefling, while today it is on the heavier beast which escapes the penalty for the overweight carcass. Early in the period heavy root feeding, mainly mangolds, was practised, and 5 lb. each of linseed and cottonseed cake were fed during the finishing process. By 1935–36 the concentrate feeding had changed to the balanced ration based on imported maize and decorticated groundnut cake. In 1948 the concentrate had been reduced to 3 lb. each of tail barley and tail oats daily. Sugar-beet tops and pulp are now the basis of feeding, and the big stores which are purchased in October are fed outside for ten weeks very largely on sugar-beet tops and straw, during which time they put on about 1 cwt., *i.e.* the grow at the rate of 1½ lb. per day. They are not yarded till the New Year, but they are kept in yards till they grade in the early spring when maximum prices are paid. The residues of the sugar-beet crop have become the corner-stone in this feeding programme, and reliance on expensive or specially grown foods has been reduced to a minimum.

This is but one example of how winter-feeding methods are evolving. Another interesting development is that reported in a farming journal,[1] where a Cotswold farmer practises folding of marrow stem kale in the autumn/early winter period to supplement summer fattening on grass. Unfinished cattle in October are folded behind an electric fence with such good results that they grade out satisfactorily in December. Such a method appears to have much to commend it on well-drained soils which permit folding of kale. Once it is cut and carted kale becomes a very expensive crop.

Another interesting development is the growing use of silage for beef production, which follows its successful adoption in dairying as a counter to the scarcity and expense of concentrates. Morrison (1951) has reported feeding trials in Northern Ireland, where over a 9-week period 9½-cwt. stores which were fed on a sole diet of silage, amounting to 118 lb. daily, made live-weight gains averaging 2.41 lb. per day and graded very satisfactorily. Comparable stores over the same period which received 60 lb. of silage, 8 lb. of hay and 6 lb. of oats averaged to 2.44 lb. per day, which is not materially different. In this trial the surplus on the silage bullocks after allowing for labour and silage (at 34s per ton) amounted to approximately £6 10s per beast compared with £4 17s for the control group. The actual margin in this trial is not the important finding, which is that very satisfactory gains can be made when stores are fed on a diet mainly or almost entirely consisting of good grass silage.[2] The question whether the feeding will be profitable or not, other things being equal, depends on how cheaply silage can be made and fed. In the Northern Ireland experiments the cost of silage at 34s per ton was creditably low, but if expensively made silage is used the feeders margin will soon be swamped. There are very few operations on farms which exhibit a greater range of costs than those for silage making, which vary from less than 30s per ton where the silage is made with a minimum of wastage, either of material or labour, by the clamp method using a buck-rake to hand-forked material which is badly consolidated, where the final edible silage may cost more than £5 per ton.

---

1 *Farmers' Weekly*, 19 January 1951

2 Dodsworth and Campbell at the North of Scotland College of Agriculture have also demonstrated the value of good silage for bullocks, obtaining rates of gain of 2½ lb. per day.

The use of silage for winter feeding ties in admirably with grassland fattening. Inevitably, when stores are expensive in the spring, and especially when there is a growthy season, there is a surplus of grass which, if it is left in the field, will deteriorate and depress growth. Where flexibility is secured in utilisation by having adequate subdivision to permit withdrawal of units from grazing, surpluses can be saved not just in the interests of winter feeding but in the interests of good grassland management as well. Such silage, unlike arable silage, is made from cheap material, for the overhead of ley establishment is spread over several years of grazing and conservation, whereas the silage from an arable crop has to bear the full costs of cultivation, seeding and fertilizing, and is not generally such good fodder as leafy pasture silage. The use of this silage need not be confined to winter feeding, for it is there as a reserve for droughty seasons when grass fails and saves recourse having to be made to expensive concentrates. Even home-grown mixtures such as oats and beans will cost over £20 per ton when prepared for feeding, *i.e.* about 3½d per lb. of starch equivalent, while quite moderate silage with a starch equivalent of 10 if made for 37s 6d per ton costs only 2d per lb. of starch equivalent.

Unfortunately not all trials with silage feeding have been as successful as the Northern Ireland trials, but it has to be remembered that there is silage and silage. There are some people who regard ensilage as a fairy-godmother process where pumpkins are turned into gleaming carriages. The quality of the silage depends primarily on the quality of material used and the efficiency with which temperatures are controlled and leaching is minimised. The buck-rake has taken the backache out of silage-making, and all that the average farmer needs is confidence in his methods of ensiling and in its use. One pictures in winter feeding a streamlining of operations whereby the tractor and trailer moves straight from the clamp to the point of feeding, so that the silage is fed with only a single handling as it is with modern yard layouts for dairying. It is not enough to make silage cheaply–it must be fed cheaply as well.

One must not forget in the discussions of cheap bulks for winter fattening the value of hay, the quality of which, like costs in silage making, is subject to extremes of variation. High-grade material cut from a general purpose ley made on tripods can have a starch-equivalent value of over 45 and a crude-protein value of over 12 per cent even in bad seasons. Efficiently organised tripoding need not cost 15s per ton more than ordinary methods in a good season, and quite possibly less per ton in a bad season when hay is repeatedly handled in an effort to save it. Meanwhile each handling and each wetting reduces food value and increases costs. Ten pounds of good hay (with an S.E. of 45) is equal to 10 lb. of poor hay (with an S.E. of 30) plus 2½ lb. of oats. Disregarding protein values, if it costs £8 per ton to make the poor hay, one can afford to spend £12 making gold hay. This leaves a very nice margin in favour of tripoding and reduces the necessity of dipping one's hand deeply into the expensive concentrate bag to finish wintered cattle.

Summer Fattening

When one thinks of summer fattening one's thoughts turn immediately to the renowned fatting pastures of the Mid-lands, which will fatten up to two bullocks to the acre in a season–but not in a year. There is an old saying that in the winter a bullock on pasture has five mouths. The reference here is to the poaching during the winter months which will lower carrying capacity very materially in the following season. The Midland fatteners attitude is, 'Make your pasture and your cattle will get fat on it' (Astill, 1940). They, like their Romney Marsh counterparts with sheep, have been making their fatting pastures for hundreds of years, and one wonders whether the conditions imposed by man, as opposed to natural conditions such as soil type and climate, are mainly responsible for the quality of these pastures. Certainly on Romney Marsh one sees fatting pastures alongside breeding or store pastures where the soil type is substantially the same in both cases.

The Midland grazier, and generally graziers of good bullock pastures throughout the country, prefer big mature stores at least 2½ years old which are capable of thriving on the rich herbage. Younger cattle tend to scour on such pasture and make poorer live-weight gains. The preference, too, is for stock that have not been too softly wintered, and usually the spring demand is for cattle with rough coats. At the same time there is no point in buying stores which are all skin and bone because they take a very long time to get moving, and will miss the good price period in the early summer. Probably the best course for a fattener, and this task is made much easier by the proportion of arable which is now found in most farms, is to buy stores rather more cheaply in the autumn for wintering on the farm.

They can be used before Christmas to clean up rough growth on pastures while the turf still has some holding capacity, and for the rest of the winter they can either be kept in open yards or in a well-sheltered sacrifice field which is intended for subsequent ploughing. The liberal plaster of dung and urine well benefit the subsequent crop, while the mechanical damage done to the soil is not so serious in these days of adequate tillage implements and power to draw them. At all costs one should avoid wintering the animals too well, for if they go out to cold showers and easterly winds they will scour and lose condition which has been put on expensively. The transition from hard to grass feeding should be as gradual as is practicable, and the use of a succulent such as silage in the winter diet is an aid to this.

A very interesting development in this wintering problem is the winter grazing of foggage obtained from S143 cocksfoot grown in rows which has been reported by Hughes (1949). Fourteen acres were closed up in July 1948, following summer grazing, and were given 6 cwt. of complete manure and 3 cwt. of sulphate of ammonia. The area carried 17 store bullocks averaging 10 cwt. from 18 January until 5 April, and they maintained their condition without other feed. The area provided what was substantially rather more than a ton of good standing hay to the acre, which was cheaply utilised by folding with an electric fence. It is suggested that better results still would have been obtained if the cocksfoot had been utilised by the end of December, because it is inclined to winter burn, and grazing for the rest of the winter had been provided by leafy timothy and meadow fiscue which are not so subject to burn. It is not implied that grass should be grown especially to provide such winter grazing but that it should be integrated in the general farming plan. There is evidence to show that grazing of cocksfoot to the end of the year can be done without serious depletion of yield if the field is subsequently closed for seed production (Hughes, 1949). Alternatively, the grass could be utilised for summer grazing. One interesting feature is that the grazing of plants sown in rows reduces the ill effects of poaching and fouling very markedly. The soil on which the above trial was completed is one of the most difficult clays we have in Britain, and yet poaching was not serious because the cattle kept to the rows.[1]

---

[1] The growing of lucerne and grass in rows is an important recent development of this work.

Usually the field size of these fatting pastures is not large. This is important because it gives the grazier flexibility in his management and assists him in obtaining a full and even utilisation of the sward. He is able to size his stores fairly evenly and keep animals of a kind in the one group so they can all be marketed in a bunch. He endeavours to reduce to a minimum the introduction of strange cattle into a field to keep up the required intensity of grazing, and usually fields are stocked as early as possible in the spring to their full grazing complement. On the best fields this will be at the rate of 1 to 1½ beasts to the acre, rate of stocking being decided from experience of the normal carrying capacity of the field. Both good and bad growing seasons have to be catered for, but rather than disturb the cattle once they settle, adjustments in rate of stocking are made mainly with sheep, which may be increased or decreased in number according to the state of growth on the pastures, and a field may be cleared of stock by August when it can be rested before restocking in September. Some of the best of these autumn cattle will also grade out, possibly with some small assistance from concentrates, while the remainder will be carried over the winter, but not on the good pastures, for finishing in the following spring. Sheep, however, will be used to trim up good pastures so roughage will not impair fresh growth in the spring. Usually lambs are bought in for this purpose, and they are sold fat as two-tooths in the summer when they have completed their task of controlling the flush of growth. Alternatively a breeding flock can be used.

The live-weight increase obtained from these good pastures is high. Davies and Williams (1948) report figures from cattle grazing alone in one of the most notable of fatting pastures at Medbourne of 301 lb., 388 lb. and 376 lb. per acre in the three years 1945, 1946 and 1947 respectively. However, this very careful attention which is paid to the smaller proportion of a farm which is composed of fatting pastures is generally to the detriment of other parts of the farm, which are maintained as a reservoir or holding area which may be mismanaged by overstocking or understocking in order to preserve the right rate of stocking on the favoured pastures. One wonders just how much greater output of meat from the whole farm would be if it was all subjected to good management. It must be remembered that the traditional system of management dates from a period when there were no artificial fertilisers and when there were no bred strains of leafy pasture grasses such as we have today, and so the need for

Plate 14: Higher Prices for Artificials will put a New Emphasis on F.Y.M.

Plate 15: Herefords Grazing Cocksfoot Drills in January at the Grassland Improvement Station

these carefully managed pastures is not so great. Why is some pasture closely adjacent to fatting pastures only good enough to be classed as store land if it is substantially on the same soil type and is subject to the same climatic conditions? Perhaps it is a question of phosphate or lime. These can be applied to achieve the state of fertility which high-producing pasture associations demand. Perhaps the limiting factor is management which discourages high producing species to allow poorer grasses to achieve dominance. It is well recognised that fatting pastures will deteriorate quickly if they are mismanaged, *i.e.* subjected to the same kind of management which is the lot of store land. Great improvements can be made in our second-rate grassland by making good the deficiencies in biotic conditions which are essential for maximum productivity. In many cases most rapid progress will be made through ploughing up and reseeding to replace poor species quickly with improved strains. In other cases fertilising, liming and drainage combined with correct grazing management will be sufficient to lift the status of the sward from mediocrity to high productivity.

One visualises an overall plan of management for the whole of the grassland area of the farm whether it be permanent pasture or ley, based on subdivision and controlled grazing. The most forward cattle would be given first pick of the pastures and would be followed by stores, which are capable of making gains on inferior food because of their less-advanced stage of fattening. They, combined with sheep, are the cleaners-up which convert uneaten herbage into dung and urine to grow more grass. The chain harrows would follow to spread droppings, and the mowing machine would be used judiciously to prevent grass going to head. As pastures get ahead of the stock some fields would be withdrawn from the grazing rotation to provide silage and hay to fill the winter gap. By cutting early silage a strong aftermath can be provided for grazing as pasture growth declines. In this way, combined with reduction in stock numbers as cattle and sheep are graded, very good equation of pasture growth and stock appetite will be obtained. The relative inflexibility of the permanent pasture can be countered by the use of special leys. Really early grazing can be provided by short rotation rye-grass sown in association with S100 white clover and S23, which comes in later in the season to give a prolonged flush. Timothy and clover leys, suitably managed, will produce well when rye-grass is losing its bloom, and will also make another worth-while contribution in the back end. In this way, and by appropriate fertilising, weeks can be carved off both ends of the winter.

It is not suggested that these first-class fatting pastures should be sacrificed in this plan. There is no need for them to be subjected to haying or even silage, for they can remain as the mainspring of grazing. However, the view that it is sacrilege to break a fatting pasture, which was so strongly held at the commencement of the war when the ploughing campaign was at its height, has not received support from trials which were initiated by the Royal Agricultural Society of England, which Davis and Williams (1948) have reported. In no instance was it shown that permanent pasture had an advantage over well-managed leys established alongside on comparable land. Even in the Medbourne instance, referred to previously, where the comparison was made between a renowned fattening pasture and a rye-grass clover pasture which followed two crops of potatoes and one of wheat, the only conclusion that could be drawn was that the ley appeared to have a better autumn performance. Elsewhere, with comparisons between inferior permanent pastures and leys productivity was much in favour of the ley, in some instances 50 per cent higher. Most revealing is the fact that in several cases productivity of these leys, measured in terms of live-weight increase of cattle per acre, was higher than it was on the permanent pasture at Medbourne.

However, it is academic to discuss whether good pastures which constitute only 6 per cent of the total permanent pasture of England and Wales should be ploughed up. Ploughing and reseeding has plenty of scope on the millions of acres of low-class permanent pastures which are amenable to improvement. We have the 'know how' to effect improvement, but apparently we have not yet, in spite of economic pressure, the inclination to do so, but we may have it if the national belt has to be drawn up another notch or so.

To those that suggest that removal of stock in a process of rotational grazing will be so disturbing that they will not thrive, it may be answered that there is much evidence accumulating to show that the reverse result obtains. In the final chapter reference is made to the colossal live-weight gains per acre which Davis (1951) has obtained from rotationally grazed sheep which similarly are said to react badly to movement. McMeekan's work with rotational grazing of dairy heifers has already been referred to, and here the conclusion, very strongly, is that young stock benefit very materially from frequent changes to good clean pasture. It is not just a question of effect on stock but effect on pasture too, for Woodman *et al.* (1928) in their classical studies nearly a quarter of a century ago showed that too frequent defoliation was detrimental to production of nutrients. Whether we set stock on traditional lines or adopt controlled grazing we come back to that same conclusion, 'Make your pasture and your cattle will get fat on it.' Certainly the system of rotational grazing outlined is easier for the beginner to follow than it is for him to pick up the art, or is it the science, of managing a fatting pasture on traditional lines. It is important, however, that cattle approaching prime condition could not be pushed too hard in order to secure full utilisation of pasture. Like milking cows given the same task they will show an adverse response. Store cattle and sheep are more appropriately used to clean up the uneaten pasture so that the fattening animals are maintained in the contented state which is characteristic of stock which are making good live weight gains.

Chapter 13
Beef Cattle on Hill and Marginal Land

Contributed by A.G. Davis

Historical

History records that cattle were bred and raised in the west and north of Britain on our extensive regions of hill and mountainous country, and that the descendants of these stock are our present distinctive breeds of Welsh Black, Highland and Galloway cattle, the only breeds whose mature animals can stay out during the severest winter weather on the hills. The pages of history tell us all too little about the ancestors of these famous breeds and how they were managed. They were summered on the higher country–the 'sheilings' in Scotland, the 'hendre' in Wales, where the family moved for the duration to tend them. They were wintered in the sheltered valleys close to the steadings and croftings–on the edge of the ffridd in Wales, on the inbye land of the north of England and in Scotland–

with some of the cows bedded indoors on bracken litter. Within reasonable proximity *Molinia* was scythed for the winter's hay supply, as it is today in some parts. It is stated that on Highland crofts when the cows dried off, as they did early in the winter, they were bled in order to supplement the diet of oatmeal and fish, with the result that by spring the cows literally had to be hand-lifted out to grass. Large numbers came out of Scotland and Wales, but they were small and hardy animals which had to walk every step of the way to the butcher's yard. We may hazard, a shrewd guess that the meat was mighty tough and anything but juicy.

It is possible that the cows had a long life for their fertility rate was low, with a calf reared every other year or even less often. Growth was very slow, for the stock did not have enough to eat during the long winter. Artificial fertilisers were unknown, and lime or chalk was available only where it could be carried by boat to the nearest point and carted a day or two's journey when the tracks were dry, or carried in small quantities over great distances in baskets on ponies. The grass at its best is most likely to have been a very mixed herbage of bent, fine-leaved fescues, Yorkshire fog, field woodrush, bedstraws, creeping buttercup, sheep's-sorrel and the like on the inbye field, at its worst on the open moor, fescue, *Molinia, Nardus* and the more tender shoots of rushes and *Scirpus* and cotton grass, where the peat would carry the stock. If we are to accept the concept (Johnstone-Wallace, 1944) that a beast grazes for approximately eight hours in twenty-four, and that his ancestors did likewise, their nutrition on mountain herbage must have been very meagre indeed.

Despite all these handicaps the hills and mountains produced large numbers of cattle (Stewart, 1949), and probably therefore supported a substantial human population. They, too, must have been a hardy lot, living under exceedingly primitive conditions on a bare level of sustenance with the fear of famine always in the background, and, in unsettled times, the threat of raids upon their stock. Today there is much talk of restocking the hills. We can put the cattle there, we can improve the vegetation, and of both more will be said, but how do we stand as regards the men, women and children who must, if it is to be a success, live among the hills and mountains to look after the cattle? For generations folk have been leaving the hills either for employment outside of agriculture or for lowland farms. This depopulation of the hills is a matter of grave national concern. Grand schemes are afoot to resuscitate the hill-farming community, to bring cattle back and to aid the flock master, but it is doubtful whether people will go back to live on the hills unless life there is made more attractive for them. The clock cannot be put back except at a price which the country may not be prepared to pay, or, alternatively it may prefer to invest in lowland farming. This human problem must be tackled with bold and far-sighted imagination, for until solution is found the contribution to the national meat larder which could be made by hill land will never get past the planning stage.

Hill and marginal land in Britain comprises about 34 per cent of the total area, one-third of it in England and Wales and two-thirds in Scotland. In some counties hills and mountains predominate, as for example in Merioneth and in Sutherland, where agricultural land which is in rough and hill grazings amounts to 63 and 97 per cent of the total respectively (Stapledon, 1937). Again, there are quite extensive areas where sheep and possibly deer may range, but not cattle by reason of altitude (2,000 to 4,000 feet), lack of shelter, inaccessibility and paucity of herbage. On individual holdings often the entire area is hill country, although there will be a few inbye fields alongside the steadings, where the pasturage is good in comparison with the moorland herbage on the other side of the wall. The herbage on the open hull is poor–poor in species, seasonality of growth, nutritive value and mineral content. The complete replacement of cattle by sheep which took place during the nineteenth century, and the long period of supremacy of the sheep industry, were accompanied by a deterioration in the type and quality of herbage. This change of management was intensified during the first half of the twentieth century, when lambs were sold straight off the dams and older weathers were no longer maintained on the mountain, and as a result of this practice the rate of loss of calcium and phosphorus removed on the hoof was increased. Mismanagement of the grazings through using only the one type of stock was, however, by far the most important factor in this process of deterioration.

Methods of Improvement

There are a variety of methods of improving the herbage, and therefore the carrying capacity of hill and marginal land. The key to the whole sequence of operations is the crawler tractor. In the first instance drainage by means of open ditches is essential on some lands and highly desirable on others, both for the benefit of the herbage as well as helping to avoid losses from cattle over-reaching on wet areas and becoming bogged. Bennett-Evans (1949) has stressed this and called attention to the new drainage plough which cuts a clean ditch 2 ft. 6 in. deep by 2 ft. 6 in. wide at a cost then of 2s 3d to 2s 9d per chain. In the second instance liming and phosphating are essential. Milton (1940) has shown that lime alone over a long period of years, provided it is accompanied with judicious grazing, will completely replace the poor herbage with lowland species and wild white clover, but that does not take into account the need of phosphorus by the stock. This may be circumvented by the feeding of a bone meal supplement which, as Dunlop (1947) demonstrated, improved the breeding efficiency of cows on hill pastures in Scotland.

Under the guiding hand of Stapledon, Griffith on the Cahn Hill Improvement Scheme, Ellison in Montgomeryshire and Hughes in Staffordshire effected a complete transformation of the herbage by pre-discing, ploughing and burying the old mat, pioneer cropping and reseeding with a seeds mixture including leafy pedigree persistent strains. Griffith (1950) has outlined his ideal rotation for a scheme of reclamation:

1st year: rape, turnips plus Italian rye-grass
2nd year: rape, very light seeding plus seeds mixture
3rd year: 1st year seeds for grazing young cattle
4th year: 2nd year seeds for grazing young cattle
5th year: pasture for mature cattle
6th year: pasture for mature cattle and breeding portion of the sheep flock
7th year: grass for ensilage and pasture
8th year: grass for ensilage and pasture

Bennett-Evans, the pioneer hill farmer of central Wales, has made great improvements by surface treatments and cattle grazing, as well as by ploughing and reseeding, and he rather favours the former technique despite its comparative slowness. He, as well as many others, including those on enclosed marginal land, has been disheartened by the super-abundance of rushes which make their appearance where the plough has been used, whereas they are markedly less evident where surface improvement is in progress. It is an ecological problem, the answer to which is probably very simple, as is so often the case, and all too little research has been carried out. Moore (1948) and his colleagues in Yorkshire were favourably impressed with a leafy multi-tillering strain of timothy as a successful competitor with the rushes. Frequent mowing if it can be done will suppress them; the operative word is 'if.' The same technique must be used to check and eliminate bracken on thin or stony land where it cannot be ploughed under. Hoof cultivation by cattle is a further aid to the destruction of frond-buds while still in the soil (Braid, 1947).

Surface improvements carried out by Heddle and Fenton at Boghall on the Pentlands have illustrated the importance of cattle in stopping the spread of useless *Nardus* or mat grass. Where only sheep have access mat grass will replace fescuebent down the slope and encroach upon heather up the slope. It is not quite such a simple ecological process as this statement suggests since many other factors are involved, but that is what occurs. Likewise *Molinia* is checked and then reduced in the glens by cattle grazing, and this in turn enables the sheep to work the whole area which otherwise they could not have done.

McDougal (1946) in Berwickshire states that ploughing and reseeding after cropping or at once is a success, and that he has been doing this for over forty years. He has made a long and close study of species and seeds mixtures, which are summarised in his words, 'Cut down the rye-grass and sow plenty of cocksfoot, fescues and timothy with wild white.' This is supported by Wells's (1950) experiences, following up the work of Hughes at Mixon Hay, Staffs, where they are placing increasing reliance upon a hay or silage mixture based on timothy and meadow fescue. Griffith's (1950) favourite mixture for the drier land is based upon the leafy S143 cocksfoot.

By and large the type of tractable hill land which has a good depth for ploughing and carries extensive stretches of *Nardus* with rushes, or *Molinia* or heather or bracken invading heather is also far from habitation, and, worst of all, very exposed. On broken land with steep slopes where stock may find shelter in bad weather, the soil is often thin, stony or strewn with outcrops of rocks, and it is

Plate 16: Modern Methods must be Applied in Order to Lower Handling Costs

Plate 17: This was a Marginal Farm

Plate 18: The Key to Development is the Crawler Tractor

Plate 19: Glenlochay Flats have been Drained and Semi-permanent Pastures have been Established

there that the existing vegetation must yield to surface treatment, largely brought about by the cattle. The first method not only demands lime and phosphates but also nitrogen on the seed bed–lime in two dressings before and after ploughing to rot the mat, and with the phosphates and nitrogen to aid in feeding the new crop. Ellison (1949) states that 'soil analyses have shown that on most marginal lands, especially in upland areas, there is usually a deficiency of lime and phosphates equivalent to 30–40 cwt. of ground limestone and 6–10 cwt. of medium-grade basic slag per acre.' By the second method it will not be possible to get lime and phosphates on the whole area owing to the topography, but the transference of fertility which accompanies stocking together with browsing of the cattle will promote improvement of the herbage of the area as a whole. It may be that the initial amounts of lime and phosphates must continue to be applied in the traditional manner, although now we all have hopes that the aeroplane can be made to spread subsequent top-dressings, particularly of phosphates, which should be given at regular intervals.

An important feature of the surface treatment technique of improvement is the spectacular manner by which valuable species make their appearance in the midst of vegetation which previously showed absolutely no sign of their presence. This is largely due to a sufficiency of buried viable seeds of in the more desirable species (Milton, 1936), and also to the seed in the dung of the stock introduced from lowland areas or from good swards or from the hay fed out in previous winter, *e.g.* wild white clover. The broadcasting of seed cleanings containing wild white clover hastens the change towards *Agrostis* and white clover sward. If the plough goes in and reseeding follows it is very desirable to sow pedigree leafy strains in order that the sown species shall persist (Griffith, 1950).

Large blocks of improved areas, none of them enclosed and each with a different aspect, were developed by Stapledon on Cahn Hill in order that the sheep and cattle might have access to good quality herbage all the time, irrespective of the weather, and on the assumption that man knew what was best for the stock. Boulett (1939) found that in wet weather and early in the day when the dew lay heavy on the grass, sheep browsed the unimproved areas. Of course by doing so they transferred stock fertility from the improved to the unimproved area. Altogether then there is a strong case for carrying out improvement of the vegetation on the hills and marginal lands by both surface treatment and ploughing, pioneer cropping and eventually reseeding on different areas of the same estate, using whichever is the more suitable, the former on steep slopes and shallow or stony soils, and the latter on more level, deeper soils with the final result of improving the vegetation and fertility of the area as a whole.

Bennett-Evans (1949) has stated that 'sheep must remain masters of the mountain,' and they will certainly keep that place if wool prices remain high. Since it is recognised that improvement of the herbage can be maintained only with the aid of cattle (Ellison, 1949) the two are complementary to one another, for cattle in the hills enable the carrying of more sheep. Historically it is interesting to know and appreciate that in the Highlands and Islands both cattle and sheep were kept in large numbers, and in this connection Fraser (1950) has debunked any present-day misconception that only the former were in evidence there. Our contemporary appreciation of the decline in stock-carrying capacity and deterioration of the grazings of the upland regions associated with the absence of cattle is less than it is in New Zealand, where extensive areas of hill grazings which were carved out of bush and forest by pioneers of the Victorian generation have since rapidly reverted to fern and scrub, when cattle were removed from the land. McGuiness (1947) has produced figures to show that a workable ratio of cattle to sheep on hill country of the North Island is 1 to 7.6, which in terms of stock-carrying equivalents closely approaches half and half. Cattle by themselves, that is of the hardy breeds, are unlikely to pay sufficiently, nor is it a good practice to have all the eggs in one basket apart from the fact that mixed stocking is essential to maximum production. There are of course always exceptions of which Lord Lovat is one, although his system relies upon the importation of Irish heifers on which he uses beef bulls, and the cattle are only summered on the higher country.

Possibly one of the best recent examples of cattle being used in Britain to improve the quality of sheep grazings is that provided by Stewart and his associates on Glenlochay near Killin in Perthshire, where rainfall exceeds 100 inches annually. The property, approximately 15,000 acres in extent, was taken over in 1941 when the total stock amounted to 2,200 Blackface ewes plus the requisite ewe hogs and rams. The lower slopes of the glen were covered with bracken and *Molinia,* while the flats at the bottom were badly drained and infested with rushes, with the result that the sheep flock kept to the hilltops to neglect the lower and potentially more productive land. Nine years of sound management have, however, effected a transformation as the following figures show. In the winter of 1950–51 the sheep flock being carried in the Glen, mainly Galloway-type Blackface, amounted to 4,100 breeding ewes, 400 2- and 3-year wether hoggs, and 120 stock rams. In addition there were 130 hardy Cross-Highland cows and heifers, which were being carried with only a limited amount of supplementary food, amounting to not more than 12 cwt. of hay and straw per beast, which has been brought into the Glen. A thousand ewe hoggs are wintered off the Glen but return in the spring.

The enclosed flats have been drained and seeded down to a semi-permanent mixture after a pioneer crop of rape and Italian rye-grass, and the quality of these swards compares very favourably with lowland pastures. They are specially valuable for wintering rams and for fattening a proportion of lambs. Amounting as they do to only 100 acres or 0.66 per cent of the total area, they cannot be given the credit for the lion's share of the improvement, which must be attributed to the Cross-Highland breeding cows which are mated to high-quality Shorthorn sires to produce first-class weaners in September, which are taken away from the Glen. During the summer months these cows, with their calves at foot, graze the lower slopes, and now they have got right on top of the *Molinia* to allow more valuable species to achieve some measure of dominance. As a result the sheep now work over the slopes which they used to neglect. The cows, after weaning, do not stick to the lower slopes but move to the higher ground to continue their good work of eating out rough growth. Usually they will continue to get sustenance from the hill until the new year, when supplementary feeding with oat straw or hay is commenced, but in early winters this feeding may have to commence at the beginning of December. Normally it is caried on till the first or second week of May.

Bracken cutting and drainage of the lower slopes have also contributed to the improvement plan. Normally bracken cutting has to be done twice in the season, commencing in June, for three years in succession, and it will require further attention four or five years later. This work combined with that of the cattle has now brought the herbage close to the point where the move expensive methods of improvement–liming and phosphating–are justified. It is pointless pouring fertility on to old man *Molinia,* but it is a very different story when more valuable elements such as Yorkshire fog, *Agrostis* and wild white clover start to appear.

In regard to the number of cattle that have been used, Stewart (1951) states that the breeding herd has consisted of about 100 cows. A larger number were put on the ground in 1941, but some of these had to be sold because of age or unthriftiness in the ensuing years. Replacements have been hard to find, and only quite recently has it been possible to increase the herd size, Eventually, with fencing, in order to keep cows on the blocks where they are most needed, it is hoped that the herd will increase to 200 cows, or 1 to every 75 acres, On lowland standards this is a very unimpressive figure, but on high hill farms it is a performance with a real significance.

Bennett-Evans (1949) has courageously kept a Welsh Black herd on Plynlimmon in mid-Wales since 1931 without recourse to the services of a veterinary surgeon apart from attestation with cows reaching a good age and still breeding. Duncan Stewart (1949) has outlined the cattle required for the 'high wild open country of central, west and north Scotland,' as well as for regions of kinder climate north of the border. The Highland, or Cross-Highlander cow with a Scotch or beef Shorthorn bull as one of its parents, will forage, thrive and rear its calf on the poorest region. On the drier hill country of the east the Cross-Highlander or Aberdeen Angus Shorthorn cross may be carried. In the south-west, the Galloway is at home, and when put to a white Shorthorn bull gives the hardy Blue-Grey, which in turn may be crossed with an Angus bull, Although the more rapidly maturing beef breeds, Angus, beef Shorthorn and Hereford will stand up to long cold winters, as for example on the Canadian prairies, they cannot contend with winter's driving rain on upland Britain. In mid-Wales, even during the summer, the Welsh Black make better gains than cattle with Hereford or Angus breeding (Griffith, 1947), On marginal farms where all the stock can be wintered under cover or removed to nearby lowland farms after summering on the open hill, there is a sufficiently wide range of beef, dual-purpose and crosses, as well as stores derived from the dairy industry to satisfy the stockman's fancy. In fact, it is from this class of cattle and from marginal upland farms that we must endeavour to obtain any immediate increased meat ration, for however necessary and valuable hardy cattle are on the open hill, their present numbers are so small and the rate of increase so slow their contribution to our meat supplies must be of a long-term order.

At the risk of repetition it is emphasised that lime and phosphates are essential for both the improved health of the stock as well as for the production of more and better herbage. The low intake of these minerals, as well as the low level of sustenance during long periods of the year, probably accounts for the decline in size of cattle beasts kept on the hills throughout their life. If improved blocks are fenced then water must be provided. But the former, in the interests of good management, and the latter are expenses which might wait upon financial returns from initial improvements.

The Problem of Winter Keep

The greatest problem, though, facing the hill and marginal upland farmer is the acute shortage of winter feed, both in quantity and in quality. Adaptations of the old system of summering on the open hills away from the croft and hafod, which lessened this problem and made good use of the mountain grazings, have received merited publicity. The cattle agistment scheme developed by the Montgomeryshire Committee during the war not only assisted the small low-land farmer by carrying some of his stock during the summer months, thereby enabling him to increase his acreage of hay, but also has contributed to the improvement of the hill. The successful running of an estate combining mountain grazings and a productive lowland farm with the financial backing associated with post-war lowland farming, which enables the development of cattle raising along with sheep on the open hill, contrasts with the position of self-contained upland sheep farms which have not enjoyed a comparable degree of post-war prosperity. Hay or other fodder produced on the lowland part of the farming organisation can be made available on the associated hill farm, or alternatively, stock may be easily drafted down if the feed position is tight.

Gregor (1946) in Scotland has advocated the ploughing, reseeding and manuring, in particular heavy dressings of nitrogen, of the small areas that are tractable in difficult country. These are accessible to the stock at all times, and they can satisfy their nutritional needs in terms of minerals and proteins from the reseeded area and their bulk and carbohydrate from the hill herbage. Such complementary grazing provides them with a balanced diet.

Without an agistment scheme the high hill farmer is at the mercy of a wet hay and harvest period as in 1950 and/or a winter which slaughters livestock such as early 1947. I recollect such a winter in western Canada where cattle died even in the sheds, and on most mornings a team was put on to drag out the carcasses. Those who have not seen it at first hand just cannot appreciate the tragedy which smites the cattle owner. At the present time the only certain means of providing a sufficiency of winter fodder in advance is to buy oat straw and hay and to make silage, but the former are far too expensive while the latter is difficult to feed out at any distance in deep snow. We must not blind ourselves, however, by the present price structure, for by a stroke of the pen officialdom can alter the price received for store cattle, and bought hay might no longer be too expensive. Buying of hay, therefore, must not be ruled out, especially when the amount required to winter a beast is probably less for hardy outwintered cows than it is for those kept in steadings, for the former are free to forage except in deep snow. Bennett-Evans (1949) feeds about 5 lb. a day to his Welsh Blacks, a quantity which is doubled when snow lies heavy, whereas Stewart (1949) advises 7-10 lb., with the possibility of having to feed it from January to mid-May–that is, 10–12 cwt. per mature beast. Good oat straw may be used, particularly during the early part of the winter, or oat sheaves instead of hay, but they, too, are at a premium in the west and north because of wet harvests. The cattle should be free to range when and where they wish, and if hand-fed this is best done at the same time each day. Because the winter may arrive early or stay late, it is necessary to have a supply of fodder on hand, which is accessible in blizzard weather. Exponents of silage for feeding to cattle outwintered on the open hill are apt to overlook the difficulties the need for a permanent waterproof cover, and the siting of the pit or clamp in relation to where the herbage is produced, and where it will have to be fed, points which may be some distance apart, for in deep snow it may be impossible to cart it at all, let alone any distance. Hay can be man-handled to the stock, but not silage, nor is the latter anything but unpalatable if it becomes frosted in below-zero weather.

On enclosed marginal farms with some building accommodation or shelter, the position is different, and probably much more use of grass silage could be made. Too much must not be made of the difficulties, and one feels that if a Rex Patterson could be persuaded to embark upon a hill-farming venture, a technique for making and feeding silage would soon be forthcoming. Concerning this attitude towards difficulties I am reminded of my own brother's attempt to substitute a tractor for some of the teams of horses maintained during the winter on the cattle ranch in southern Alberta. Father was adamant that it would be impossible to start the tractor when the thermometer dropped to 30 deg. F. below zero, and he was right until my brother overcame the difficulty by draining the oil every evening and putting it on the kitchen stove every morning prior to starting–all, of course, very much to my mother's disgust.

The National Farmers' Union promoted a scheme in 1950 to help their hard-stricken brethren in the west by making available some dried sugar-beet pulp, which is normally retained for dairy stock in the east. At £20 a ton plus cartage it is probably cheaper than hay on a basis of its starch equivalent value. It is to be hoped that this effort is a forerunner of some scheme whereby home-grown feeding-stuffs could be made available in high-rainfall areas where they cannot be produced. It is puzzling why the sugar-beet industry, which received Government assistance, should bring benefits to the arable lands of lowland Britain alone, while the stock-raring uplands struggled along without any assistance until the arrival of the Milk Marketing Board. The contrast of prosperity between the two systems of farming is very striking, and now that the former is well established it should turn to and lend a hand to the latter, the more so in view of the forthcoming restrictions of dairying premises, which will squeeze out quite a number of dairy-cow keepers in upland areas. Furthermore, the arable man with his yards is dependent upon the supply of store cattle from the upland regions, and it would appear to be to his own advantage in the long run to assist the producer with some assurance of a supply of feeding-stuff as well as a reasonable monetary reward.

On enclosed land herbage can be made accessible to stock for part of the winter's day. Such rationing of the grass was carried out pre-war on the Cahn Hill by Griffith (1947), where S48 timothy was grown in drills as for seed production, and 70 ewe lambs were successfully wintered on 7 acres in conjunction with 9 acres of rough pasture. Hughes (1948) adapted the technique for wintering Hereford bullocks on heavy lias clay at the Grassland Research Station, using an old seed production stand of S143 cocksfoot sown in wide drills. Wastage due to treading was negligible, and some hay was fed to maintain them in good condition. Some such method of making use of winter green leafy strains of pedigree grasses deserves further investigation to enable more stock to be carried on marginal farms.

Management of improved areas either on the open hill or in enclosed fields must take into consideration the needs of the plants and the balance of species in the sward. An early species like rye-grass will not survive in the face of repeated hard grazing in the spring to be followed by under-grazing in the summer, when a later species like bent grass will compete unduly and white clover too will suffer. In practice the sheltered and enclosed areas are overgrazed in late winter and spring and undergrazed in summer, when the stock are either away on the hill or there is too much growth for their needs. In both instances the less-desirable species rapidly dominate the sward. On-and-off grazing by cattle during the summer, with periods of rest in order that the better grasses and white clover can replenish their root systems is necessary to prolong the life and production of the sown sward.

Hay making for one reason or another in upland regions is late, not being commenced until after shearing, and even then the weather may turn against the farmer. Silage enthusiasts point to the fact that they are less dependent on, the weather, but probably what is even more important, silage making is good grassland management. The herbage is cut early rather than late, and less desirable species are kept in check and prevented from seeding, and there is little opportunity for smothering the white clover. Of course on the vast expanse of the open hill, where either it has been reseeded or surface treated, the cattle will do much of the work of mowing machines.

Productivity of the Improved Hills

Griffith (1947, 1950) and Ellison (1947, 1950) have published details of production to be obtained and the expenses and returns entailed in improving hill and marginal land. The data are quite extensive–more than sufficient for a chapter of their own, and a mere summary must suffice. The former states 'the reseeded pastures can produce from 150 to 224 lb. per head live-weight increase in cattle, and some barren heifers have been fattened without any hand-feeding'; furthermore, 'on reseeded pastures the stock-carrying capacity has been more than trebled'–this largely in terms of sheep, but without the cattle it could not have been achieved. The latter reporting upon the 6,000 acres which were tackled in Montgomeryshire, states that the average return per acre up to the end of the third harvest year for two improved hills totalling 880 acres managed under the cattle agistment scheme was £12 8s. The margin of profitability per acre in relation to the investment entailed is very small if only the agistment of cattle is considered. There is, in addition, the sheep stocking, in this case one ewe and her lamb per acre, and the benefit derived by the small farmer of being relieved of some of his stock for the summer period at a low charge of £6 less the £3 hill-cattle subsidy.[1] Rearing of calves on the hill out of Welsh Black heifers crossed with white Shorthorn or Hereford bull was more profitable, and also more risky (Ellison, 1949). In Scotland, with their £7 subsidy per cow kept on the hill throughout the year, rearing has been made a profitable venture when the cost of wintering has been successfully overcome. Even in pre-war days Wilson (1936) demonstrated in Boghall Glen that by introducing Galloways with calves there was no reduction of sheep and lambs, and they fetched a much better price while the cattle paid their way.

Unfortunately and as already stated, a substantial proportion of any immediate increase in the meat ration must come from the cattle that can be carried by the small marginal farmer; cattle which he must either buy as weaned calves from the open hill, or what is more likely, rear himself, and sell as stores for fattening at 18 months to 2 years to the low-land farmer. Many of these farms have come to rely upon the monthly milk cheque which will not be easy to replace, and they will require financial assistance to change back to rearing cattle and improving their grassland.

Government Assistance

Direct Government assistance to the hill-farming industry has taken various forms–subsidies for keeping cattle and sheep on the hills, calf-rearing, ploughing, liming, manuring, drainage and, more recently, grants towards these and other operations, and to buildings, machinery, roads, electricity–in fact in any manner that will aid

---

1 1952–£5 for breeding cows and heifers and £2 15s for other eligible stock.

Britain's hill and marginal farms. The programme has culminated in a Livestock Rearing Bill, which aims to extend the grant of the 1946 Hill Farming Act to £20 million plus a possible further £2 million. Such assistance may check the drift of the human population away from a hard and isolated life and put more stock–both sheep and cattle–on the hill and marginal farms; but the area deserving of improvement is vast. The area capable of improvement, conservatively estimated at 5 million acres (Griffith, 1950), would eventually carry thousands of more stock, necessitating more labour, cottages and amenities. Government must tackle the whole problem very cautiously, for that labour may not be forthcoming. Since it is more likely to be the farmer and his family who must do all the work, as is done on so many small stock farms today, it is imperative that they be given immediate help before they leave to seek a kinder way of life. These two contradictory sentences are intended to call attention to the very great task facing the Government in its efforts to produce more cattle to augment the week's meat ration. Men will put up with the rigours of hill farm life, whereas women folk will not, and they are to be respected for their attitude. Today there is many a young man who would jump at the opportunity of taking a marginal hill farm, but his fiancee or young wife would examine the house, the amenities if there were any and the degree of isolation, with the result that in all probability they would seek elsewhere for their prospective farms. Lament the fact as all too many people do, amenities must be provided or the wherewithal earned to provide them. A pioneering spirit, such as opened up the Dominions and Colonies was fostered by prospects of wealth and power, although few attained such heights, and many lived a hard existence, but today the reward will be certain crippling taxation and a few more eggs to eat than the average person can obtain.

The Agricultural Act of 1947 provides for security of tenure for the good farmer, yet many farmers in hill country live in fear of eviction or dispossession of part of their holding by the Forestry Commission. The co-operation, or rather lack of co-operation, between the two interested parties is a very sad business which smacks with injustice, and any revival of farming in areas which are easily amenable to planting will have to be heavily financed by the State, *i.e.* you and I, dear reader, because private capital and enterprise are unlikely to risk such a venture.

The Need for Research

Before concluding this chapter on the improvement of hill and marginal grazings and the part that. cattle must play in that improvement, it is fitting that some comment should be made about the need for further research. A great deal of the present achievements on hill country throughout Britain owe their initiation to the pioneering work of Stapledon and his colleagues on the Cahn Hill Improvement Scheme, ably supported by hill farmers like Captain Bennett-Evans and landowners like the late Stanley Bligh. Even statesmen assisted, as, for example, Lloyd George's financial support of the Survey of the Agricultural and Waste Lands of Wales. It is therefore a sad state of affairs that the research work on the Cahn Hill has ceased, and at the present time research concerned with the problems of hill and marginal land[1] is of a very limited nature and directed by a number of independent authorities. Research by scientists on fundamental problems, and efforts by farmers to find new and more economic ways of improving their husbandry must go forward hand in hand, for as has often been stated 'the history of the earth records numerous civilisations which perished because of their failure to meet changing circumstances with new ideas, new and successful methods of dealing with those changing circumstances.'

---

[1] An authoritative review of this subject will be found in *Marginal Land in Britain*, by W.E. Ellison, published by Jeffrey Bles.

Chapter 14
Economic Considerations

Production and Consumption of Beef

Prior to the war the consumption of beef in the United Kingdom amounted to 24 million cwt. annually or 55 lb. per head of population as compared with 33 lb. in 1951. If we were to return to the pre-war rate of consumption the above total would have to be augmented by a further 1½ million cwt. to cover the interim population increase. In the present circumstances, such a suggestion is just wishful thinking, for there are not the available supplies of beef at the sort of prices we can afford to pay.

Before the war the United Kingdom, with the help of Eire, produced slightly more than half her total requirements, but during and just after the war, as a result of the emphasis placed on dairying and direct food crops, home production fell and in 1948 was just under 10 million cwt. Since then there has been a gradual recovery, and in 1951 output at 13 million cwt. was above the pre-war level, quantitatively, if not qualitatively. Output is likely to increase over the next few years as a result of Government measures to make beef production more attractive, notably higher prices as compared with other animal products and the payment of a £5 per head subsidy on young heifers and steers suitable for beef production. Such increases will be very necessary to compensate for the reduced level of imports which in 1951 amounted to less than one-third of the pre-war level.

It is most unlikely that we shall be able to obtain much in the way of additional supplies from abroad in the foreseeable future. Eire, with a climate so very well suited for pasture production could undoubtedly expand her output if we were able to pay a price that stimulated a fuller development of her pastoral resources but, as it is, Irish beef is now being exported to the Continent and even to the United States. New Zealand, too, could increase beef production, for she is not yet using her land resources to the full. Today beef production is only a very secondary adjunct of sheep farming. The average sheep fanner is not encouraged to keep cattle beyond the minimum needs for keeping pastures in order for sheep. In 1951 farmers were being paid under 100/- per cwt. of export beef of good quality, *i.e.* the equivalent of about 55/- per live cwt., which is appreciably less than half the price paid to British producers for beef of similar quality. Admittedly there is a considerable difference between home-produced fresh and New Zealand frozen, but not the sort of difference implied by these prices. From the consumers' point of view the tragedy is that a small but fairly reliable source of beef is not being developed because the price offered is insufficient to stimulate expansion. This increase, it is considered, would not be at the expense of dairying or fat lamb production.

Meanwhile efforts have been made to conclude trade agreements with the Argentine, which for many years was the main source of supply. Normally about 7 million cwt. or two-thirds of all imports came from the Argentine, but since the war supplies have been most uncertain and at times shipments have been suspended completely. In 1952 a new trade agreement was made, but Britain had to pay substantially higher prices and to make available by way of payment items such as oil that can ill be spared from Britain's economy. There were suggestions that the Argentine was holding a pistol at our heads, but such criticisms are neither fair nor realistic. Beef is in short supply, and it is meeting a seller's market. In the United States, where supply and demand are operating without impediment, the ruling prices have been nearly double those which are being paid to the Argentine. On a seller's market even bulk-buying cannot achieve bargain prices, and in fact the position may be aggravated as compared with free marketing. Admittedly the prices being paid for beef are well in advance of the pre-war levels, but since then the purchasing power of sterling has fallen markedly. The importing country today is interested less in the sterling value of the produce she sells and more in the return in the shape of goods and services that this produce realises. If the wherewithal to live well must come from abroad then it must be paid for by equivalent goods. In the ultimate, British industry will determine how much imported beef we shall be able to eat, and as beef gets scarcer so then will industry have to become more efficient.

But to return to immediate sources of supply, Australia is a country with a considerable potential which is far from being realised, though there are plans for developing a beef industry in the North. They are still plans, however, though one cannot be unduly sanguine over tropical development schemes which abound with more problems than those remote from them are able to comprehend. Particularly is this the case where there are considerable husbandry, adaptation and transport problems to be resolved. Unfortunately Australia is very subject to droughts and this causes very considerable fluctuations in the volume of export surpluses from year to year.

Unquestionably Africa has possibilities for beef production, but prospects are very long term. Furthermore any increases obtained may be required to satisfy African rather than British needs. Apart from massive disease problems which are aggravated by the conditions under which cattle are kept there are enormous social and economic barriers to progress. The owning of cattle is a mark of prestige with natives, and quantity rather than quality is the criterion for assessment of status. Under such conditions it will be difficult to implement a cattle improvement plan based on the exploitation of proven sires!

The more one examines the overseas supply situation the more one is forced to a realisation that a politician's promise that there shall be more red meat is going to depend more and more on home production. Taking the shorter view there is considerable scope for increased production, some of which might be diverted to Britain if we were able to pay the price, but, in the ultimate, export surpluses are bound to fall. Every year there is a greater pressure on world food resources for there are an additional 22 million mouths to feed, and this means that land will have to be diverted from specialised beef production to the production of higher priority foods. Gradually beef production throughout the world will be reduced to the status it now occupies in this country, namely that of an adjunct to other more essential lines of farming contributing to total output but complementing and not competing with the primary objectives. Though beef cattle are much too inefficient to be given much in the way of oilseed residues or rough grains, which must be reserved for the pig and the hen and the dairy cow, there is a tremendous amount of other food which is available or can be made available for beef stock without in any way competing with the needs of dairy cows, sheep or cash crop production. It is considered that with the assistance of Irish stores, beef and veal output could reasonably be raised to at least 17 million cwt. annually, which is about 40 per cent above the pre-war level of production. Apart from the capital tied up in stores and fattening beasts it could be achieved with relatively little in the way of other capital investment. It will, however, mean an intensification of effort and it won't be the easy pattern of farming as we know it today. It must be farming with fewer rabbits and more fertilisers and certainly much more of that intensity in management which is an essential of high farming.

At the top of the scale one envisages the hill country being developed, not necessarily in a spectacular way with regiments of ploughs and batteries of bull-dozers, but in the gradual, almost imperceptible way, if measured over a short period of time, which has been demonstrated by men like Bennett-Evans,[1] who use cattle as the primary implements of reclamation. Such a procedure keeps pace with the natural increase of the herds and flocks which are capable of exploiting the improvements which are effected. Though initial progress is slow, it eventually gathers momentum and a point is reached where more intensive efforts are justified–the greater use of the plough and the application of lime and fertilisers, probably by aeroplane. Not many years ago this was a fat-fetched notion, but today it is a practical one, and in New Zealand private operators are making a good living satisfying the demand for this service.

---

[1] See *Proceedings of British Society of Animal Production*, 1949.

The output of stores from the hills, which Griffith (1950) estimates could reach 400,000 annually, if we really get down to the job, can be augmented by not less than 1,000,000 from a more efficient dairy industry made up by coloured-marked calves from cows which are not required to contribute to herd upkeep, dual-purpose males surplus to breeding and Friesian steers which have been properly reared. In addition there are the stores from Sussex, North Devon, Hereford and other breeds, which are run on farms not particularly well suited to dairying. If they alone were used to utilise leys and permanent pastures they would not be economic. Their natural association is, of course, with sheep, for together these two classes of animal under proper management do not compete, but complement each other as records at Cockle Park have shown. Mean live-weight gains over a period of 21 years there were twice as great from a mixed stocking of permanent pasture with sheep and cattle as they were from sheep alone. The increased output was not entirely due to the direct contribution of the cattle, for the ewes and lambs made better gains when they were associated with cattle than they did alone (Bywater and Robertson, 1946).

Shaw (1949) has estimated that 40 per cent of the domestic production of beef, *i.e.* 4 million cwt., is accounted for by discarded dairy cows. This quantity cannot be maintained if we are to have an expanded beef industry, for a dairy industry exerting unduly heavy pressure on our limited land resources would hamper development of beef production. We have got to increase the life of our dairy cattle, and thereby reduce the demands on food from replacement stock. A five-year life in the milking herd as opposed to the present four years would substantially reduce the contribution made by cow beef to 3 million cwt. This leaves a balance of 14 million cwt. to be provided by the variety of stores which will be reared for beef. This means substantially a supply of 2½ million stores annually, which will average 700 lb. dressed weight when they are eventually slaughtered. This is probably well beyond our home potential, but we have in addition the contribution that Eire can make, certainly not less than half a million stores annually. It is not envisaged that these extra stores could be obtained within a few years, but they could be got within a decade provided the incentives were there, and we had an agricultural policy designed to remove the barriers, both physical and mental, which limit expansion.

Now the question arises, how will this increasing volume of stores be fattened? The answer is by better farming of our cultivated and cultivable land, by a full use of the by-products of cash cropping and by the growing of special forage crops, especially catch crops. We will still have a pressure on our good land for crops for direct human consumption, *e.g.* bread grains and potatoes–probably the demand will be even greater–and so our beef production must be integrated with this priority. Indeed, it can be a factor in increased crop production, for as work at Sprowston (Rayns and Owers, 1950) has shown, better yields of arable crops result from the application of bullock manure, which on arable farms can be produced substantially from the by-products of cash cropping, including the hay or silage of the seeds shift.

The Potential of Grassland

Foremost among the measures which must be taken to provide sustenance for fattening cattle is a wholesale improvement in our grassland. Davies and Williams (1948) estimate, conservatively, that if four-fifths of our permanent grass were replaced by well-farmed leys that output would be increased by well over 50 per cent. Their conclusions are based on a number of trials they conducted in which leys were compared with permanent pasture, The sort of permanent pastures they are referring to are not the few thousand acres of good permanent pasture which is to be found in the Midlands, on Romney Marsh and in well-drained, fertile river valleys throughout Britain, but the millions of acres of low-grade stuff which is deficient in clover and is dominated by daisies, buttercups, bents and other rubbish, There are no physical barriers to the improvement of much of this land. Drainage, liming, reseeding with the recognised strains of superior pasture plants, and the building up of fertility to the point where these high-producing plants can compete with invading weeds and weed grasses, coupled with proper grazing management and an elimination of the rabbit menace could transform British agriculture. Altogether in the United Kingdom there are 13 million acres of permanent pasture, apart from rough grazing, and much of this is amenable to improvement along the lines which have been suggested. Most of it remains in its semi-productive state, to constitute the biggest challenge we have in British agriculture, and until we have taken effective steps, as a nation, to answer this challenge we have no right to complain of the poverty of our meat ration.

Currently at Wye a colleague, A.G. Davis, is investigating strain differences in white clover grown in association with S23 rye-grass on a piece of really good land which lies alongside a small piece of permanent pasture which has been mismanaged for many years. It symbolises much of the permanent grassland of Britain, and normally it yields a meagre hay cut of about a ton to the acre and a few weeks of indifferent grazing. The experimental area, by way of contrast, has, over four years, been responsible for the highest live-weight increases which have ever been recorded in Britain. Where good clovers such as S100 and Grade A Kent wild white have been associated with S23, average live-weight gains from sheep have averaged 800 lb. per acre annually, but where short-lived Dutch white clover has been used production has fallen after the first harvest year to under two-thirds of the level of the good swards. A difference of a few shillings per acre in initial seeding costs has resulted in a loss of over £50 gross in worth of sheep grazing in four years.

The above high productivity has not been obtained through excessive rates of top-dressing. No artificial nitrogen has been applied, for this would have confused the clover picture, the sole dressing after seeding being an annual dressing of 3 cwt. of superphosphate, and 1 cwt. of muriate of potash. Undoubtedly the main factor in this high production has been the system of grazing management which has been adopted. The fattening tegs are always moving on to good fresh feed, which is quickly and effectively utilised. A lawn-like effect is preserved throughout the year, and grass is not allowed to run to stem to lose its nutritive qualities and its capacity for growth. After the sward has been eaten out, generally within a period of four days, it is rested for twelve days so that there is a good recovery. Under such conditions there is a very much greater production of nutrients, probably 50 per cent more than there is where grass is constantly defoliated or allowed to run to head, as it is under a system of set stocking.

Rotational or change grazing is equally applicable to cattle fattening as it is to sheep fattening. It does not now involve expensive fencing costs to secure subdivision. Folding with the electric fence is possibly the most important advance in the technique of pasture management and utilisation which has been made in the past decade, for it provides a cheap means of securing a more even plane of nutrition for stock, more complete utilisation of pasture and allows surplus feed to be concentrated in one area, where it can be cut for conservation instead of being spread in patches of neglected growth over a grazing area where not only is it an eyesore but a depressor of subsequent growth. If one regards these clumps of rough growth as weeds, then one has the right attitude to such manifestations of mismanagement of pasture.

It is beyond the scope of this work to proceed further with this topic of pasture management beyond saying that the meat production recorded in the above trials required a utilisation of not less than 4,000 lb. of starch equivalent and 800 lb. of digestible protein per acre, which is equivalent to a yield of over 3 tons of oats and beans. These are exceptional figures, which can be achieved under experimental but not practical conditions of farming, but they give some measure of the green gold we are neglecting in Britain through a failure to apply techniques which are now very well established.

By-products of Arable Farming

Another great source of nutrients for bullock feeding is the variety of by-products of arable farming which are ploughed in or burnt each year. When one sees at the end of harvest the pall of smoke from burning straw, or, later in the year, the ploughing in of thousands of tons of beet tops, one cannot but reflect on the crazy state of affairs which permits such a waste of potential stock food to take place. (These remarks are not directed against the individual farmer, who obviously will adopt his most profitable course of action according to prevailing circumstances, but against a system which permits such waste.) Rayns and Owers (1950), reporting on work conducted at Sprowston, show that there is no depression of yield in the subsequent rotation of crops when beet tops are folded off as opposed to being ploughed in, and they have shown also that these tops make a very worth-while contribution to the winter feeding of bullocks. Their work comparing the application of dung with the ploughing in of straw with sulphate of ammonia, a growing practice, shows a material advantage in favour of muck. With present prices for hay, sugar-beet, wheat and barley, which are the crops used in the trials, a ton of F.Y.M. on their estimates has a value of 62s over a full rotation. Apart from the fact that it is immediately good business in these areas to produce and apply F.Y.M., even if it does involve a small loss in bullock feeding, the important point that has been established is that the utilisation of crop residues in bullock feeding enhances and does not depress yields of crops, while there is a harvest of meat in addition.

Why then is bullock feeding disappearing from the arable areas, *e.g.* Rayns and Owers (*loc. cit.*) give figures for one Norfolk district with a first-class reputation for arable farming, and which was a traditional fattening area where the marketing of fat cattle has fallen by more than 40 per cent over the period 1940–48? Eleven farms in the district, comprising 3,000 acres, which fed 1,500 bullocks in 1940, were feeding approximately 250 beasts in the winter of 1950. Even in 1944, when the war-time shortages of feeding-stuffs were most pronounced, many more bullocks were being fattened than there are now. The immediate answer is that the feeders' margins are not big enough having regard to the high price of feeding-stuffs in relation to the initial cost of stores and the selling price of the fattened beasts. Wheldon and Hall (1950) have published a depressing list of economic surveys covering five different districts in Britain over the period 1944–9, where the average loss per beast in yard fattening varied from £1 6s 8d to £7 9s 6d. It is very natural that farmers should ask themselves whether it is worth the candle to invest money in bullock purchase, feeding-stuffs and labour and to lose money in the process) in order to produce muck which is expensive to handle when, very simply, they can secure very adequate crop yields by purchasing and applying artificials. They probably realise that by so doing they are not getting maximum yields, but they are producing good enough crops and making an adequate living. Increased production by the other method mainly benefits the Chancellor of the Exchequer, and it is not surprising that they should simplify their farming, for it has enough problems without adding unnecessarily to them.

It must not be accepted from the foregoing that yard feeding as opposed to yard fattening of bullocks is necessarily an unprofitable undertaking. Many farmers realising that the feeding of corn to fattening cattle is a primary cause of the losses that are occurring, have switched to cheap wintering on roughages, where the aim is to maintain stock in a forward store condition, so that they can be fattened cheaply on grass which fairly consistently has been a profitable undertaking. Dinsdale and Carpenter (quoted by Wheldon and Hall, 1950) report an average profit on 924 Northumberland farms of £8 6s per head for cattle store wintered in 1947–48 and fattened in the summer of 1948.

Such a system is admirable on ley farms with summer grass available for grazing, and crop by-products available for wintering, but in East Anglia, where the ley phase is very often represented by a one-year seeds mixture which is cut for hay and for clover seed, there is often an insufficiency of summer grass for feeding out the bullocks which can be wintered on straw, beet tops and sometimes beet pulp. It is easy to suggest that these stores should be transferred to the Midlands for grass fattening, but such transference is expensive. Apart from transport costs, there are dealer or/and auctioneer expenses to be covered by the bullocks, and there is an aggravation of the seasonal glut of beef which is becoming such an undesirable feature of British beef production. It is in this connection that the silage fattening of bullocks is particularly interesting. The development of the buck-rake and the making of silage in pits has reduced the costs of this operation to a very reasonable figure, and currently we are seeing the effects of these developments in the dairy industry where a veritable revolution in feeding is occurring, and there is no real reason why this should not be extended to winter beef production particularly in the arable districts. A proportion of the seeds which are normally cut for hay could be cut earlier to provide a high-grade silage, which along with beet tops, limited beet pulp, hay and feeding straw would constitute a very satisfactory winter fattening ration. Perhaps such rapid gains would not be made as they would if corn was fed in addition, but this is not the consideration, which is profitability and yield of F.Y.M. That we have not seen more efforts along these lines to reduce costs of winter fattening is a reflection of the depressed state of this branch of agriculture in relation to other branches. Farmers have not been sufficiently interested to evolve methods which conform to the changed circumstances. They have preferred either to go out of livestock or to switch to dairying, which has been profitable. In more respects than one beef production has been the Cinderella of British agriculture.

The Problem of Seasonal Gluts

One of the greatest weaknesses of the British beef industry has been irregularity of supply. Even before the war when purchased feeding-stuffs were reasonably cheap there was an autumnal glut which caused a sharp drop in prices. Shaw (1949) has published figures illustrating this point. The average wholesale price for English longsides in June over the period 1927–31 was 9d per lb., but in November it had fallen to 7¼d, representing a drop of 19 per cent. Over the same period the greatest monthly difference for Argentine beef amounted to only ¾d per lb., or only 6 per cent of the highest monthly price. This result is a direct reflection of the supply position which is illustrated in Figure 21. The Argentine really marketed beef by ensuring that supplies were on hand in the quantities required to meet the steady demand which such a policy created. English beef, on the other hand, was its own worst competitor. Apparently the position has not improved over the past few years despite the premium in the guaranteed price for beef marketed in the months of scarcity as compared with the months of highest killings. In 1947, for instance, more than half of the slaughterings were in the four-month period August-November. In the month of October alone there were more slaughterings than there were in the first quarter of the year (Long, 1950). Since that time there have been adjustments in the winter price schedule, but the seasonal problem still remains.

We have seen from economic surveys that it is good business for the farmer, who is protected from market uncertainties by guaranteed prices, to aim at producing cheap beef from grass rather than dear beef from conserved foods and concentrates, but though it may suit him it does not suit the consumer, who has had more than his share of a tenpenny worth of carcass meat per week in the very months of the year he has the greatest need for meat. What can be done to mitigate this position, so that both producer and consumer are protected? It is suggested that it is better to go flat out for *in situ* utilisation of grass and crops in order to produce as much cheap beef as possible on the grounds that it is better to preserve meat than feeding-stuffs. The intention here, of course, is that the immediate surplus should be frozen and stored for the months of reduced supplies. To many, a suggestion that English meat should be frozen and thereby reduced to the lowly status of the cheapest imported meat is sheer sacrilege, and yet the idea has much to commend it. If we are to be forced into eating frozen beef for five or six months of the year, it may as well be home produced as imported. There is no point in our returning to the old medieval situation where people feasted in the autumn when surplus stock were killed, and went without

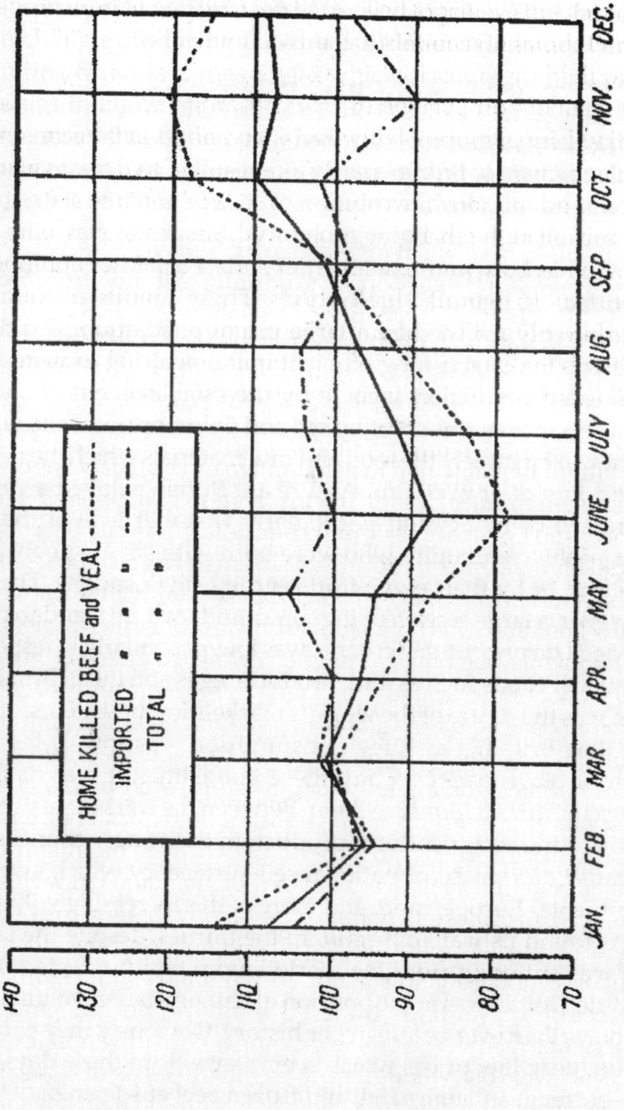

Figure 21: Indices of Monthly Average Supplies of Beef and Veal in Great Britain 1927–31 (Monthly Average, 100) (Shaw, 1949)

meat for the rest of the year. The position of course is not quite as bad as this in that the southern hemisphere is our main source of imported beef, and seasonal production there tends to dovetail with our own seasonal production. This certainly is the case with Australia and New Zealand, but the Argentine, in the past, made a feature of even monthly deliveries to maintain a goodwill for her beef.

The Future of Beef Production

The past fifty years have witnessed vast changes in the economic and social structure of Britain, partly as a result of two major wars, partly as a result of normal evolution of society in a free state and partly as a result of the changing economy of new countries, who at the turn of the century were essentially exporters of primary produce and importers of manufactured goods. These conditions suited Britain admirably for she had a large urban population, and the raw materials for establishing efficient manufacturing industries. She augmented her export income by the establishment of such services as financing, transport by sea and insurance, and she was in a position to buy freely the food and raw materials which the new countries could offer in return. As a result Britain enjoyed a very high standard of living, and particularly was that true of those members of the community who were born with silver spoons in their mouths, or by their own efforts earned silver spoons. There was, however, a large section of the community whose standard of living, judged on present-day criteria, was low, particularly in respect of high-quality foods such as milk products, eggs and meat. Britain, however, was the centre of the world's markets for these items, and the fact that Britain's average consumption was low is less a reflection of her capacity to buy these goods than it was of the exporting countries to produce them. Between the wars there was a vast increase in the agricultural production of the new countries, and, because of a phase of national self-sufficiency which swept over continental Europe, more and more of this increasing volume of exports found its way to Britain. In the thirties, despite the fact that she was suffering from the world slump which affected her export trade, Britain was in the position of having a larger volume of food imports than ever before in her history. Obviously they could only sell at very low prices which seem fantastic in these days of scarcity–butter at 1s, lamb at 8d, and frozen beef at 4d per lb.

As a result of this plentiful and cheap food, consumption rates for that proportion of the population which was in reasonable employment rose to a very high level, but there was a big section, not less than one-fifth, who were on a sub-optimum diet. Chiefly through the work of Boyd Orr there was an increasing realisation of the importance of adequate dietaries, and at the outbreak of war there were active measures being taken to give effect to this, notably the milk-in-schools scheme.

The war with its rigid rationing did not put a halt to improvement. Because of the fairer-shares policy a proportion of the population was encouraged to purchase more food than it did before the war. This was one of the psychological effects of rationing, and a greater sharing of national wealth, a consequence of war, gave such people the means of buying what was their allotted share. Food habits for many people changed, and it would have been interesting to have seen the course of consumption had meat supplies quickly returned to their pre-war level. But they have not returned. Britain's manufacturing potential has suffered through the war and her production costs have risen disproportionately. She has lost markets because her former customers, through war conditions, have developed their own secondary industries and are now more self-sufficient. Overseas investments have gone in financing the war, and Britain has become a debtor country.

This has thrown a greater responsibility on British agriculture than ever before. Obviously Britain will not cease in her endeavours to expand her export trade, but her progress in this direction is limited on the one hand by high costs and on the other hand by the international situation which has placed nearly one-half of the world behind an iron curtain. Britain's economy is now at the cross-roads. Though she will continue to export as much as she can and buy as much food as possible, after she has paid for essential raw materials she is bound to face a lower standard of living unless her own agriculture can make good the deficiencies. Furthermore, this has to be made good as cheaply as possible if Britain is to participate successfully in international trade.

Our land resources are very restricted. If we exclude rough grazings there is only about three-fifths of an acre of agricultural land per head of population. At the very worst we could turn into a nation of allotment holders and live on potatoes, Brussels sprouts and cabbages, but there is no danger of that if we really apply ourselves to the task of increasing productivity. It is recognised that many products must take priority over beef–potatoes, vegetables, bread grain, milk–but there is room for a great deal besides. Consider the milk industry, which is the greatest competitor beef has for leg-room and feeding-stuffs. If we could cut down the wastage in our herds by one-fifth and increase average productivity by 150 gallons per annum, and reduce initial age at first calving by six months–not unreasonable goals, for they have been achieved by many thousands of our more efficient farmers, as well as by whole dairying industries abroad–we could produce about the same quantity of milk for about four-fifths of the food we use at present. This is but one example of how progress can be made.

On top of this there are vast new techniques in agriculture which are not being applied fully. What proportion of our farmers record their dairy herds and use their results to advantage; how many sow only certified pasture seeds of good quality; how many take a chance with wireworm when they sow cereals though prevention is cheap and effective; how many really correct deficiencies in soil fertility? These questions could cover many pages, and invariably the answer would be only a proportion. Unfortunately so many of the difficulties operating against expanded production are human difficulties. Somehow or another we have got to speed up not only the application of new knowledge but the reaction of farmers to new circumstances. We can't get imported feeding-stuffs, so it is no use bemoaning the fact. We must do what we can to improve the pastures, or grow the crops which will replace those feeding-stuffs which made pre-war British agriculture insecure because it had to depend on the agriculture of overseas countries, who were busy mining their fertility to create a problem for posterity.

Perhaps the suggestion that with the help of Eire we could set about filling the gap of 17 million cwt. in our beef supplies is an ambitious one, but it is a goal, and even if we only get part way along the road we will have done something to increase the weekly ration that is still with us nearly eight years after the end of the war, which was responsible for rationing. If we don't we will have to resign ourselves as a nation to a much lower standard of living.

But one can end on a more cheerful note. Who would have predicted twelve years ago that the dairy industry, in a decade, could increase production by 40 per cent in the face of a decline of 50 per cent in supplies of imported feeding-stuffs? That is one of the most remarkable achievements we have witnessed in the revival of our agriculture, and one for which farmers have not been given sufficient credit. Given the incentives and provided limitations to progress are eliminated wherever they can be by statesmanship from the Whitehall sector of the battle for food, one may reasonably expect a response in beef production comparable with that in dairying over the next decade.

But Whitehall must remember that agricultural production cannot satisfactorily be controlled on an annual basis through the mechanism of the Price Review. In 1948 eggs and milk were wanted in large quantities, and attractive prices were offered. In 1951 both products were being subjected to disincentives. The thousands of poor unfortunate farmers who had invested large sums of money in free range and fold equipment, which is ideal for spring and summer egg production, found that they had to go out of poultry or switch to intensive production, using lighting if they wanted to make a profit. The situation was not quite so bad in dairying, because the dairy farmer, with his greater independence in respect of purchased feeding-stuffs, has more resiliency, but even so there are many men who are regretting their substantial investments in dairy cows, buildings and equipment.

Such a hand-to-mouth policy will destroy the confidence of farmers. The 1952 February Price Review placed an emphasis on meat; but what will be the position in 1955 if the Ministry of Food is able through some swing of the pendulum to buy large quantities of cheap beef and bacon from abroad? Will the pig and cattle producers be meted out the same sort of treatment as poultry and milk producers? That is a question which thoughtful farmers are asking, and it is one which must be answered satisfactorily if producers are going to make the long-term investments which characterise agriculture. We would be better served by strong commodity boards, such as the Milk Marketing Board, which has really looked after producers' interests, than we would by the present system with its uncertainties and its dependence on what is politically expedient. The national policy in agriculture must be comprehensive, and it must be a long-term one, so that farmers can tackle their production tasks with confidence. The beef industry needs the equivalent of the

Milk Marketing Board, not only to protect its interests and to ensure its development on a thoroughly efficient basis, but also that the margin between a fair return to the producer and the price the housewife has to pay is kept to a minimum.

Appendices

APPENDIX 1
Value of Common Feeding-Stuffs
(*Derived from Woodman, Bulletin 48, Ministry of Agriculture*)

	Per cent Dry Matter	*Per cent Dig. Prot. Equiv.*	*Per 100 lb. Starch Equiv.*
Mangolds (yellow globe)	13.2	0.4	6.8
Swede turnip	11.5	0.8	7.3
White turnip	8.5	0.4	4.4
Sugar-beet	23.4	0.5	15.0
Sugar-beet tops	16.2	1.1	8.6
Cabbage (drumhead)	11.0	0.9	6.6
Kale (thousand head)	15.8	1.4	10.3
Kale (marrow stem)	14.0	1.4	9.1
Rape	14.1	1.6	6.9
Pasture (3-weekly rotation)	20.0	3.4	14.6
Pasture (close grazing non-rotational)	20.0	4.1	14.7

Appendix I–Contd...

	Per cent Dry Matter	*Per cent Dig. Prot. Equiv.*	*Per 100 lb. Starch Equiv.*
Silage, grass (1st quality)	21.0	1.8	12.8
Silage, grass (2nd quality)	24.5	1.6	12.6
Silage, grass (hay maturity)	25.0	1.4	10.2
Silage, marrow stem kale	15.9	1.2	9.2
Silage, sugar-beet tops	23.0	0.8	9.5
Silage, canning-pea residues	23.6	1.1	11.6
Silage, vetches and oats (green fruity)	27.3	1.6	12.8
Hay, lucerne (before flowering)	84.0	10.1	32.0
Hay, lucerne (full flowering)	83.5	7.9	27.0
Hay, meadow (poor)	85.7	2.9	22
Hay, meadow (good)	85.7	4.6	37
Hay, meadow (very good)	84.0	8.8	48
Hay seeds (good quality)	85.0	7.0	40
Hay seeds (average)	86.0	4.9	30
Oat straw (spring)	86.0	0.9	20
Oat straw (winter)	86.0	0.5	21
Barley straw (spring)	86.0	0.7	23
Barley	85.1	7.3	71.4
Oats	86.7	7.6	59.5
Wheat	86.6	9.6	71.6
Maize	87.0	7.2	74.1
Beans	85.7	19.7	65.8
Peas	86.0	18.1	69.0
Linseed	92.9	18.7	119.2
Linseed cake (English)	88.8	24.6	74.0
Groundnut cake (undecorticated)	89.7	27.2	56.8
Groundnut cake (decorticated)	89.7	41.3	73.0
Flaked maize	89.0	9.2	84.0

Appendix I–Contd...

	Per cent Dry Matter	*Per cent Dig. Prot. Equiv.*	*Per 100 lb. Starch Equiv.*
Palm kernel cake (English)	89.0	16.9	73.2
Soya bean cake	85.5	36.9	68.9
Cottonseed cake (decorticated)	90.2	34.1	68.4
Fine middlings*	86.7	12.2	69.6
Coarse middlings*	86.0	10.8	56.5
Brewers' grains (fresh)	32.4	5.3	18.4
Brewers' grains (dried)	89.7	12.5	48.3
Meat meal (pure)	89.2	65.4	91.0
Fish meal (white)	87.0	53.0	58.9
Separated milk	9.4	3.3	8.3
Whole milk	12.8	3.2	17.1
Bran	87.0	10.0	42.6

* Pre-war grade.

APPENDIX 2

Supplies of Beef and Veal to the United Kingdom (1,000 tons)

	1938	*1939*	*1949*	*1950*	*1951*
Home produced*	605.0	625.0	528.1	633.6	652.0
New Zealand	51.6	55.5	50.7	67.7	40.4
Australia	114.8	113.8	53.3	54.7	42.4
Argentina	354.3	350.0	215.4	162.9	48.1
Uruguay	32.9	29.4	39.2	44.0	15.2
Other countries	31.4**	29.8**	6.1	4.7	4.9
Total	**1190.0**	**1203.5**	**892.8**	**967.6**	**803.0**

* Includes carcasses from fat cattle imported from Eire.

** Mainly imports from Brazil.

(*Source of information–Commonwealth Economic Committee*).

References

Astill, P.F., *Agriculture*, Vol. 47, No. 9 (1940).

Bennett-Evans, *Proc. Brit. Soc. An. Prod.* (1949).

Boulet, L.J., Unpublished thesis, University of Wales (1939).

Braid, K.W., *Jour. Brit. Grass. Soc.*, Vol. 2, No. 4 (1947).

Bywater, T.L., and Robertson, C.G.A., University of Leeds and Yorkshire Council for Agriculture Educ. Bull. No. 209 (1946).

Cunningham, I., *N.Z. Jour. Agric.*, Vol. 69 (1944).

Davies, W.M., and Williams, T.E., *Jour. Roy. Agric. Soc. England*, Vol. 109 (1948).

Davis, A.G., and Cooper, M.M., *Jour. Brit. Grass Soc.*, Vol. 6, No. 4 (1951); Vol. 8, No. 2 (1953).

Dodsworth, T.L. and Campbell, W.H.M., *Scottish Agric.*, Vol. 32, No. 3 (1953).

Donald, H.P., and El Itriby, *Jour. Agric. Sc.*, Vol. 36, No. 2 (1946).

Dunlop, G., *Agriculture*, Vol. 53, No. 12 (1947)

Edwards, J., *Jour. Farmers' Club*, Pt. 6 (1950).

Ellison, R., *Proc. Brit. Soc. An. Prod.* (1947); *Jour. Farmers' Club*, Pt. 3 (1949).

Ernle, Lord, *English Farming Past and Present* (Longmans, London 1936).

Fawcett, E.J., *Bull.* 138, N.Z. Dept. of Agric. (1929).

Fenton, E.W., *Jour. Ecol.*, Vol. 25, No. 2 (1937).

Filmer, J.F., and Underwood, E.J., *Jour. Dept. Agric.*, Western Australia (1936).

Fraser, Allan, *Farming for Beef* (Crosby Lockwood, London 1950).

Garner, F.H., *Cattle of Britain*, (Longmans Green, London 1944).

Greenwood, A.W., and Blyth, J.S.S., Official Report, 8th World's Poultry Congress, Copenhagen (1948).

Gregor, J.W., *Scot. Jour. Agric.*, Vol. 26, No. 9 (1946).

Griffith, Moses, *Proc. Brit. Soc. An Prod.* (1947); *Jour. Farmers' Club*, Pt. 3 (1950).

Hagedoorn, A.L., *Animal Breeding* (Crosby Lockwood, London 1939).

Hammon, John, *Growth and the Development of Mutton Sheep* (Oliver and Boyd, Edinburgh 1932); *Farm Animals* (Arnold, London 1941); *Proc. Nutrit. Soc.*, Vol. 2, No. 8 (1943).

Henderson, A.E., Unpublished thesis, Wye College (1950).

Hiner, R.L., and Hankins, O.G., *Jour. An. Sc.*, Vol. 9, No. 3 (1950).

Hirzel, R., *Onderstepoort Jour. Vet. Sc. and An. Industry*, Vol. 12, No. 2 (1939).

Hughes, G.P.H., *Agriculture*, Vol. 55, No. 3 (1948); *Agriculture*, Vol. 56, No. 5 (1949).

Johnstone-Wallace, D.B., and Kennedy, K., *Jour. Agric. Sc.*, Vol. 34, No. 4 (1944).

Kelley, R.B., Australian C.S.I.R. Pamphlet No. 27 (1932); Australian C.S.I.R. Bull. No. 172 (1943); *Principles of Animal Breeding* (Angus and Robertson, Sydney 1946).

Knapp, B., *Farm Quarterly*, Report of Montana Cattle Breeding Station (1950).

Knapp, B., and Clark, R.T., *Jour. An. Soc.*, Vol. 9, No. 4 (1950).

Krallinger, quoted by Lush, *Animal Breeding Plans* (State College Press, Ames, Iowa 1931, 1936).

Long, W.H., *Farming*, Vol. 4, No. 4 (1950).

Lush, Jay L., *Animal Breeding Plans* (State College Press, Ames, Iowa 1947).

Mansfield, W.S., *Proc. Brit. Soc. An. Prod.* (1949).

Marshall, Quoted by Stewart, A. Unpublished thesis, Oxford University (1950).

McDougal, R., *Jour. Farmers' Club*, Pt. 8 (1946).

McGuinness, S., *Proc. N.Z. Soc. An. Prod.* (1947).

McMeekan, C. P., *Jour. Agric. Res.*, Vol. 30 and 31 (1940–41); *Proc. N.Z. Soc. An. Prod.* (1943); *Proc. N.Z. Soc. An. Prodc.* (1947).

McMeekan, C.P., Campbell, I.L., Cooper, M.M., and Ward, A.H., *Principles of Animal Production* (Whitcombe and Toombs, Wellington, New Zealand 1943).

Milton, W.E.J., Welsh Plant Breeding Station Series H. 14 (1936).

Moore, H.I., and Burr, S., *Jour. Brit. Grass Soc.*, Vol. 3, No. 4 (1948).

Morrison, I., *Farmer and Stock Breeder* (6 Jan. 1951)

Nihlsson-Ehle, Quoted by Babcock and Clausen, *Genetics in Relation to Agriculture* (McGraw Hill, New York 1923).

Orr, John Boyd, *Food, Health and Income* (Macmillan & Co. London 1936).

Phillips, R.W., *Breeding Livestock Adapted to Unfavourable Conditions*, F.A.O. Agric. Series No. 1 (Washington 1948).

Price, O.T.W., *The Farm Economist*, Vol. 3, No. 3 (1949).

Rae, A.L., *Sheep Farming Annual* (Massey Agric. College, New Zealand 1947).

Raynes, F., and Owers, A. C., *Farming*, Vol. 4, No. 6 (1950).

Rendel, J.M., and Robertson, A., *Home Farmer*, Vol. 16, No. 4 (1949).

Rhoad, A.O., *Proc. Amer. Soc. An. Prod.* (1940).

Robertson, A., *Animal Breeding Abstracts*, Vol. 17, No. 1 (1949).

Shaw, T., *Proc. Brit. Soc. An. Prod.* (1949).

Shrode, R. R., and Lush, Jay L., *Advances in Genetics,* Vol. 1 (Academic Press, New York 1947).

Sjollema, B., *Jour. Brit. Grass Soc.,* Vol. 5, No. 2 (1950).

Stapledon, R.G., *The Hill Lands of Britain* (Faber, London 1937).

Stewart, D., *Proc. Brit. Soc. An. Prod.* (1949); Private Communication (1951).

Swett, W.w., *Jour. Agric. Res.,* Vol. 37 (1928).

Wallace, L.R., *Jour. Agric. Soc.,* Vol. 38, Nos. 2,3 and 4 (1948).

Walton, A., and Hammond, J., *Proc. Roy. Soc.,* B125 (1938).

Ward, A.H., *Twenty-second Annual Report N.Z. Dairy Board* (1946); *N.Z. Dairy Board Sire Survey Register* (1949).

Wells, H.E., *Agriculture,* Vol. 57, No. 3 (1950).

Wheldon, R.W., and Hall, J.S., *Farming,* Vol. 4, No. 7 (1950).

Wilson, A.S.B., *Scot. Jour. Agric.,* Vol. 19 (1936).

Wilson, James, *The Evolution of British Cattle* (Vinton, London 1909); *The Breeding and Feeding of Farm Livestock* (Methuen, London 1921).

Wood, T.B., and Newman, L.F., *Beef Production in Britain* (Silcocks and Sons, Liverpool 1928).

Woodman, H.E., *Rations for Livestock,* M.A.F. Bulletin 48 (H.M.S.O., London 1948).

Woodman, H.E., Norman, D.B., and Bee, J.W., *Jour. Agric. Sci.,* Vol. 18, No. 2 (1928).

Wright, S., *Jour. Heredity,* Vol. 10, No. 9 (1923).

Index